Also by Michael Sokolove

THE TICKET OUT: DARRYL STRAWBERRY
AND THE BOYS OF CRENSHAW

HUSTLE: THE MYTH, LIFE, AND LIES OF PETE ROSE

Warrior Girls

Protecting Our
Daughters Against
the Injury Epidemic
in Women's Sports

Michael Sokolove

Simon & Schuster
New York   London   Toronto   Sydney

Simon & Schuster
1230 Avenue of the Americas
New York, NY 10020

First Simon & Schuster hardcover edition June 2008

SIMON & SCHUSTER and colophon are registered trademarks of Simon & Schuster, Inc.

For information about special discounts for bulk purchases,
please contact Simon & Schuster Special Sales at
1-800-456-6798 or business@simonandschuster.com.

Designed by C. Linda Dingler

Manufactured in the United States of America

1   3   5   7   9   10   8   6   4   2

Library of Congress Cataloging-in-Publication Data

Sokolove, Michael Y.
Warrior girls : protecting our daughters against the injury epidemic
in women's sports / Michael Sokolove.
p.   cm.
1. Sports for girls.   2. Sports for women.   3. Sports
injuries—Prevention.   4. Sports—Safety measures.   I. Title.
GV709.S64   2008
796.083—dc22   2008012176

ISBN-13: 978-0-7432-9755-4
ISBN-10:   0-7432-9755-5

For Ann

Contents

Warrior Girls

PROLOGUE

A photograph of my nineteen-year-old daughter, a college swimmer, serves as the screen saver on my computer. I suppose I could have put up her senior prom picture, but I chose one in which she is breaststroking through the pool, her face taut with determination and her powerful shoulders rising high above the surface of the water, hard-earned musculature built in many a predawn practice. It showcases the strength, confidence, and indomitability she has developed through sport. It catches her authentic spirit, one that will remain even when her days of athletic competition are over.

Athletic girls seem happier, more confident, more in control of their bodies and their destinies than girls who do not put themselves in motion, who do not compete, who do not experience all the highs and lows and disappointments and exultations that have long driven boys onto the field of play.

In many regards, sports are *better* for girls than for boys. Sports too often socialize boys in the wrong ways, promoting misogyny, overaggression, entitlement. They give boys more of what they already have, or at least push them toward what they are susceptible to. The most toxic of male sports cauldrons, the National Football

League, has a parallel, police-blotter narrative that consists of strip club brawls, shootings, motorcycle crashes, and serial cases of spousal abuse.

Girls, through sports, gain the joy of physicality and spirited play that has long been the staple of a boy's childhood. They get to compete in a wide range of sports through high school and college, no longer just field hockey and softball and a handful of others, and they play the games well—better, in fact, than the boys if the measure of quality is team play. Girls indulge in far less posturing than boys, less look-at-me chest beating, less taunting of opponents. Athletics help shape girls into women who are both competitive and collaborative, a formidable combination that most management experts now recognize as the best model of leadership. They take ownership of their own bodies. They go after what they want. Their strength gives them power.

In 1972, the year Title IX was enacted, about 300,000 girls participated in high school sports. The number is now just above 3 million, a tenfold increase. Thirty thousand girls played college sports before Title IX; about 205,000 now play. The numbers for participation for girls at the youth level have soared in even greater measures.

What you will read about in the pages that follow is the unforeseen and largely invisible consequence of the women's sports revolution: girls and young women are injuring themselves in astonishing, alarming, depressing numbers. This disturbing reality has been overlooked amid the good feelings generated by all those ponytailed girls bursting into competition, and the noisy celebrations of such watershed moments as the soccer World Cup captured by Mia Hamm, Brandi Chastain, and a team of spirited U.S. women. The enterprise of women's sports is flourishing, but the athletes are hurting.

Girls suffer a whole range of injuries at greater rates than boys—shin splints, chronic knee pain, back and hip pain, stress fractures—and too often a chain of these injuries takes them off the field for several weeks, a season, a career. The most serious problem, by far, is the routine incidence of major knee injuries in girls—mainly tears to the anterior cruciate ligament, or ACL, the rubber-band-like fiber that stabilizes the joint. If girls tore their ACLs at just twice the rate of boys, it would be notable. Four times the rate would be astounding. But some studies have shown that in sports that boys and girls both play, and with similar rules—soccer, basketball, volleyball—girls tear their ACLs at rates as high as *eight times* that of boys. And plenty of girls do it repeatedly—to one knee, then to the other, or to the same knee multiple times.

The reconstructive surgery is complicated and the rehabilitation long and arduous. Multiple ACL tears leave scar tissue and other damage, so many girls are exiting their sport battered and broken—candidates for artificial knees before they reach menopause. "I don't think there's a real understanding yet in the general public of what's going on," Dr. Jo Hannafin, director of the Women's Sports Medicine Center at New York's Hospital for Special Surgery, told me. "We are going to see more and more knee replacements for women in their forties, and even thirties."

And these former athletes needing artificial knees won't be like NFL players who knew and willingly accepted physical risks in return for big paydays. They'll just be women who once played a sport they loved, but didn't get the right information and training, and ended up with shredded knees.

There are other vulnerabilities crying out for attention, and I have written about them at length in the chapters that follow. To give one example: for all the justifiable attention paid to concussions suffered by football players, you may be stunned to learn, as I was, that female collegiate soccer players suffer concussions at a statistically identical rate to college football players. (And don't even ask about female ice hockey players.) Much of this book deals with immutable facts of anatomy and physiology. In the case of concussions, girls have smaller heads and weaker necks than men, so it takes less force to give them a concussion.

I have devoted, as well, a great deal of thought to the new culture of women's sports—to the Warrior Girl, personified by the ultra-aggressive players of perennial NCAA soccer champion North Carolina and their celebrated coach, Anson Dorrance. Speed of play, intensity of play, and ferocity of play are directly related to injury rates. Dorrance's players are, by design, ferocious. He proudly calls them "savages and blunt instruments."

Dorrance all but invented women's soccer in the United States, and he reimagined the female athlete. He expanded her capabilities and changed her mind-set, for better and for worse. Success like Dorrance's—eighteen NCAA national championships and, at one point, 101 consecutive victories—has a trickle-down effect. To compete with him, you must adopt his methods. If his team plays with a heretofore unseen fury, yours must too. This ethos trickles all the way down to the youth level and into multiple sports. Any girl hoping to get to the next level—the travel team, the high school team, the college scholarship—knows that today's female athlete does not back down from anything, including physical risk and pain.

THE IDEA that girls should play sports at all is relatively recent. The earliest women's basketball games, played a century ago in a few New England colleges, were conducted amid an atmosphere of illicitness. Men were not allowed into the gyms to watch, as if women competing, exerting themselves, and (God forbid) perspiring were so unladylike that the games had to be played in secret. Increases in female participation in the Olympic Games were slow, steady, and almost always achieved over the opposition of male sports executives. "I am fed up to the ears with women as track-and-field competitors. Their charms sink to less than zero," Avery Brundage, the president of the American Athletic Union and later the longtime president of the International Olympic Committee, said at the 1936 Summer Olympics in Berlin.

It has been thirty-five years since Congress passed and President Richard Nixon signed the sweeping civil rights bill that became known simply as Title IX, which mandated greater opportunities for female athletes. The National Collegiate Athletic Association, which now proudly sponsors and markets a women's basketball Final Four and other high-profile women's events, opposed it and feared its consequences. "Impending doom is around the corner if these regulations are implemented," then NCAA director Walter Byers said.

He was wrong, of course. The notion that young women not only should be allowed to play but must also be granted *equal access* to organized sports—the same opportunities as boys—became the only major social revolution of the last half century in America to be supported by every segment of society, cutting across all the usual divides. Yes, there are critics, persistent ones, some of them at high levels of government and politics. But they are a tiny (if loud) minority. The daughters of all races, all classes, all political and religious persuasions—from the most secular households to home-schooled evangelicals—play sports in huge numbers.

Female athletes are emblems of our modernity. What do we think of those few nations left in the world that will not let their girls play or that drape them in such restrictive clothing that they can hardly move? They are backwards, right? Not societies we generally admire.

Fathers, perhaps even more than mothers, crowd the sidelines of girls' athletic events in communities all across America. I think it's no accident that they are often the primary soccer parent—or basketball or lacrosse or softball parent. Men don't always easily share interests with their daughters, but sports we get. More than any other social force, it is Title IX that has brought a welcome revision to the father-daughter relationship. Millions of dads have come to see their daughters as strong, rather than as delicate flowers who need their fierce protection. But strong is not invincible.

●   ●   ●

KNEES ARE where the biggest problem lies, and they are the site of the most dire long-term consequences. They are the focus of an intense, well-funded, many-faceted research effort to identify the causes of and solutions to what is crippling so many young female athletes—a search for answers that is a medical detective story, a tale of brilliant doctors, dogged researchers, competing theories, and clashing egos.

Knees are the source of utter heartbreak. Amy Steadman was going to be one of the great American soccer players of her generation. In her junior year in high school, in Brevard, North Carolina, *Parade* magazine named her the top high school defensive player in America, "the best of the best." She was captain of the U.S. women's under-nineteen team, a future star of the women's national team. But by the time I met her, Amy was twenty-one and had torn the ACL in her right knee three times. She had undergone, by her count, five surgeries. (Her mother counted eight including certain minor cuttings that Amy did not put in the category of actual surgeries.) She was done playing.

As Amy walked toward me the first time we met, she moved like an old woman. Her right leg was stiff and her whole gait crooked. If I hadn't known her history, I would never have believed she had been an athlete, let alone an elite one. She told me about her final surgery, recalling that when she came out of anesthesia, the surgeon looked like he was about to cry. He was silent for what seemed like a long time, trying to compose himself. Finally, he told her, "Amy, there was nothing in there left to fix."

In the two years I spent researching this book, I returned again and again to a dense set of data disseminated by the NCAA: its Injury Surveillance System, tables and charts based on the reports of athletic trainers at colleges and universities around the nation. The frequency of certain injuries is calculated by the number of occurrences per thousand "athletic exposures"—practices and games.

I looked at the rate of ACL tears for women's soccer: 0.25 per

1,000, or 1 in 4,000. The Injury Surveillance System puts out commentary in addition to the data, and in a 2007 report, the authors cautioned readers not to make too much of the ACL tears sustained by male and female collegiate athletes across a range of sports, as their frequency should be considered in proper perspective. "Although serious (as measured by time loss, pain, disability, and costs), in terms of both frequency and rates, ACL injuries are not epidemic," the NCAA report says. Applying statistical probability standards, the report added, "The actual probability of ACL injury would be considered a rare event."

A rare event? Perhaps when comparing the number of ACL injuries to all injuries together. But not when looking specifically at some of the most popular sports for young women.

I dwelled a bit more on the numbers and then did some figuring of my own. A young woman playing college soccer can easily generate 200 exposures a year between her regular season in the fall, off-season training in the spring, and club play in the summer. Plenty of younger players, girls in their mid- and late teens, will accrue well in excess of 200 exposures between their high school seasons, their club seasons—which often run year-round and overlap with school seasons—multigame tournaments on weekends, and soccer camps in the summer.

And the ACL injury rates for these younger girls may be higher—perhaps much higher—than they are for college-age women because of a spike in the injury that seems to occur as girls hit puberty. So let's imagine a hypothetical high school soccer team of twenty girls, a fairly typical roster size, and multiply it by the conservative estimate of 200 exposures a year. The result is exactly the magic number: 4,000 exposures. That means that in our cohort of twenty spirited soccer girls, one each year will tear an ACL and go through reconstructive surgery, long and painful rehabilitation, and the loss of a season—an eternity for a high schooler. Over the course of four years, four of the twenty girls on our team will rupture an ACL. (Again, perhaps a conservative estimate, since it is based on the ACL injury rates of older players.)

Each of them will likely experience what Hannafin calls "a grief reaction." "They've lost their sport," she says, "and they've lost the kinship of their friends, which is almost as bad as not being able to play."

If you are the parent of an athletic girl and live in a community that bustles with girls playing sports—especially the so-called "jumping and cutting" sports like soccer, basketball, volleyball, and lacrosse—it may seem that every couple of weeks you see or hear about some unfortunate young woman hobbling off the field and into the operating room. The first time, you think, What a stroke of bad luck. But you figure it won't happen to your daughter because, after all, what are the odds?

After a couple more ACL tears in the neighborhood, you get worried and think, Gosh, we must be in a really bad cluster for these injuries. Why here? But in all likelihood, what you are witnessing is not a freakish run of misfortune but rather the law of averages playing out.

Why do girls suffer knee injuries at greater rates than boys? And what can be done about it? Researchers are making progress on both those tracks, but the information has been slow—far too slow—to reach coaches and parents.

Amy Steadman is a particularly unfortunate example of all that can go wrong, but by no means a singular one. Young women with histories like hers are easy to find. I sat in a Starbucks in Rockville, Maryland, one day with Rachel Young, another former high school and college soccer player. She was wearing shorts, so when she turned in her chair, I could plainly see how much bigger her right knee was than her left.

She showed me all her surgical scars, a map of pain. "This is the first one," she said, pointing out a diagonal mark. "And here's where they took the patellar tendon," she said, showing me another mark where a surgeon had cut to extract tissue to use as raw material to construct a new ACL. "And here's these two tiny marks here. I'm not sure what they are, but I think that's just where they put in the arthroscope. And here's the other one" — another big diagonal scar, for a second ACL reconstruction. "It's pretty ugly, isn't it?" she said, wincing.

Rachel had recently undergone another surgery, a new and as yet unproven procedure to try to regenerate cartilage so her knee would no longer be what doctors call "bone on bone," which is just as bad as it sounds. She told me she wanted yet another surgery, "just so they can clean up the scar tissue and it won't look like this and I won't have as much clicking and popping."

I didn't really know what to say. I told her that my knees sort of click sometimes, from a lifetime of playing various sports. "But I'm just twenty-one," she said. "Mine shouldn't do that."

OF NECESSITY, female athletes and their advocates have had to keep a laser focus on one thing: making sure they have equal access to high school and college sports. Any thought that perhaps girls *were* different had to be banished from the collective groupthink, understandably, because it would be seized upon by the troglodytes who preferred women not to be equal. See? They can't go into battle. See? They can't hold office. And what about their mood swings when they get their period? They can't dunk, so what's the point of women's basketball?

It's pretty hard to battle these stereotypes while also broadcasting alarm about injuries that seem to suggest women are too delicate to play certain games or to play them at a high level of intensity. There are parallels in the workplace, where gender differences can easily be perceived as weakness. A woman must have maternity leave. She is the one more likely to press for on-site child care or ask for a quiet room to nurse her baby or pump milk. In high-powered settings like law firms, she may be less likely, over time, to want to work eighty hours a week. She does not always conform to the model of the default employee: a man.

A female athlete, similarly, is a different being from a male athlete, with different strengths and needs—but she must exist within an almost entirely male model. In adolescence, a young woman's body undergoes a general widening and softening process. Her weight-to-strength ratio is changing in a distinctly nonathletic way. This is as true as it is impolitic to say. For a boy, just the opposite occurs. With puberty comes a burst of testosterone. He adds lean muscle and, even without any particular effort, gets stronger.

Significantly, this divergence of the sexes occurs just at the age that we ask more of young athletes, especially if they show promise: play more, play harder, play faster, play for higher stakes. And we ask this of boys and girls equally—unmindful of physical differences.

This book will likely provoke argument, which I welcome. It may make some people angry, which is fine too. It might, in certain cases, be used by boys' wrestling coaches and other opponents of Title IX who believe, wrongly, that the revolution in women's sports has been a zero-sum game—that girls' gains have come at the expense of opportunities for boys. It is not my intent to further their argument. More boys are playing high school and college sports now than ever before. Title IX should be strengthened and enforced more vigorously, not less.

What *does* threaten women's sports, more so than a handful of wrestling coaches, is that far too many girls and young women are leaving the field broken up and in chronic pain. It's time for a mature, more informed, and more nuanced advocacy of women's athletics. Political correctness on this issue must be jettisoned. It gets in the way.

Experts in biomechanics know, conclusively, that many girls, even highly athletic ones, *run* differently than boys—with less knee bend and a more upright gait. They land harder from jumps and do not decelerate as safely when slowing down to cut. This difference appears to be a factor in ACL tears and almost certainly in other injuries as well—to the ankles, hips, and back.

There are programs that teach girls to run differently—that reprogram them, essentially, to run like boys. If you are the parent of a girl who plays sports, you need to know about this.

As important, we all need to think more deeply about the insanity of our youth sports culture, with its focus on early specialization in one sport and, especially, its seasons without end. Part of it is aspirational—deriving from parents' aspirations for their children. If a kid does one thing to excess, he'll get better at it, right? And part is connected to our culture's "more is more" ethos—our houses with ever more square footage, TVs with ever wider screens. So if a four-month season of one's sport of choice is good, then six months is better. Ten months is better yet. And twelve months: optimum. Except that it's not.

Young women in adolescence should keep playing sports and keep playing them hard. But they need to train better and smarter—and in ways that target gender-specific vulnerabilities. And they need to play fewer games. Shorter seasons. More varied sports.

The way children play sports in America is not particularly good for either sex. For the girls, though, it is all too often disastrous.

CHAPTER I

AMY

Amy Steadman was no cosseted suburban child. She grew up in the far western part of North Carolina amid scenic waterfalls and rugged rock formations, an excellent setting for a girl of her temperament. "She was wired at birth," her father, Ned, a high school science teacher, recalls. "She was inconsolable until she could walk, and as soon as she could walk, she ran. If she saw a hill, she took off and sprinted up it. It was just something within her."

Three-hour car trips took six hours because of the stops required to give her time to burn off energy. Her birthday parties were always the same: an overnight camping trip to a favored spot where she liked to dive off a fifty-foot ledge into a lake. For show-and-tell one day in the fourth grade, she came dressed as the football coach Knute Rockne. She begged her parents to visit the campus of Notre Dame, in South Bend, Indiana, until they finally relented. "She wanted to see the temple of football," her father says. "She loved football. She would have played that if she could."

She played sports in the school yard with friends, often as the only girl, and was not happy unless she returned home scraped up and caked in mud. She joined her first organized team in fourth grade, a boys' squad because her area had no girls' soccer, and it was not long before the coach was telling her parents they needed to find her a higher level of competition.

Don Scarborough, a college soccer coach who happened to be coaching Amy because his son was on the team, believed she played as if the game had been preprogrammed into her. "It was almost like she could play soccer before she ever got on a soccer field, you know what I mean? You could throw a ball at her feet or body or head and she intuitively could handle it. She didn't need to train to learn a skill; she got it the first time. She needed something beyond what our county parks-and-recreation league could offer her."

Ned Steadman had run track and was still an avid hiker, but neither he nor his wife, Carol, had ever been high-performing athletes. Their daughter was a marvel and a mystery to them. Where had she come upon those bountiful gifts? Carol's father and two brothers were good ballplayers, so the Steadmans joked that maybe the athletic genes had skipped a generation and Amy got them.

At first, they had had no interest in rearranging their lives just for the sake of Amy's soccer. They had another child, a younger son. Ned had his teaching, and Carol worked as an aide at the local elementary school. It took two years for them to finally put her into a girls' league in Asheville, which was forty-five minutes away. There they almost immediately began to hear the same refrain from coaches: This isn't enough for her. You need to put her with better players.

"It all began mushrooming," Ned Steadman says. "Other people saw what was coming way before we did. She was probably in the third grade when the pediatrician said after he examined her, 'I'll see you in the Olympics.' I said, 'Please don't say that.' I'd been around high schools and heard that said of kids, and it was never true."

In junior high school, Amy began playing for the Greensboro Twisters, a top club team halfway across the state, two and a half hours away. By the time she reached high school, she was playing for a team in Atlanta, four hours away. Don Scarborough teased Ned: "You didn't want to take her to Asheville, and now Amy's playing in Atlanta?"

Ned Steadman took most of those long drives with his daughter— all through the Southeast and as far away as Dallas. He would try to talk about the game on the way home—to rehash and analyze it and perhaps learn more about a sport he knew little about—but she was rarely interested. Sometimes Amy would say, "I played OK," which Ned learned to translate as "I played great." Usually she was quiet in the car. She listened to music on her headphones or slept. It was not false modesty on Amy's part or even teenage sullenness. She was spent. And truly not interested in the periphery of sport, the rankings and the awards and accolades. That was for others. For her, it was all about the personal competition, not the postgame commentary.

Ned and Carol Steadman were immensely proud of their daughter's accomplishments but ambivalent about her fierce independence. They certainly had not pushed her into soccer, and she was the opposite of one of those kids of whom you had to wonder, Is she playing to please her parents or because she truly loves it? She loved it.

But as Amy rose into the elite levels, she inhabited a world her parents could not enter. She was guided by coaches, mentors, and her own passion. It was not that different from what happens with a lot of good young athletes as they climb the ranks of their sport— their decisions, increasingly, are directed from outside the home. Often mothers and fathers hesitate to be too involved, not wanting to be seen as clamoring or insistent—as stereotypical sports parents. It is a difficult thing to balance: coaches may know a sport, but they are rarely the best judges of what is best for a child.

The Steadmans watched and listened from a respectful distance, picking up what they could. Amy was not a mystery to them: they knew what she cared about and what motivated her; they knew that her deepest passion was her sport. It was just that she kept the details to herself. "We didn't know too much about the soccer," Carol said. "She was her own person." Ned adds, "That's the way she wanted it, and we respected that."

The local newspapers—the *Transylvania Times* in her hometown of Brevard and the bigger *Citizen-Times* in Asheville—picked up on her story as she began to climb the ranks of U.S. soccer and make national teams. "She Packs a Big Kick," one of the headlines said. After she set conference records at a track meet and was named "high school athlete of the week," the story noted how remarkable her performance was, considering that all her soccer travel barely left her time to train for sprinting. She just dropped in on track meets and dominated.

Amy, as always, was thoroughly unimpressed by it all. She cared about the next game, about winning every single "one v. one situation," as she called them—every race in which she and an opponent were in furious pursuit of the ball and the victor would be determined by speed and heart. That's what soccer was for her: one challenge after another, each of them deeply personal. "All those write-ups and other hoo-hah, they don't mean anything," she told her father. "They don't get you playing time."

Anson Dorrance loved everything about Amy's game. "Her discipline was off the charts," he says. "She had speed and a high pain threshold. She took physical risks—she was fearless. This is a positive problem. You want players who are hell-bent for leather. And she had a sophistication to her game. She knew how it was supposed to be played. She had everything you could possibly want. She was a coach's dream."

He got a particular kick out of Amy's being a state high school sprint champion, observing, "Not bad for a white chick."

For all her love of mixing it up on the field, Amy was a wholesome-looking beauty, unadorned and natural looking, very much the girl next door if the girl next door would bury you on her way to a soccer ball. Her loveliness made the nickname she acquired playing soccer all the funnier: "the Killer."

In addition to being a fast runner, Amy was a young woman in a big hurry. In the middle of her sophomore year of high school, she took the SATs and scored a perfect 800 on the math portion. She decided early in her junior year to forgo the rest of high school and enroll at North Carolina. Other talented female players had done the same at various NCAA schools, including former UNC star Mia Hamm, who arrived in Chapel Hill in what would have been her senior year of high school. While it would be difficult for a boy that young to compete on equal footing with a twenty-two-year-old college senior, it is far easier for young women, who by that age are further along in their physical maturity.

Amy's force of will was so strong that no one could ever really stand in its way. One of her elementary school teachers told the Steadmans they had never seen such a focused child. "She was intense in everything she did," Ned says. "She set getting the 800 in her math SATs as a goal. As soon as the scores were available, we had to call the test center to see if she had accomplished it."

By the time Dorrance suggested that she leave high school early and come to Chapel Hill, her parents were accustomed to letting her make her own choices. The coach assured them that she was ready athletically and academically. "I realized at that point that Amy's dreams are going to be realized," her father recalls.

All her parents asked was, Are you sure this is what you want? But they knew she had already made up her mind.

By that time, Amy was already a seasoned veteran of youth national teams and had competed internationally in England, Sweden, and the Netherlands. She had been playing with the American team that would compete in the first women's under-nineteen World Cup in Vancouver, and although a final roster for that tournament was not yet set, she was one of the core players and seemed to have a guaranteed slot. "I kept doing well at every one of the training camps," she says. "Some girls would be invited in once, but then not for the next one, but I never really had that problem." When she wasn't training with the national team, she still played for her club team in Atlanta — and it was in a game for her club, before she could set off for Chapel Hill, that she first hurt her knee.

AMY RECOUNTED her injury history for me as we sat on a couch in a lounge area of the Dean Smith Center, UNC's indoor athletic complex. She was twenty-one years old, five years past her first ACL tear. She lived just a short walk across campus, but her boyfriend had dropped her off because she was not moving comfortably. Later, when she could not reach him by cell phone for a ride, I asked if she wanted me to drive her back, and she said, quietly, "Yeah, I guess I do."

That first day we talked for close to three hours. Her tone at first was flat and unemotional, which I soon realized was her way of trying to maintain her composure. What caught me off guard was my own reaction: I can remember no other time in three decades in journalism when I have had to fight back tears of my own during the course of an entire interview.

"It was a miserable game and we weren't playing well," Amy began, describing the club game in Atlanta. "So my coach just decided to throw me up top" — move her from defense, her usual position, to striker. "There were like ten minutes left. With me being fast or whatever, he wanted to see if I could make something happen.

"It was really surreal the way it happened. A ball was being played in to me, and I jumped in the air because it was high. As I kicked it, the defender pushed me in the back. It wasn't a real hard push, but I landed on one leg, my right leg, and I could just feel it hyperextend. I didn't hear anything, but I felt something. It was more than a pop."

She had probably landed in similar fashion—on one leg and off balance—dozens or perhaps hundreds of times before with no negative result. But this one time would be life changing.

"I lay on the ground, but it didn't hurt that much. So I got up and tried to keep playing, but every time I came down on my right leg, it was like there was no support. It collapsed underneath me. There were like five minutes left in the game, so the coaches took me out and helped me over to the sidelines, and people were saying that maybe I'd just strained it. I didn't know enough to think differently, so I was hoping that was the case."

She sat on the bench for the few minutes until the game concluded, then hobbled to the car for the four-hour drive home with her father. About halfway, they made a rest stop. "I didn't notice my knee swelling until then," she recalled. "But when I got up to go to the bathroom, it was just huge and I couldn't walk. I knew I had done something pretty bad, but I didn't know too much about ACLs. I figured I would get it looked at and they'd tell me what the problem was. In Brevard, things move kind of slow, so it took like two weeks to get an MRI and for them to tell me I'd torn my ACL. So at that point, I had to call Anson and the national team coaches and tell them what happened."

Amy underwent reconstructive surgery in early November 2001, a couple of months after turning seventeen. Her surgeon grafted a new ACL from part of her patellar tendon in the same knee. The U-19 World Cup was scheduled for late the following summer, less than ten months away. And after that, she was to begin her first season as a Tar Heel—a member of the famed UNC women's soccer team.

"To be on that World Cup team was my ultimate goal at the time," Amy says. "I just wanted it so bad. I had ten months to recover and get back to close to 100 percent, or I wasn't going to make the team. I still had two months at home before going to UNC. I couldn't run yet, but I rode the bike and I swam. I worked out like three or four hours a day. I was really determined, and being so young, I didn't know anything about patience. So I was doing this really, really aggressive rehab program."

In her understated way, Amy says that she had "a lot of complications with that first one." What she describes sounds more like a nightmare than a set of complications. "They give you pain pills, and basically, I unknowingly got addicted to them. I was in so much pain that I couldn't sleep without them, so I took them regularly. I couldn't go to school for like two or three weeks, because I couldn't keep anything down. Everything I put in my mouth came right up.

"I finally had to be hospitalized and get an IV because I was dehydrated, and I got a huge lecture from the nurses about how I had to eat. I went down to a hundred and five pounds from a hundred and twenty pounds. I could do upper-body work at the gym, but I felt like all the weight came out of my legs because I couldn't do anything with them yet. It was like my legs were wasting away."

After that first injury, Amy says, "I probably screamed at my parents a couple of times. It's not like it was their fault, and I should have never done it. But I was just overall angry."

Her parents watched in awe as she pushed herself through rehabilitation, even as they had misgivings about her pace. The trainer for the UNC women's team, Bill Prentice, had sent an "accelerated rehab schedule," Ned Steadman recalls. "The physical therapist here in Brevard looked at it and said, 'Whoa.' But she wanted to be back on that U-Nineteen team, and that's what was necessary."

In the initial couple of weeks after surgery, ACL rehab consists mostly of excercises to restore the range of motion in the injured leg.

One example: lie on your back, grasp the backs of both thighs, pull them to the chest—easy for someone with a healthy knee but painful for a patient just off surgery. The exercises are meant to be done intermittently throughout the day, starting out with relatively few repetitions, so that the recovering patient can gain strength and flexibility while leaving time for rest and healing. But Amy made her accelerated regimen even more ambitious by doubling or tripling the recommended number of repetitions for each exercise. It was the same with the stationary bicycle. When she was allowed to start pedaling it an hour a day, she went at it hard for two hours.

Ned remembers thinking, I'm tough, but I'm not as tough as she is. Asking her to back off would have been pointless.

Amy says, "If anyone would have told me after that first one that I should stop and do something different, play a different sport or whatever, or slow down my rehab, I would have said, 'You know what? The hell with you. I'm going to do this.' Nobody could have stopped me. Girls are so strong-willed when they're young, and to explain to them that they have this vulnerability—it wouldn't work. We're like guys in that way. Even girls I know who have had their first or second ACL—they think it won't happen again, and that they'll be back one hundred percent and it won't affect their lives."

After the lecture from the nurses, Amy began to put weight back on and regain her tone and strength. At the turn of the year, she moved to Chapel Hill to begin classes, during what would have been her junior year of high school, and she now had new teammates, as well as Dorrance, to push her. The UNC coach believed deeply in international soccer and wanted his players to compete for the U.S. teams, so Amy's ambition to get healthy in time for Vancouver was Dorrance's goal for her as well.

"The things I needed to get back were my speed and agility, and I worked a lot in the weight room," she says. The day she was cleared to finally begin running, she didn't set off on a light jog; she did a full sprint set. After five months of being unable to touch a ball, she felt that she had lost timing, so Dorrance took her back out on the field and personally put her through workouts. "Once they started letting me play," Amy says, "I just played every chance I could get. The thing I needed to do was get back my speed and agility. In Brevard, I had to do everything on my own, but here I had Anson and all these team-mates to help me. I just felt so thankful."

That summer, the U-19 team gathered to train for a couple of weeks in Chula Vista, California. Amy needed not only to make the team but also to win back her starting position. The coach had changed the team's formation into a more attacking mode, so there were only three rather than four spots for defenders. "They said to me, 'We pretty much have our back three set.' It was disappointing."

Instead, she was given an opportunity to play left midfield. She wasn't sure about the position, because it involved much more run-ning of the field, but she quickly grew to like it because it gave her an opportunity to score goals. "But it was heartbreaking for me because the girl who was supposed to be in that spot, she tore her ACL and she was out for the tournament. So that's how it became open for me."

There were other ACL victims and survivors. Out of the original forty in the "player pool" under consideration for that U-19 team, ten suffered ACL injuries in the two years between the time they were put into the pool and the tournament—one out of every four. Some, like Amy, had made it back onto the field; others were still rehabbing and out for the tournament.

In Chula Vista, twenty players competed to be among a final eighteen who would compete in Canada. Amy remembers being called into a room after the final decision had been made. "They said to us, 'You're the team.' At that point, you start to bond with those girls 24/7. I was so excited."

She had not only won back a starting position but was named captain, a remarkable accomplishment for a young woman who not that long before had been so debilitated that she needed to be hooked up to an IV. Amy felt as though she had climbed an enormous mountain. All the pain had paid off. The team flew from its training camp to Seattle, then took a ferry into Canada. "I was so excited," she says. "It was just going to be the coolest thing ever."

CHAPTER 2

WARRIOR GIRLS

Just outside Anson Dorrance's office at the University of North Carolina is a sort of wall of fame, a long hallway hung with retired jerseys of some of his former players. Mia Hamm. Kristine Lilly. April Heinrichs. Carla Overbeck. Trisha Venturini. Legends of U.S. women's soccer. As we talked one afternoon, he gazed out his open door toward this gallery. "She would have been one of those jerseys out there," he said, referring to Amy Steadman. "She didn't get to play nearly enough while she was here, but she was one of the greatest players I ever coached."

Dorrance, like any coach, appreciates skilled play and is thrilled to have any young woman who through pure wizardry with the ball can weave her way through a thicket of defenders and place a shot into the corner of the goal. But he puts as high a value on players who will run over, rather than around, opponents. At the top levels of sport, Dorrance believes, skills even out, and the teams that prevail do so on pride, courage, and a willingness to put their bodies in harm's way. He comes from a military family, and his outlook on life and sports is distinctly martial. He recalls that as an undersized and not overly skilled soccer player, "I absolutely loved crashing into people."

As coach of U.S. national teams in the early 1990s, Dorrance did not initially take to Brandi Chastain, who scored the deciding penalty kick to defeat China and win the World Cup in 1999 and then, memorably, stripped to her sports bra. "He preferred the thundering, lashing muscularity of Michelle Akers and April Heinrichs to the clever, aesthetic, nifty skill of Chastain," Jere Longman wrote in *The Girls of Summer*, his account of the 1999 World Cup.

Dorrance did not coach that 1999 World Cup team—Tony DiCicco did—but eight of the twenty players on the roster had competed for him at North Carolina, and he coached another three on various national teams. The squad consisted largely of Dorrance's players, and his *kind* of players—Warrior Girls to the core. Ponytails, yes. Spunky and spirited, check. Marvelous teammates to one another, absolutely. And above all, immensely appealing to an American public hungry for role models for their active, empowered daughters. Here were women who knew what they wanted and knew how to go get it. And if someone else had what they coveted, they were not shy about seizing it.

When the women on that World Cup team praised one another, they rarely mentioned their teammates' skills. "She reminds me of a football player. She just wants to get in there and make contact," one teammate said of Kate Sobrero. The great Michelle Akers, who fought through numerous injuries as well as chronic fatigue syndrome, was known, admiringly, as "a beast, a savage warrior." And Carla Overbeck, the team captain: "Her eyes could burn through your soul."

Colleen Hacker, who was the team psychologist for the 1999 World Cup squad, observes that "from the earliest levels in girls' sports, up through the elite and Olympic level, how one plays the sport, how one comports oneself, is talked about in specific ways that transcend technical or tactical expertise. It is more overt with the girls than the boys. Character counts. Physical toughness, mental toughness, and handling adversity count."

Not every suburban soccer mom would have wanted her little girl eavesdropping on the pregame conversations among Mia Hamm and the gals. Here was team captain Overbeck, as reported by Longman, before a grudge match against Norway: "The only thing between us and the trophy is that team. Let's go fuck 'em up."

Toughness and raw, primal aggression are an essential part of sport—men's or women's sport, boys' or girls'. Watch from the sideline of a game of five-year-olds playing soccer. The kid who is willing to plow into the pile—risking his own bloody nose or skinned knee, and more than willing to inflict that fate on others—dominates. Sports, at a base level, is always war. Competitors battle for the ball and fight to advance it toward a goal. Games are hard fought to the point of violence. Who will keep going beyond exhaustion and who will quit? Who will be the intimidator and who the intimidated? Who will shrink from injury and who will play on? You can't play the game, any game, unless you can take a little pain.

There is a difference, though, between playing through some pain and worshipping pain. The latter is a distinctly male model, and a pretty old one—the model of the National Football League, circa 1958, in which pain that cannot be denied is dulled with a pill or a cortisone shot and then, after the contest, quieted with more pills, chased by Jack Daniel's.

Writer Tim Crothers spent nearly four years observing Dorrance for a book on the coach and his program, *The Man Watching,* at one point even serving as an assistant coach. He quotes the North Carolina coach at a season-end event at which he reads aloud from letters he has written to departing seniors, recalling memories of their previous four years, including this one to Amy Whittier, who had defied doctors and returned to competition after a broken back. "The next image was you as a sophomore on a stretcher after they put those rods in to repair your broken back," Dorrance says. "And where are you? You're not in the hospital. You're on the sidelines with us. Part of our team.

"The most recent image brings it all back together. It was this year, and like your freshman year, we were wondering out loud if any of our starting forwards would take any kind of risk to help us win. We asked you if you would take a risk. You survived Lyme disease as a child, a broken back on the soccer field as a young college kid, and a medical dismissal as an old college kid when doctors told you that you could never play again. So if you did not want to take the risk anymore, it was OK. You earned the right to quietly decline, but you said yes, you'd take a risk to help the team win."

I asked Dorrance why he would congratulate a kid for ignoring medical advice. "She wanted to play," he explained. "We weren't going to get in her way. She wanted to take risks. That was the definition of who she was. In contact sports, that's the dimension that separates the truly extraordinary. The people who make these choices and take these risks are valuable athletes. To be completely honest, it's one of the things I like about contact sports. It's exciting. The willingness to take a risk is basically someone living an incredibly passionate life."

Even now, women's sport is still in its formative stage. Toughness and courage cannot be assumed; that's why those qualities are so talked about. You can sink the three-pointer or execute a mind-blowing crossover dribble? Fine, but can you take an elbow to the mouth, or give one? At the highest levels, even in Dorrance's program, which attracts the best of the best, female athletes must still prove their bona fides. How much can they endure? Who will step up and who will back down?

Crothers observed a preseason scrimmage in which new arrivals to Dorrance's program are roughed up by his older players. One of them explains her reasoning for basically picking a freshman up and throwing her to the turf. "There was a message," she says. "This is our program and this is how we play. How are you going to deal with it?"

More often it is Dorrance delivering the messages, and they are often raw. As Crothers relates at halftime of a game in which his team is performing poorly, Dorrance tells them, "Stick your head in there so they're leaving their fucking teeth in the back of their skull, and then look at that girl and say, 'How does that feel, bitch?' "

DORRANCE'S MANTRA, what he tells his players at the start of each season, is this: The UNC women's soccer team does not pass the ball backward. It does not pass it "square," side to side. He could recruit mediocre athletes to play like that. They're a dime a dozen, he tells his teams. "We play the ball forward," he says. "We attack."

Any female soccer player of Amy Steadman's caliber is almost sure to either enroll at North Carolina to play for Dorrance or give it strong consideration. For Amy, there was never really a question. UNC was her state school, and she was Dorrance's kind of player: a superior athlete with more grit than polish. Even now, she downplays her technical abilities. "My skills were not very good," she says, although others would disagree with this assessment. "Other girls came from different kinds of areas where they started playing younger and had all this coaching before I did. I was just faster than everyone. That was my main quality. I ran track, and I won like eight championships. And I was always a tomboy growing up, and playing soccer I was really aggressive. It didn't bother me to get bruises or rip my shirt or that type of thing."

Across the board, women's sport is moving in Anson Dorrance's direction. In Amy Steadman's direction. They may be extreme, but they are not outliers.

Nancy Theberge, a sociologist at Waterloo University in Ontario, Canada, is among the most provocative writers on gender and sports.

In *Higher Goals: Women's Ice Hockey and the Politics of Gender*, a book she wrote after following a women's team for two years, she observes, "Historically, femininity and athleticism have been constructed in opposition, yielding the conventional wisdom that great sport was men's sport and the corresponding view that women are intruders in the world of sport."

So how do women prove their merit and earn a place on the field? How do they justify their scholarships, their inclusion on the sports pages, their paychecks in pro leagues, and even a piece of the endorsement money? The same way men do. They suck it up. They indulge in what Theberge calls the "normalization of injury and pain."

Playing hurt, Theberge writes in an article in the journal *Sport in Society*, has long been recognized "as a way for men to validate their masculine and athletic identities." Women's sport increasingly dwells in "the valorization of pain and injury," she says, "compelling evidence of the incorporation of women into the dominant model of men's sport."

Is it possible, I asked Theberge, that women have actually become *more* accepting of injury than men and more willing to endure pain and risk lifelong consequences? "It is," she said. "What's that old expression from the sixties? A woman needs to be twice as good as a man."

Leslie Gaston, another former UNC player, has a history of knee troubles like Amy Steadman's, only even more extensive. Leslie became legendary for what she could endure. The *Durham Herald Sun* in 2002 ran a feature story on her under the headline "Unbended Knees: Despite 11 Operations, UNC's Leslie Gaston Refuses to Bow to the Numerous Knee Injuries That Have Threatened to End Her Career."

The story itemized parts of Gaston's anatomy that had been used to form grafts to repair her knees: snippets of her left and right hamstring tendons, a part of her right quadriceps tendon. A teammate complimented her as the "ultimate gladiator," and Leslie referred to herself as a "medical miracle" and someone who is able to "react very well to physical pain."

By the time I met Leslie, she was twenty-six years old, working as an advertising saleswoman at the *Atlanta Journal Constitution*, and coaching a couple of girls' soccer teams. Miraculously, she had managed to play four seasons of college soccer, rotating back into the lineup just as quickly as she could recover from her latest surgery.

Like Amy Steadman, Leslie Gaston arrived for her first semester at UNC fresh off an ACL injury suffered in high school soccer. Her surgeon, at the same time he was reconstructing her right knee, began what he believed would be a minor procedure on her left knee to carve away some loose cartilage. He discovered that the ACL in that knee too was ruptured; one week later, he reconstructed it. "It was like two birds with one stone," Leslie says. "Double ACL surgery. I went to college two weeks later and started class with full leg braces. I couldn't bend either knee. I had lost about twenty-five pounds."

Leslie sat out her freshman season. Back on the field in the spring, she tore an ACL again. "I think the left one," she says. "This is where it all gets foggy."

She played the following fall, suffered yet another ACL rupture—her fourth—decided against immediate surgery, and played with a bulky brace stabilizing her knee. UNC was driving toward another national championship, and Gaston was able to contribute a useful, if painful, ten or fifteen minutes a game. She didn't want to miss the experience or let the team down. "I was what they call ACL deficient," she says, "but I wasn't really risking any further long-term injury. That had already happened."

A player who competes without an ACL is called a "coper." They usually cannot play at their former level in that condition, or for very long.

Leslie tried to catalog the rest of the knee injuries she incurred during her time at UNC. Meniscus tears. Two more ACL reconstructions. A few "minor things" she could not put a name to but that required surgery. She would call her parents each time she learned she needed more surgery. They took it harder than she did. "That's the last thing a parent ever wants for their children, more operations," she says. "But they knew I wanted to play and that it was the thing that made me happy."

Dorrance's program at North Carolina is obsessive about fitness; he wants players who can run endlessly, who will win balls after their opponents have wearied and quit. He gives fitness tests in the preseason—distance runs as well as a crushing series of sprints on short rest. His players take pride in how they stack up against their teammates. Leslie rarely did well on these tests, and often did not pass and had to repeat them just to earn playing time. "When you have to make them up, it's not really the punishment of doing it again as much as the peer pressure you feel," she says. "Everyone knows you didn't pass. It's a bad feeling."

One explanation for her unsatisfying performance was that she rarely was healthy enough to train. She could not build aerobic capacity. But she saw it another way—she blamed herself, deciding that the *reason* she kept getting injured was that she wasn't fit. She began training like a madwoman. "Going into my junior year, I wanted to play and I didn't want any more injuries. I trained my butt off. I was determined I was going to pass those tests. It was a personal goal. I ran. I lifted. I went at it like four or five hours a day, and then I played pickup games in the afternoon."

Leslie won a starting position and by her junior season was no longer just playing for short stretches. She played in the NCAA championship game against Santa Clara. The team lost, but for Gaston, it was a quiet, personal victory—she was on the field for all ninety minutes. Her teammates voted her cocaptain before her senior season. She played injury free until just before the NCAA tournament. "I think it was a meniscus tear again. I took a couple of weeks off and was able to play through it."

Miraculously, after she graduated, Gaston even played a couple of seasons of pro soccer. Her surgery count eventually reached twelve—or possibly more, since she is not sure she remembers them all. Some biomechanical or anatomical flaw led to her series of injuries. An immense pain threshold and iron determination—along with prodigious powers of recovery—allowed her to keep going.

"I hung up my cleats a couple of months ago," Leslie said in 2007. "I decided it was time to focus on my quality of life twenty years down the road. I can't say I'm a hundred percent pain free, but I think I've developed a high threshold for pain. Different people handle pain in different ways, and I have been able to handle it pretty well. Does it interfere with what I want to do? Not really. I went to Paris and all I did was walk for seven days."

I asked if she had knee pain. "I have no cartilage left. Both ACLs are deficient. So I do. It's inevitable in my case. But if I had to do it all over again, I wouldn't change anything. I know that sounds strange. But all the injuries have shaped my character and life in a way that I never thought something as devastating as having five ACLs could. I know whatever obstacles I face, I can get through them."

Dr. William Garrett, who performed some (although not all) of the surgeries on Amy Steadman and Leslie Gaston, is a pioneer in ACL research. He's short, strong-looking man with a helmet of graying hair that makes him look like the former Dallas Cowboys football coach Jimmy Johnson. Younger colleagues tend to revere him. I have heard him described as "the godfather of ACL research" and as the progenitor of a kind of informal ACL think tank, a web of researchers who either trained under him or expanded on his research. He serves as the medical director for the United States Soccer Federation and is a past president of the American Orthopaedic Society for Sports Medicine.

Garrett is self-effacing, comfortable enough with his stature to project the friendly, down-home manner of a country doctor who just happens to have found his way to the nearest big city. He grew up in the tiny town of Bahama, North Carolina, north of Durham. "Where I live now," he says, "is less than thirty miles from any other place I've ever lived."

He is currently a professor of orthopedic surgery and coordinator of sports-medicine research at Duke. Garrett began doing ACL surgeries after his residency, at age thirty-two and figures he has performed well over one thousand of them. His research grew out of his clinical practice. In the early 1990s, he began noticing that an increasing number of his ACL patients were young women. At the time, ACL tears were still considered primarily a football injury, something that occurred after a shoulder pad or helmet came slamming into a running back's knee. The injury was so devastating that it seemed intuitive that it had to be caused by something pretty violent. But most of the women who were streaming into his office—sometimes he saw several new cases a week—had suffered noncontact ACL tears.

At most, they had experienced what the medical literature on ACL injuries refers to by a strange word—*perturbation*. The root of this word is *perturb*. In this context, it means that an athlete has been thrown off balance, or perturbed—physically or even just mentally—in the instant just before the ACL rupture. She is pushed, or even just jostled slightly, so that she lands awkwardly. Or there has been an element of surprise—an intercepted pass or an opponent breaking free—that prompts a sudden stop and a change in direction. It all happens in a flash.

The nature of the injury explains why it occurs so frequently in two sports: soccer and basketball. They are what I would call

360-degree sports—panoramic field games in which the action can be occurring from any direction, including from behind. A greater number of variables are at play than in a more scripted game like, say, softball. There are more unexpected changes of direction, more opportunities for perturbation, than even in a jumping, high-speed sport like volleyball. (Skiing, gymnastics, and cheerleading are also sports with high rates of ACL tears and other major orthopedic injuries. But they also are sports with well-known risks, featuring movements like skidding down icy mountains, somersaults off human pyramids, or cartwheels on thin balance beams.)

Garrett studied men's and women's soccer in the Atlantic Coast Conference and found that women were suffering ACL ruptures at a rate at least eight times that of men, based on their injuries per athletic exposure. The article was published in the *Southern Medical Journal,* after being rejected elsewhere. "I submitted it to one of the more famous journals," Garrett says as he sits behind the desk in his office, with pictures of his children and grandchildren on a shelf behind him. "The reaction was, 'Who cares?' This was some years back, keep in mind. Maybe the thought was that it's just a bunch of girls playing sports."

To the extent that there *was* research about ACLs, it tended to focus on surgical techniques. "What gets emphasized is what somebody gets paid for," Garrett says. "They are not paying doctors to prevent ACL injuries. There's no money in it."

A cynic might question Garrett's surgical artistry, since the knees of Steadman and Gaston kept ripping back apart after he had surgically reconstructed them. But no one I talked to expressed any doubt about his skills, and I came across numerous other young women—patients of other highly regarded doctors—with the same pattern of repeated tears. The first three of Leslie's surgeries were not even performed by Garrett, but were done in her native Alabama, while she was still in high school, by the most renowned orthopedic surgeon in America—James Andrews, a name familiar to any regular reader of a newspaper sports page. Andrews operates on and offers second opinions to scores of multimillionaire pro athletes, many of whom do not feel they have exhausted all possibilities until they have paid him a visit in Birmingham. (His patients have included Michael Jordan, Derek Jeter, and Jack Nicklaus.)

Surgeons like Garrett and Andrews are highly skilled practitioners, not miracle workers. They have refined their techniques for repairing ACLs to the point that most athletes believe that within a year of surgery, they will be as good as new. "The horror stories like Amy's and Leslie's are not huge in number, but nevertheless they exist," Garrett says. "I just had a gal who was six months out from her first ACL. She just started playing again, and did the other one in her first game. That's not uncommon, I have to tell you. It's not the norm, but it's not one in a million."

LESLIE GASTON is one of Anson Dorrance's favorite players. "I respect a lot of athletes who come through here, but no one do I have greater admiration for than Leslie Gaston," he told me. "She has unbelievable physical courage. If I had to go to Iraq, she's the one I'd want on my left shoulder and the one I'd want to be in a foxhole with. I wouldn't pick some Navy SEAL. She is that tough. She's who I would want to go to war with."

When I repeated this to Garrett, he winced. "Maybe now he would want to be in the foxhole with her," he said. "But in twenty years or so, he would probably have to help her out of that foxhole."

CHAPTER 3

INCONVENIENT TRUTHS

A young woman who suffers a serious athletic injury responds in an intensely personal way and has a limited capacity for reflection or self-protection. She is in pain—physical as well as emotional, because she has lost the thing she loves—and her response is to rehab as quickly as possible and get back on the field. "Even when I learned more later on, whatever facts or statistics somebody brought up, I didn't think any of it applied to me," Amy Steadman says. "I thought, I'm different. I can do it. Just let me get through this and I'll be good to go."

I asked Rachel Young, the former Virginia Tech soccer player, how many other young women she knew who had suffered ACL tears. She started tabulating the various players from her high school team, club team, and college team with the injury, along with young women from other teams that she knew less well. But she quit when she ran out of fingers. Did her teammates and friends ever talk about what was happening or wonder about the reasons or possible prevention strategies? "Not really," she said. "ACL is like a curse word. You just cringe when you hear it."

The most ardent advocates for women's sports—who know how important competition is for girls and have long been on the front lines of the fight for full inclusion—are the ones who should be out front sounding the alarm. They should be campaigning for more research and more education of female athletes about what steps to take to reduce the risk of injuries. But many of those most heavily invested in the cause of women's sport have been silent on this subject.

Donna Lopiano has been perhaps the most prominent activist for women's sports, an icon of the movement. She was a terrific athlete herself, having participated in twenty-six national championships in four different collegiate sports—softball, basketball, volleyball, and field hockey. For seventeen years, she served as athletic director for women's sports at the University of Texas, and she led the Women's Sports Foundation from 1992 until retiring in 2007. When Title IX came under attack, it was Lopiano who trudged to the Hill to testify before Congress, and her forceful, cogent voice was quoted frequently in the media.

But when I talked to Lopiano, the issue of injuries was of no urgency to her. Yes, she's seen some of the research indicating that women have some specific vulnerabilities, but she is not moved by it—certainly not moved to action. She is waiting for better science.

"The foundation's concern is that there be solid science," she told me. "There is reason to question the assumptions that women as opposed to men are more susceptible to injury, for whatever reason. You have to keep in mind, women have been exposed to all kinds of myths. It was said if we ran, we would damage our reproductive system. So there has to be caution."

Lopiano told me that when she was in charge of women's athletics at the University of Texas, back in the early 1990s, there had been a "spate" of ACL tears among female athletes—right around the time it was first suspected that women were especially at risk. "We had a research group put together to see if there were common factors, and the answer was zero. They could not find a cause and effect. The only suggested link was fatigue over time. Here were women who had never had access to a weight room, and all of a sudden we put them in an Olympic-quality training program, which they tolerated really well, but they suspected the outcome was fatigue. It wasn't definite, but they said we should think about that."

The Women's Sports Foundation is not sponsoring or participating in any research on sports injuries. "We don't fund physiological research," Lopiano explained, adding that it tends to be too expensive. "We have not gone into that piece. We do signature research ourselves, mainly on social and cultural differences in terms of treatment of the sexes and public policy."

When the Women's Sports Foundation gets inquiries from female athletes on injuries, it refers them to the National Athletic Trainers' Association or to the women's sports clinic at the Hospital for Special Surgery in New York. It has no resource information on its Web site specifically about ACL injuries, other than a single article entitled "Women More Susceptible to ACL Injuries." There is also an indirect mention, oddly, in a question-and-answer section under a link dealing with "Issues Relating to Pregnancy and Athletic Participation":

Q: What are an athlete's rights to eligibility for obtaining, renewing, or maintaining a scholarship in event of a pregnancy?

A: Pregnant female athlete should receive the same treatment as any other athlete with a temporary medical condition (such as an ACL injury), in regards to eligibility and scholarships.

That's it. One article and one parenthetical phrase—and a questionable phrase at that, since an ACL injury is probably not best described as a temporary medical condition. (Nor, for that matter, is pregnancy best described as that. They both have long-term consequences.)

Lopiano believes that if, in fact, an imbalance in injury rates between the sexes exists, it is not unexpected. "Not when you look at the relatively recent admission of girls into high-powered sport," she says. Her hope is that the imbalance will even out over time as women gain more experience, have better access to training, and get stronger and fitter.

There is some logic to what she says, but it would seem to apply more to sports that women have just started to play and that do not have strong organizational foundations or a base of trained coaches — women's ice hockey, for example, or lacrosse. But the sports-medicine community has known about the high ACL rates for almost twenty years, as two generations of young women have cycled through youth, high school, and college athletics. "We know more, but it's made no difference in the injury rate," says U.S. Air Force Major Anthony Beutler, an ACL researcher and assistant professor at the School of Medicine of the Uniformed Services University, in Bethesda, Maryland, which trains doctors for the military.

One reason it has made no difference, I believe, is that while the information is well known to certain sets of people — college coaches, orthopedic surgeons, physical therapists and athletic trainers, regular readers of *The American Journal of Sports Medicine* and *The Journal of Bone and Joint Surgery* — parents of girls are still in the dark. Their daughters play constantly, but they have no idea of what may happen and how to lessen their risk.

I asked Lopiano, Isn't there a need for someone to loudly broadcast to female athletes that they may face specific peril — and that there are preventive programs targeted for them?

"You're going to do that," she replied.

•   •   •

"NOT EVERYONE wants to talk about this," says Sandra Shultz, who teaches graduate courses in athletic training and sports medicine at UNC Greensboro. "It depends on what side of the fence you're on. If your job is to encourage inclusion of more women in sport, maybe you are not going to accentuate the negative. You don't want to paint women in a negative light and tell a girl that if you play sports, your knees, by the time you are twenty-five, may be in bad shape.

"But intuitively, people know it. You can't hide the elephant in the room even if you want to. As a researcher and a clinician, I'm willing to talk about these things so we can do something about them. That's the goal. We don't want to tell girls not to play and have them become fat. We already have a terrible obesity epidemic. But we don't want to just accept some of these injuries."

Shultz, codirector of the Applied Neuromechanics Research Laboratory at Greensboro, has conducted some of the most extensive research on ACL injuries, including studies of whether hormones play a role in the higher rates among women. As an athletic trainer, she has seen a full range of injuries.

I asked her about injuries other than ACLs that women athletes also seem to suffer in greater measure than men—chronic ankle sprains, patellofemoral syndrome (pain around the kneecap), hip pain, and back pain. She believes that all of them, including ACL ruptures, likely flow from some of the same causes: women's lesser strength, particularly in the muscles that control the hips; a tendency toward a more upright running posture; and a more anterior tilt of the pelvis, which can cause the knees and back to hyperextend.

Shultz, like many other researchers I talked to, was highly critical of the current youth sports culture—the year-round play, particularly—and its impact on girls. "It's all about skills acquisition and early specialization," she said. "But just because a kid is good at a sport does not mean she has the foundational strength or movement patterns to stand up to constant play. What I'd like to be able to say is, 'Before you engage in sport, I am going to teach you to move. And I am going to give you strength.' We know some of the things to do now, but we need more research to know the risk factors and how to modify them."

She mentioned *knee valgus,* or knock-knees, the tendency of the knees to cave inward when a person runs or lands from a jump. Spend some time at your local athletic fields or inside some gymnasiums and watch groups of boys and girls competing. You will see a great many more obviously knock-kneed girls. Or just watch teenage girls walking along the sidewalk and you may see the same thing.

"What pressure is being placed on the kneecap by that?" Shultz asks. "To me, if girls are going to play sports at their current levels, it goes without saying that we need to find out."

It is not unreasonable to want to steer clear of the whole volatile subject of gender difference. Women almost always have come out on the losing end of it, victimized by a long, sorry trail of psychological findings that follow the same crackpot trajectory as research on variations between the races. The "data" produced almost always equate differences, to the extent they exist, with weakness and deficiency.

Women, it was said, had smaller brains and therefore less intellectual capacity than men. They were emotional to the point of hysteria. They lacked physical courage, decisiveness, and resolve. They were inferior in nearly every way except those specifically in, or assigned to the feminine realm: having babies, mothering them, cooking, cleaning, teaching young children, decorating, making social arrangements. Women in America were not granted the right to vote until 1920, with the passage of the Nineteenth Amendment—144 years after the founding of the nation. To deny a right as fundamental as suffrage absolutely demands a scientific, or pseudoscientific, basis.

Beginning in the 1970s, feminist-minded academics, both men

and women, basically said: Enough. Noting gender difference only comes to no good. Let's stop. Studies of sex differences were called "battle weapons against women" and "prescientific." The trend was either to cease doing such research or to highlight "null" findings, work that disproved differences and made the point that men and women are essentially the same. "Should we stop studying sex difference at all?" asked psychologist Roy Baumeister in a 1988 article in *American Psychologist,* noting that findings were frequently used to "justify discrimination and oppression." One of the only reasons to continue, he wrote, would be to counter psychological inquiry that demeaned women in order to "prevent the resurgence of masculinist biases."

At this point, psychologists were no longer making declarations about brain size or issuing blunt judgments of inferiority based on gender. Their inquires were on such subjects as how people cope with stress. How often they smile. What they value in mates. How well they work in groups; how adept they are at decoding nonverbal cues; to what extent they are empathetic, optimistic, collaborative, dominant, task-oriented; whether they are verbally, spatially, or quantitatively inclined. Such data are easily sorted by sex, with the result being that just about any psychological experiment can be construed as an inquiry into sex differences.

When the results of such research get published, nuance is easily lost—in the media and within the general public. Women smile more? OK, in any group of a thousand women, more might be described as smiley than in a similar group of men. But some women don't smile at all and some men do all the time. Or consider the example of quantitative ability: Yes, in high school, boys generally outperform girls in the math portions of standardized tests. But that is no reason to discriminate against a woman with ambitions in mathematics, since there are, in fact, brilliant female mathematicians. And it is not only dolts who trip over some of the subtlety: In 2006, Harvard president Lawrence Summers lost his job not long after opining that the university did not have more women professors in math and the sciences because women were not biologically as gifted as men in those fields.

Alice Eagly, chairman of the department of psychology at Northwestern University, was among the scholars who wondered whether gender difference should still be studied. But as she looked at the recent research, she concluded that much of it was biased in a different way—toward *not* finding, or minimizing, real differences. In a 1995 *American Psychologist* article (title: "The Science and Politics of Comparing Men and Women"), Eagly wrote that the newer research "reflected two missions: revealing people's damaging stereotypes and attitudes concerning women and displaying the absence of stereotypic sex differences in behavior, traits, and abilities." She continued, "Caught up in the passions of a burgeoning social movement, many feminist psychologists"—and here she included herself—"had a relatively uncomplicated vision of what empirical research on sex differences would yield."

Eagly alleged that some scholars were watering down findings by inserting what amounted to politically correct warning labels into their work. When they did discover actual, statistically significant differences—of the magnitude that social scientists sometimes call *nontrivial*—they quickly backpedaled and added caveats. "Although it would be accurate to describe sex differences and similarities as located along a continuum of magnitude, the writers of psychology textbooks often accompany any reports of sex comparisons by the warning that the differences are small," she wrote. "They seem not to realize that many of these differences are on the whole comparable to the other findings they have reviewed in their textbooks, findings not accompanied by any warnings about their small magnitude."

Eagly's article was a meta-analysis, a comprehensive review of all the available research on a given subject. Her most important conclusion was this: most of the serious sex difference research still being done, work she judged to have scholarly rigor, was making women look pretty darn good and, in some important ways, casting them as *superior* to men.

In a modern world, and especially in the realm of high-status work, pure physical strength is not greatly valued. (And neither is brute, top-down management.) Amid ever greater complexity and more information, no one person can effectively lead by hoarding power and information. To read a sampling of the hundreds of books written in recent years on the subject of leadership is to understand that men are basically being urged to behave in ways that are more stereotypically feminine. Men are counseled to be less command and control, and more relational.

"The hope that research would counter cultural stereotypes was central to ... many feminist empiricists because of the power that gender stereotypes possess to foster traditional roles for women," Eagly wrote. "Contrary to this hope, the results of quantitative syntheses have produced findings that conform to people's ideas about the sexes. ... In general, women tend to manifest behaviors that can be described as socially sensitive, friendly, and concerned with others' welfare, whereas men tend to manifest behaviors that can be described as dominant, controlling, and independent."

WE HAD a party at our home not long ago to celebrate our daughter's high school graduation, a gathering of family and friends that included about fifty teenagers. The girls, in colorful garden party dresses, congregated on our back lawn holding small plates of food as they talked. The boys, more haphazardly attired, pressed close to the serving tables and fed in near silence before quickly moving on to the next party on the circuit—where I assume they behaved in the same way.

The adults commented on the obvious contrast, and one of the other fathers made a hunter-gatherer reference, the clear subtext being that we were glimpsing man in his primitive, not fully evolved state. I don't remember anyone objecting to his crude stereotyping. Here, after all, were boys tearing into large platters of grilled meat (no salad, please) and then moving, en masse, to descend on another killing field.

The part of the public that is not in academia tends to be receptive to the idea that girls and boys have some significant differences, which is one reason that books like Deborah Tannen's *You Just Don't Understand* and John Gray's *Men Are from Mars, Women Are from Venus* sell in the tens of millions: they serve as confirmation of popular belief, some of which is formed by what we observe anecdotally.

But *why* do boys and girls behave differently? The debate—nature versus nurture? Is behavior programmed from birth or learned?—is ongoing and perhaps never-ending. Did the boys and girls at our party act differently because they are essentially different, or were they responding to signals sent since birth and conforming to the behaviors we expect of them?

The Enlightenment philosopher Jean-Jacques Rousseau framed the question as a sort of conundrum: Men and women, in his estimation, were the same—a progressive idea even now—except in the ways they were different. And those differences were not entirely knowable.

"The difficulty in comparing them comes from the difficulty of determining what in the constitution of both comes from sex and what does not," he wrote. "By comparative anatomy and even by mere inspection one can find general differences between them that seem unrelated to sex. However, these differences do relate to sex through connections that we cannot perceive. How far such differences may extend we cannot tell. All we know for certain is that everything in common between men and women must come from their species and everything different must come from their sex. From this double point of view we find so many relations and so many oppositions that perhaps one of nature's greatest marvels is to have been able to make two beings so similar while constituting them so differently."

(Rousseau was enlightened up to a point. Men should be "active and strong," he believed, and women, who were meant to serve and please men, "passive and weak.")

New medical knowledge—specifically the beginnings of an understanding of the hormone testosterone in the nineteenth century—provided explanations of sex differences that to this day buttress the arguments of the nature (as opposed to the nurture) crowd: Men are driven by testosterone. They are more naturally aggressive. They're the athletes, the warriors, and on the margins, the criminals and psychopaths. Women, by contrast, are softened by the "female" hormone estrogen. They are nurturing and noncompetitive. If they work outside the home, their temperaments are best suited to fields like nursing or teaching—although, in the latter case, preferably teaching younger children whose lessons are on a lower intellectual plane.

Freud's theories were also nature-based, although less concerned with body chemistry than anatomy—specifically the penis. Girls do not have one, so for Freud their psychosexual behavior is predicated on penis envy. Boys have their own penile-related hang-up that leads them through stages of development: castration anxiety.

The relatively new field of evolutionary psychology is a sort of middle ground between nature and nurture. Its practitioners hold that because tissue in living organisms is "functionally organized" by natural selection to perform a particular job, the brain is best understood in that context. If women think and behave a certain way, the evolutionary biologist argues, it is because they have had distinct roles to play in human history. So if studies show that women still seek taller, more aggressive males as mates, the evolutionary psychologist would say they are still programmed to seek optimum hunters and protectors.

The social psychologists hold the competing theory: that sex differences are mainly a social construct. Think of it this way: What do we want to know right after a child is born, after (maybe) first inquiring about the health of the mother and child? Boy or girl. From that point on, a child is treated according to gender: boys and girls are talked to differently, dressed differently, sometimes given different household chores and a different set of expectations. Often we divide the world between male and female without even thinking about it. When the sociologist Barrie Thorne spent time observing classes in elementary schools, she noticed that teachers' instructions often began, "Boys and girls," when "people" or "students" would have served just as well.

In the social psychologists' view, if boys are task-oriented and spatially and quantitatively inclined, and girls more social and verbal, they are responding to different societal expectations. (Maybe some girls would prefer to stand by the serving table and eat plates full of food in silence but feel compelled to be social.)

To defy sex-based social expectations takes courage, and it almost always comes at a cost. The tomboy was a staple of literature — in almost all cases, a spirited figure of rebellion trying to unshackle herself from a confining world. The classic tomboy in fiction, Jo March, complains in Louisa May Alcott's *Little Women,* "It's bad enough to be a girl, anyway, when I like boys' games, and work, and manners. I can't get over my disappointment in not being a boy." (*Tomboy* is no longer a word in common use. A high school girl who is physical in nature and plays sports is known by her peers as a jock, the same as a male athlete, an interesting word in that it refers to a male article of clothing that protects specifically male anatomical parts.)

Some literary critics have chosen to view Jo as a frustrated or soon-to-be lesbian, but I don't see why that has to be so. It makes more sense that she's just pissed off at living in a society that lets boys have all the fun. "Fictional tomboys chafe at the restrictions of imposed femininity and 'girly-girl' ways," Barrie Thorne writes in

Gender Play. The authors root for them, but only up to a certain point. Eventually, the characters come back to the fold—they find a man who tames them, who almost literally domesticates them, and they marry, have children, and keep house. "The stories always conclude with the girl's entry into adolescence and young womanhood, when she ultimately succumbs, at least partially, to that which she has struggled against and begins to value traits and activities associated with 'the feminine.'"

Until the last few decades, the real-life tomboy surrendered in the same way, largely because she had no choice. As a young girl, she played tackle football with the boys. She wrestled with her brothers' friends. She played kick the can in the street, hiked to the woods to climb trees and down to the creek to skip stones. But when it came time to play organized sports, boys and girls marched off in opposite directions.

The boys got teams with coaches, uniforms, and referees. One of the local men, a retiree or a fellow who worked the early shift at the mill, came out hours before game time to lovingly prepare the field, a ritual that honored the males of the community. He wheeled this wonderful machine out of a shed that drew thick, virgin-white lines with chalk to denote the yard lines in football or the foul lines in baseball. He set down plump bases in the infield and raked the batter's box so it was nice and smooth. It was all very official and exciting and exalted, and it made boys feel like real boys.

The girls, at the same point in their development, went inside and learned to wear dresses. If they were inclined toward sports, they shed an entire part of themselves, an identity. To do otherwise was a radical act of rebellion.

For three decades beginning in the 1930s, the great Babe Didrikson excelled in track and field, baseball, basketball, and, finally, golf. She is often called the greatest woman athlete ever, but a case can be made that she was just the best athlete, period. The sportswriter Grantland Rice wrote of her, "She is beyond all belief until you see her perform. Then you finally understand that you are looking at the most flawless specimen of muscle harmony, of complete mental and physical coordination, the world of sport has ever seen." Didrikson was once asked, "Is there anything you don't play?" She replied, famously and defiantly, "Yeah. Dolls."

The same dialogue, more or less, has been passed down the generations, a thread of the same, ongoing story: to be an athlete is to reject more passive forms of play. At the age of four, former University of Tennessee women's basketball star Teresa Geter was asked by her parents what kind of doll she wanted for Christmas. "I don't want a doll," she declared. "I want a basketball."

MEN PLAY sports to attain the rank of exalted beings—the high school quarterback, the big man on campus, the pro star. It is a dream sequence: the local ball field, newly chalked, Mom and Dad in the bleachers. Fade to the high school football field on a Friday night, bathed in light, the whole town watching. Then to the college football stadium on a Saturday afternoon, swelled with 100,000 adoring fans. And finally to the NFL or NBA or big-league baseball, and all that money and status—life as a series of rides in stretch limos.

The National Basketball Association's all-star weekend is a sprawling, three-day party. The sport's biggest stars—Shaquille O'Neal, Allen Iverson, LeBron James—compete to see who can have the most famous performers headline their events, and the clothes-horsing, dancing, and drinking continue till dawn. Last year in Las Vegas, caravans of limousines and Hummers ferried celebrants between such events as a celebrity poker game, a bash sponsored by Moët Hennessy USA, and a massive party hosted by Miami Heat player Dwyane Wade and featuring the rappers Rich Boy and Slim Thug.

It is very nearly the opposite for women: they play not to be exalted but to be included as full citizens of their world—within it, not above it. The feminist aspect of women's sports is more muted now, partly because of a perception that the battle has been won but also, undeniably, because overt feminism does not play well on every suburban soccer field. But at heart, women's sports have always been a political, even a radical, movement—the determined quest to participate in an activity that men, until very recently, considered their own.

"Sports have freed women, and continue to free women, from restrictive dress, behaviors, laws, and customs—and from the belief that women can't or shouldn't achieve or compete to win," Mariah Burton Nelson, an author and former Stanford basketball star, writes in the anthology *Nike Is a Goddess*.

In 1909, mountain climber Annie Smith Peck became the first woman, at age sixty-one, to scale Mount Coropuna in Peru. At the peak, she planted a banner that said, "Votes for Women"—which would not occur until 1920. The American suffragists were great proponents of sport, especially bicycle riding. "Many a woman is riding to the suffrage on a bicycle," Elizabeth Cady Stanton wrote. Susan B. Anthony believed that "bicycling has done more to emancipate women than anything else in the world. I stand and rejoice every time I see a woman ride on a wheel. It gives women a feeling of freedom and self-reliance."

Men, not surprisingly, had issues with women on bicycles. Nelson writes: "Cyclists' saddles . . . were said in the early days to induce menstruation and cause contracted vaginas and collapsed uteruses. Further, while appearing to enjoy an innocent, healthful ride, female cyclists might use the upward tilt of the saddle to engage in the 'solitary vice' of masturbation." A book published in 1837, *Exercise for Ladies*, by Donald Walker, put the supposed problem of bicycling for women more delicately: the activity was said to "deform the lower part of the body."

Men who opposed women's entry into sport, the top Olympic officials and other sports nobility, may have been pigheaded, but they were not, by and large, stupid. They understood sport in precisely the same way Mariah Burton Nelson does — as a beachhead, a territory that could be seized and used as a base for further incursions, and one that therefore had to be defended. If all those feisty tomboys would no longer conform when the time came, if they refused to put on ladylike clothes and adopt a ladylike manner, what rebellion might they stage next?

One of the showcase events for the women of the WNBA occurs during daylight. It is the All-Star Salute: Inspiring Women Luncheon. Last year, the honoree was Secretary of State Condoleezza Rice. With most of the all-star players in attendance, she recalled that as a girl in Birmingham, Alabama, she had played the old style of women's basketball, which restricted players to a third of the court so they would not have to run too hard or overexert themselves. Rice's childhood passions later turned to playing the piano and figure skating.

Rice stood at the podium, with her perfect posture and proper manner, and said she "envied" the WNBA stars and this generation of women because they had team sports they could play, which allowed them to "sweat, maybe even swear a little bit, and look like they were playing a sport. If you don't think Title IX has made a difference, just talk to those of us who were born before Title IX."

IN 1972, after the passage of Title IX but before it had much of an impact, *Ms.* magazine printed a plaintive letter from a young reader playing on her high school basketball team. She was the captain and led the team in scoring, steals, and assists, but it didn't add up to much. "During our whole season," she wrote, "we had only five games. We had to furnish rides to the games ourselves; we had to play in our gym suits because we had no uniforms in which to play; we were able to use the gym only when the boys were through with it; and we had a total of about thirty spectators at all our games combined. Everyone seems to think girls playing basketball is a big joke, but I am dead serious. If we are good enough to be called varsity, aren't we good enough to be respected?"

Dot Richardson, the great American softball player, now an orthopedic surgeon, grew up in the 1960s ardent about her sport but utterly frustrated by the obstacles put in her way. "I would actually pray at night, 'God, why did you give me this talent when there's no opportunity?' " she recalled. "As much as I had this desire to play, society threw back to me, 'Well, you're a girl. You're not supposed to want to play.' "

There were only boys' baseball teams where Richardson lived in Florida. A coach who knew of her skills suggested that she cut her hair short and call herself "Bob." She told him to forget it; she didn't want to have to deny who she was in order to participate.

The desire of women to compete in sports goes back a long way, but evidence of their actually doing so is scant and sporadic. To some degree, the same can be said of male sports; before industrialized society provided a certain amount of leisure time, few could devote themselves to games.

A single written account, by the second century A.D. Greek traveler Pausanias, tells of a sports festival for unmarried women that occurred every four years alongside the men's games at Olympia. Known as the Heraea Games, in honor of Hera, wife of Zeus, they fell short of today's standards of rectitude. The women competed in running events while wearing low-hanging tunics draped over the left shoulder and breast, leaving the right breast exposed. The attire seems to have been of keen interest to Pausanias, who does not provide much detail of the actual competition. He does add that the competitors were allowed to watch the men's and boys' games, while married women were barred, upon penalty of death, from the Sanctuary of Zeus while the male competitions were taking place.

Mary Queen of Scots might be considered the patron saint of

women who are determined to compete—no matter the circumstances or consequences. She was the first woman known to play golf, and she was so devoted to the game that in 1567 she caused a scandal by playing just a few days after her husband, Lord Darnley, was murdered.

The Olympic Games were resurrected by a Frenchman, Baron Pierre de Coubertin, and the first modern Olympiad, in 1896 in Paris, included no female competitors. Four years later, in 1900, twenty-three women competed (out of about one thousand total athletes) in five sports—lawn tennis, sailing, croquet, golf, and ballooning—although their events were not officially sanctioned by the International Olympic Committee. For the next eight Summer Games, all the way up to 1936 in Berlin, the last prewar Olympiad before a twelve-year hiatus, female participation rarely increased by much more than a trickle: the number dropped to 6 in 1904—then went back up to 36 in 1908, 57 in 1912, 77 in 1920, 136 in 1924, 290 in 1928, 127 in 1932, and 328 in 1936—about 12 percent of all participants.

And even those small gains were hard-won. Women were barred from track and field, the centerpiece of the games, until the 1928 Olympics in Amsterdam. They competed in the 800-meter run in 1928—and then not again until 1960, because a distance that great was deemed too strenuous to be safe. In the most recent Olympiads, women have never accounted for more than 40 percent of the athletes.

Elsewhere, women athletes were making gains, then seeing them grabbed back. Women's soccer in England was so popular in the first part of the twentieth century that a match between two top teams in 1920 attracted 53,000 fans, and another 8,000 were turned away from the sold-out stadium. A women's team from the Dick, Kerr and Co. munitions plant, which produced many of the best players, toured the United States and played a series of six games against men's teams, winning three of them. But the English women were flagged as a threat to the men's game, and in 1921, England's powerful Football Association barred them from all the biggest football grounds, effectively ending an era.

The arc of women's sport in the U.S. was more gradual. Before team sports became popular, a few individual athletes gained some acclaim, most notably Babe Didrikson, who was a celebrated star both before and after World War II. Swimmer Esther Williams, tennis star Althea Gibson, sprinter Wilma Rudolph, and, in the 1960s, figure skater Peggy Fleming were nationally known figures.

Team sports bubbled up, quietly, from the women's colleges in New York and New England. Matthew Vassar, a self-made, self-educated brewer, founded Vassar College in 1865 with half of the $408,000 fortune he kept in a tin box along with the deed to two hundred acres of land in Poughkeepsie, New York. He was inspired to open a women's college by his niece, Lydia Booth, who herself was educated at a school that operated on the principle of "republican motherhood," which held that women need advanced education because they are responsible for the moral and intellectual development of their children.

Matthew Vassar added the element of physical education. He made sure the college opened with a School of Physical Training that taught classes in riding, swimming, boating, skating, and "other physical accomplishments suitable for ladies to acquire bodily strength and grace." The next year, Vassar fielded two of the first women's amateur baseball teams.

It was Senda Berenson, a physical education instructor at another of the country's first women's colleges, Smith, who invented the separate game of women's basketball in the 1890s and loomed over the sport for many years as the longtime editor of the annual *Spalding's Official Basketball Guide for Women*. Her rules restricted individual players to a third of the court and allowed just one dribble before a pass. Defenders were not allowed to steal the ball from an opponent, as that was deemed overly aggressive.

Berenson believed the game that James Naismith invented at the Springfield YMCA in 1891, and that she modified eight years later, was the ideal sport for women. It was physical, social, tactical—a complete workout for the body and mind, introduced "at the right psychological moment in the development of the American girl. It is not so long ago that the mere word *athletic* applied to women seemed rather out of place. It had a disagreeable sound and brought up visions of maidens in padded trousers and nose protectors. Not long after this, however, educators began to appreciate the value of physical training. . . . It began to be considered quite in keeping with womanly qualities to play tennis, to ride, and to swim. This very enthusiasm for games, this natural outlet of the play instinct, created a need for a game that should require teamwork, organization, scientific development. . . . And out of a clear blue sky came basketball."

Berenson's version of the game, which lasted into the 1970s, when men's rules were widely adopted, is a source of derision now, an artifact of a bygone era. Even the uniforms were limiting: players wore bloomers and thick black stockings. So it comes as a surprise to find that Berenson's writing, now collected at Smith—speeches, academic papers, and old *Spalding's Guides*—serve as a considerable source of modern-day wisdom.

In contrast to many of today's women's sports advocates, Berenson saw little in men's sports to emulate. The male model was to be avoided. What Berenson wanted to replicate was the right to play. But she thought women could create something of their own, something better.

Berenson's writing occurred in a larger context, a moment in American history, perhaps the *last* such moment, when men's sports came under powerful attack. (The current doping scandals may yet produce a similar reassessment of sports.) In October 1905, President Theodore Roosevelt summoned the presidents of Yale, Harvard, and Princeton to the White House to discuss the level of violence in college football, which in its formative years resembled unregulated boxing in its sheer bloody brutality. In 1905, eighteen players died from injuries suffered in games, some after so-called flying wedges of players crashed into and pummeled one targeted player on the opposing team. The sports-reform movement that emerged from this meeting eventually widened its concerns beyond violence: it recognized that football was increasingly a force unto itself on campuses, apart from the central mission of educating students in the arts and sciences.

Berenson wanted no part of a sports culture that was disconnected from the wider society, and one way to avoid that, she believed, was for women to stay in control of their sports. In the 1916 edition of her *Spalding's Guide,* she recommends "the superiority of women's coaches for women." But over recent decades coaching has gone in the opposite direction. The better a female player is now, and the higher the level she reaches, the *less* likely she is to be coached by a woman and the more likely to be led by a man, who may view her as just a smaller, less explosive model of a male athlete. And why wouldn't he? A male coach's reference point will always be the athlete he is most familiar with: himself.

In 1972, the year Title IX passed, 90 percent of coaches of women's teams at colleges were women. Since then, that number has dropped precipitously, to a present historic low of 42 percent in 2006. At the youth and high school levels, the stakes are higher than ever before, so the unspoken feeling in many settings is that men know sports—they've been at it longer—so if you want your daughter's travel team to succeed and the girls to get scholarships, you'd better have a male coach.

Every few months, it seems, the newspapers run a story about the rare woman coach of a boys' high school team. It's the stuff of feature stories, because it's unusual. But it is the other syndrome, the rare woman coach of top female athletes, that needs to be examined.

"The history of this is relevant," says the author Mariah Burton Nelson, who is also executive director of the American Association of

Physical Activity and Recreation, which promotes lifelong fitness. "It used to be the women coached girls, and men coached boys, and that was it. Now more than half the coaches of women's high school and college teams are men, and women coach only two percent of men's teams. This has had a big influence on the way women learn to play sports—through male values and male habits. These men learn from other men, passing along that style and attitude.

"To be fair, it's not just a gender issue. You can find plenty of female coaches who are militaristic and seemingly unconcerned about the long-term impacts, health and otherwise. Tough women coaches can be demanding, setting higher goals for people than they might set for themselves. Sports have always been an ideal setting for that kind of toughness. My concern is when the body is breaking down, and the athlete, pressured by the coach, is ignoring those signals."

To Berenson, whose brother was the influential art historian Bernard Berenson, the connection between women's sports and women's rights was obvious. "One of the strong arguments in the economic world against giving women as high salaries as men for similar work is that women are more prone to illness than men. They need, therefore, all the more to develop health and endurance if they desire to become candidates for equal wages."

Her reasoning for why young women should compete is eloquent and timeless: "Many of our young women are well enough in a way yet never know the joy of mere living, are lazy, listless and lack vitality. Let such a person try this game, she will forget herself at the first throw of the ball, will take deep draughts of air with the unaccustomed exercise and tingle and throb with the joy of this game."

Writing nearly a century ago, Berenson seemed to anticipate a plague of overuse injuries, emotional burnout, and even what is now called the "female triad": a combination of eating disorders, suppressed menstruation, and osteoporosis that afflicts highly trained female athletes. "We still would point to the danger of over-fatigue which comes from playing the game too often or too long at one

time," she wrote. "All the symptoms of malnutrition and lack of vitality seen in people who take no exercise are found in people who
over-exercise. Each year one or two students enter Smith College
who have been distinctly injured by over-exertion in basketball
played at the lower schools under careless supervision or no supervision at all."

What Berenson definitively did *not* believe was that women's
and men's sports were equivalent. The differences were not a matter
of superiority or inferiority: she just believed women's sport should
develop on its own parallel track. "It is absurd to say that whatever
game the men play we can play. . . . Women cannot compete with
men in physical prowess. And why in the name of all that is sane
should we? Why not rather have our ambition go into sport for
health, endurance, and the mere love of it?"

CHAPTER 4

"WE CAN BRING IT"

B erenson's insights seem all the more progressive when
compared with the precepts of American sports culture
some seventy years later.

"Athletic competition builds character in our boys," a Connecticut judge wrote in ruling against a girl who wanted to join the boys'
cross-country team at a high school that offered no team for girls.
"We do not need that kind of character in our girls, the women of
tomorrow." A young woman today might assume that this opinion
was handed down some time in the distant past, but the year was
1971, not all that long ago.

The revolution in women's sports has been so sweeping as to
render prerevolution times difficult to grasp for the current generation of girls. Their mothers may have benefited from the gains of
feminism and the liberation of the Pill, but before Title IX, if they
wanted to get on the playing fields, they had to be scrappy, defiant
trailblazers. Today's girls live in a sort of sports paradise. They join

their first organized team at age five. Practices and games are catered, with parents providing halftime and postgame juice boxes and orange wedges. The menu of sports keeps expanding beyond the old standbys—softball, field hockey, track and field, basketball—to offerings that may include lacrosse, water polo, crew, ice hockey, and fencing.

The current generation's struggle is to choose from amid this plenty; it can't conceive of not having options. The smorgasbord of sports choices is wrapped into a wider culture of abundance—our hundreds of channels of TV; the ever-expanding Internet; modes of communication that quickly become obsolete, with e-mail morphing into instant messaging and then into wall-to-wall contact on Facebook or MySpace. A time when girls couldn't climb into the minivan and lace up their cleats and mix it up? Please. It never existed.

Tennis star Jennifer Capriati, asked at the 2002 U.S. Open about reports that the Bush administration was seeking ways to water down Title IX's provisions, responded, "I have no idea what Title IX is. Sorry."

The passage of Title IX in 1972 was the first of three watershed events in the modern history of women's sport. The law itself is all of thirty-seven words: "No person in the United States shall, on the basis of sex, be excluded from participation in, be denied the benefits of, or be subjected to discrimination under any education program or activity receiving Federal financial assistance." Notice that sports are never mentioned, although a legacy of the bill has been to provide greater opportunities for female athletes.

The second big event occurred the very next year, the so-called Battle of the Sexes tennis match between Billie Jean King, then twenty-nine years old and still at the top of the women's rankings, and Bobby Riggs, who at fifty-five was a former champion decades past his prime. Riggs was a promoter and provocateur whose goading of King attracted a crowd of 30,000 to the Astrodome and a huge national television audience. He entered the arena like a potentate, riding on a rickshaw with several buxom young women serving as his attendants — his "bosom buddies," he called them.

The Riggs imprimatur, the 1970s vintage, and the space-age venue make the whole event now seem like something out of *Austin Powers*, but at the time, it was important. Expertly playing the "male chauvinist," Riggs served, if unintentionally, as a great ally of women's sports. King trounced him in straight sets (6–4, 6–3, 6–3), as he surely knew she would.

Depending on how you looked at it, either King affirmed some point about women's abilities in athletics or she *avoided* leaving a negative impact, which seemed to be her view. "I thought it would set us back fifty years if I didn't win that match," King said. "It would ruin the women's tour and affect all women's self-esteem."

Her reaction was telling. Female athletes, even mature, confident champions like King, rarely gloat in victory. They're just relieved they haven't let anyone down.

Writing in the *New York Times*, Neil Amdur said King had overcome the old assertions that women could not mentally withstand the rigors of sport. "Most important perhaps for women everywhere, she convinced skeptics that a female athlete can survive pressure-filled situations and that men are as susceptible to nerves as women."

Mia Hamm and the U.S. women's World Cup soccer team produced the third watershed moment, and the first that belonged, in spirit, to the twenty-first century. Their triumph was nonideological, at least on its surface. It was a coronation of women's *right* to play, rather than a plea or demand. And it was absent the absurdist, comic overtones of the Battle of the Sexes.

The members of the 1999 World Cup team were, remember, Anson Dorrance's girls, the new archetype — take no prisoners, take no shit — what young women could be and, in some senses, what they were supposed to be. They were not kids. Most members of the team were in their mid-twenties. Two of them, Carla Overbeck and Joy

Fawcett, were mothers who quickly after childbirth trained their way back onto the team.

On July 10, 1999, they took the field against the Chinese national team at the Rose Bowl, in Pasadena, California, in front of 90,185 fans, the largest crowd ever to watch a women's sporting event anywhere in the world. Forty million U.S. viewers watched on television. At that moment, about 7.5 million girls in the United States played youth soccer, and it seemed like the American women represented them all. One out of every 2.5 girls in high school played a sport—as opposed to one in 27 before the passage of Title IX.

For ninety tense, excruciating minutes, the American women ran up and down the field, shoulder to shoulder with their Chinese opponents, with not one goal scored. The game was decided by penalty kicks, with the clinching goal scored by Brandi Chastain, who in celebration ripped off her jersey, exposing her blue sports bra and her kick-ass body.

The pictures of Chastain, on her knees in jubilation, her fists clenched above her head, her rock-hard abdomen and defined upper arms on display, were the event's iconic images, the cover shots of *Time* and *Sports Illustrated*. Chastain's maneuver was controversial—why strip, some asked, at the height of such a female-empowering moment?—but she showed off less than what you'd see on any beach. And besides, male players habitually tear off their jerseys after games. Unapologetic and defiant, Chastain said she had not planned her reaction, but she was proud of it—proud of the victory and proud of a physique she had built with her own effort and sweat.

THE WOMEN'S sports revolution retains a core of critics. Prominent among them are coaches and other devotees of men's wrestling, and their sense of grievance is understandable. In the last three decades, some 170 college wrestling programs have been shut down. These people blame Title IX—specifically, an interpretation that holds that collegiate sports programs can comply by providing opportunities for male and female students that are "substantially proportionate."

Because college athletic departments at the time did not run programs that were even *remotely* proportionate, after 1972 they had to make changes (private colleges as well as public ones, since they too took federal funds). They added new women's sports. Many also cut some men's sports—not just wrestling but also, in some cases, swimming, gymnastics, baseball, track and field, or whatever else could be slashed to make the numbers closer to even. So Title IX was, yes, in some way responsible. But what was the alternative? To defy the law and *not* grant new opportunities to women who wanted to play?

Wrestling partisans could more reasonably blame men's football, which, with its massive rosters and colossal budgets, eats up a big portion of the men's share of resources and which, despite its widely held reputation as a revenue producer, only rarely turns an actual profit. NCAA Division 1 football teams carry an average of 105 players, a small army that must be coached, outfitted, housed, wrapped in athletic tape, insured, treated for injuries, transported, and fed. At all but a handful of universities, football is the opposite of a moneymaker—it's a money pit.

There is another category of Title IX critic: the political conservative who chooses to view the women's sports revolution as a front in the culture war. This critic equates expanded opportunity with *quota*, a bad word. In a 2002 *Newsweek* column headlined "The Train Wreck of Title IX," George Will wrote, "Colleges have killed more than four hundred athletic teams in order to produce precise proportionality between men's and women's enrollments and men's and women's rates of participation in athletics. . . . If participation in sports must mirror the sexual composition of the student body, why not participation in the engineering department? And why not in extracurricular activities other than sports—debating, orchestra, choir, cheerleading?"

Will's facts are wrong and his logic flawed. Even with the cuts of some men's sports teams, "precise proportionality" is still a long way off: there are about 40,000 more men playing college sports than women—even though women's percentage of undergraduate enrollment has grown to 56 percent. Men get 58 percent of the scholarship money. In high schools, about 4.2 million boys—and 3 million girls—compete in athletics. At the dawn of Title IX, 78,500 boys played high school soccer, compared with 700 girls; now it is boys, 359,000, and girls, 321,000. As for Will's question on why proportionality is not sought in other areas of campus life, is there a *men's* engineering department somewhere?

The other line of attack against Title IX argues that women are not as interested in sports and therefore don't need or deserve equal access to it. Steven E. Rhoads, a professor of public policy at the University of Virginia, advanced this argument in a 2004 book called *Taking Sex Differences Seriously,* a volume worth dwelling on for a moment because it represents the outer limits of Title IX opposition.

Watching sports, Rhoads argues, should be taken as evidence of interest in *playing* sports, as should reading about them on the sports pages, which he says men are much more likely than women to do. Women prefer viewing activities that involve costumes, he observes, and they like contests with judging rather than strict scorekeeping. He finds it noteworthy that "one half billion viewers, predominantly women, watched the 2002 Miss World pageant."

Not only are men more interested in sports, they *need* sports more, for a variety of reasons, including to mitigate their tendency toward violence. Dropping wrestling may have put more boys "in unsupervised peer groups," Rhoads speculates, and could lead to more violent crime by leaving "tough boys without a sport or other activity where they can bond with other boys and show their mettle in a rule-bound environment." He cites the example of Dennis Hastert, a former wrestler who became Speaker of the House and a prominent

Title IX critic. Hastert was "a lost boy until wrestling brought him some discipline and motivation."

Rhoads even suggests that the Title IX debate and allocation of sports resources between the sexes has something to do with the making of proper marriages, citing "mating studies" that show females are attracted to the dominant risk-taking personality of male athletes. "Thus, the high school football captain is still more likely to pursue the homecoming queen than the best female athlete." (But what if she is one and the same? He doesn't say.)

Rhoads and other Title IX critics have pushed for "interest" surveys to be the predominant way of determining whether colleges or high schools are complying with Title IX: they would poll the student population and see how many students are interested in being athletes. If more boys wanted to play on teams, they would get more of the resources. The process requires self-identification and is problematic because males may be more likely than equally active women to declare themselves athletes.

Dr. Lisa Callahan, codirector of the Women's Sports Medicine Center at the Hospital for Special Surgery in New York, treats men as well, often the fathers or husbands of the women who first come in to the practice. "A guy jogs across the street or shoots baskets in his driveway and he says he's an athlete," Callahan observes. "I have women who come in here who play ball three times a week or run marathons, and they say, 'I'm just keeping in shape.' For men, sports is more of their identity, but if you look at it objectively, they're not always more of an athlete than the woman who just has a different way of talking about what she does."

In other words, an "interest" study might identify a lot of men on a college campus who think they have the talent to play intercollegiate sports, and undercount women who may not be as vain about their athletic prowess.

• • •

You DON'T need an opinion poll to know that the public strongly supports girls' rights to play; just go out to the local fields and see the great numbers of girls competing and all the parents who drive them to games, coach the teams, officiate, keep the statistics, or just stand and cheer.

But the critics—the laughable ones, the ideologues, the Beltway players angling to water down Title IX—keep Donna Lopiano and her allies busy. I have no doubt that if the advocates for women's sports dropped their guard, gains would be rolled back. But while they keep their heads down, fighting the familiar battles over access to sports and equality of opportunity, they ignore or downplay the problem of injuries.

Without exception, when I talked to young female athletes and their parents about this book, they were supportive and thankful that I was taking on the subject. They wanted to know why so many girls were suffering serious injuries and what could be done about it. But those who had spent years in the trenches, fighting for the right of women to play, were far less enthusiastic. They feared how the book would be read—and that it might be used by their old adversaries.

"I'm not in any way suggesting that this topic should not be taken seriously and covered by the media. We need to do everything we can do to prevent injuries," said Mary Jo Kane, director of the Tucker Center for Research on Girls and Women in Sport at the University of Minnesota. "But when you look at the stories that get told, that those who cover women's sports are interested in telling or are assigned by editors, it does seem that so little coverage focuses on women's accomplishments, on their mental toughness and physical courage. There is a disproportionate emphasis on things that are problematic or that are presented as signs of women's biological difference or inferiority."

Julie Agel, a researcher at the University of Minnesota, has authored NCAA-sponsored reports, part of the Injury Surveillance

project, that clearly document the alarming incidence of ACL ruptures in women—rates in college soccer and basketball that are two
and a half to three times that of men. The NCAA numbers are far
lower than other estimates, especially in younger age groups, that
estimate the girls' rates of ACL injuries to be as much as eight times
greater than the males'. Timothy Hewett, a leading ACL researcher
in Cincinnati, has identified a "four- to sixfold greater incidence in
female athletes compared with male athletes playing the same landing and cutting sports." Dr. Jordan Metzl, perhaps the nation's leading authority in pediatric sports medicine, told students at
Georgetown University's School of Medicine in 2007, "Anterior cruciate ligament tears, unfortunately, with increasing numbers of females playing sports, are really reaching almost epidemic proportions
in the female young athlete group."

Agel told me that she was concerned about "trying to preserve
the role of women in sport. I'm not a big fan of these gender things"—
research that stratifies results by sex. She said that ACL tears are
"rare in the context of overall injury" and "rare when you compare
them to the injury everyone is ignoring, which is ankle sprains, which
we don't treat. We ignore them."

Ankle sprains are, by the numbers, much more frequent; nearly
anyone who has ever played a sport that requires running has suffered at least one, and usually more. But in the hundreds of interviews I conducted and the research I reviewed, I did not encounter
anyone who considered an ankle sprain and ACL tear to be in any
way equivalent in terms of severity. Besides, there is suspicion that
indicates women athletes are more prone to chronic ankle sprains
than men, and even that weak and chronically sprained ankles could
have something to do with ACL tears.

"I hate the focus on it," Agel continued, referring to ACL
tears and women. "If you continue to point it out, parents won't
let their kids play, and the benefits of playing sports outweigh the
downsides."

The hedging is reminiscent of the caveats Alice Eagly identified in the psychological research—qualifications that may be well-intended on some level but are inspired by something other than the numbers. The caveats diminish conclusions that can and should be drawn from the data: Frequent serious injuries to young women. Complicated, expensive surgeries. Long rehabs, lost seasons, and chronic pain.

A committee report submitted at the International Olympic Committee's 2002 Women in Sport Conference in Spain stated, "Gender-specific injuries are rare, and concerns about female participation in sport are outdated and erroneous." That, as far as it goes, is all certainly true. Long-held fears that female athletes would injure their reproductive organs were nonsense; in fact, women are at less risk for that type of injury than men, who are not as well protected.

But after dismissing the notion of gender-specific injuries, the IOC report states clearly that women are more at risk for a range of sports injuries. It uses the lower figure—four times the risk—for ACL ruptures. It adds that female athletes "may be more susceptible to overuse sports injuries," including "stress fractures, tendonitis, and bursitis."

The IOC report recommends that coaches "take measures to improve their understanding of the special considerations of the female athlete," that young female athletes develop a broad range of skills and not specialize in one sport before age ten, and that "increases in training volume are not so great that they cause overuse injury."

All good ideas—and all of them routinely ignored across the wide swath of American youth sports culture.

So WHAT does it mean to point out that girls and young women are suffering high rates of serious sports injuries? That they are too weak to play? Too delicate? Not deserving of full access to sports and all the joys of physicality and competition—and that all those things should be given back over to the boys?

No, no, and no. But the cause of women's sports will hit a road-block—and progress will come to a halt and may be reversed—if the injury issue is not aggressively confronted. And the first step is to acknowledge differences. But the women's sports culture is not headed in that direction.

No one exactly saw it coming or intended it, but post-Title IX, women ceded control of their sports to men. In the late 1970s, the Association for Intercollegiate Athletics for Women sponsored national championships in nineteen sports. The organization was led by physical educators, the heirs of Senda Berenson, who believed that sports were related to health and recreation and connected to some larger purpose. But in 1982, the AIAW disbanded, and most of the athletes, coaches, teams, and administrators still affiliated with it were subsumed by the NCAA. It was part of the price of moving on to a larger stage and benefiting from more money and media attention. James Shulman and William Bowen write in their book, *The Game of Life,* "The Title IX legislation of 1972 came as some-what of a mixed blessing to a group of women athletics administrators who were working to develop a model of intercollegiate athletics based not on equality and sameness but on opportunity and difference."

The goal of elite women's sports—and here I include everything from the ambitious travel soccer team in Any Town, U.S.A. on up to the WNBA and Olympic competition—is increasingly to be like men's sport. To play the same way and to have the same status, perks, and rewards. No one, seemingly, will step back and ask, Is the male model all that great? Has it not strayed a long way from its own beginnings—from its ideal as a builder of character, a molder of young men?

Michael Vick, the Atlanta Falcons quarterback sent to prison for his involvement in the "sport" of dogfighting, is not coincidentally a football player—he is a certified product of a culture that worships money and raw aggression and indulges antisocial behavior from its icons. Note that abuse of women in male sports does not usually result in a star's loss of status, but Vick's cruelty to dogs got him banished from the NFL even before he pleaded guilty to criminal charges.

Let me be clear: I don't think girls ought to be made to play basketball in skirts or should be prohibited from running the whole court. I don't think Smith College should have remained the epicenter of women's sports. But Senda Berenson's major points, a century later, are dead-on. Much of male sport has strayed far from its best purpose; it was headed off in the wrong direction even in Berenson's day, as President Roosevelt highlighted in his football inquiry. So why seek to mimic it?

The veteran sportswriter Shelly Smith, in a chapter in *Nike Is a Goddess*, described a 1998 dunk contest at a women's all-star basketball game at the Disney Wide World of Sports Arena in Tampa—won by a 6-foot-5 player named Sylvia Crawley. "Crawley's winning dunk came on the heels of another amazing day in women's basketball," Smith writes. "Nikki McCray, who had helped lead her professional team, the Columbus Quest, to the first-ever ABL championship, was defecting to the other women's professional league, the WNBA, for a reported $250,000-a-year contract. At a packed press conference, McCray, who was the ABL's Most Valuable Player in its inaugural season, also announced that she was signing a $1 million contract with Fila, which was designing a Nikki McCray basketball shoe." Smith goes on to enthuse that Olympic star Dawn Staley "became the first woman whose portrait was painted on a giant Nike billboard" and that "Sheryl Swoopes got her own Nike shoe the same year she became pregnant."

Big money. Defections. Shoe deals. This is the NBA replicated—

but is that a worthy goal? Smith writes, "As America prepares to enter the twenty-first century, women's basketball has never been healthier or filled with more promise."

THE FASCINATION with the dunk shot is worth lingering on for another moment. Could there possibly be a more definitively *male* act in all of sports? Stuffing something, with maximum force, into a cylinder? It is an expression of power but rarely of grace.

The dunk—taking it to the hole! as the TV announcers unfailingly exclaim—is the money shot of every ESPN basketball highlight reel. We do not need Dr. Freud back at the studio to provide halftime analysis of why that is.

Power and thrust are the athletic traits that earn our highest respect. Pure lean muscle performing its essential, biological task. Even within male sport, we narrowly define athleticism. Explode to the hoop and dunk the ball and you're an athlete; scan the defense, probe for a weakness, and make a perfectly timed bounce pass to an open teammate and you are a clever fellow, making do with meager physical gifts. Creativity, court vision, the ability to meld with teammates, are formidable athletic gifts. But we don't value them as highly.

The legendary John Wooden, the Wizard of Westwood, who coached UCLA's men's teams to ten national championships, is no fan of the dunk. His greatest player, Kareem Abdul-Jabbar (known in college as Lew Alcindor), played in an era when the shot was briefly banned, and he developed an array of other, more elegant moves. "I've never liked it," Wooden said of the dunk. "I think it brings on selfishness, showmanship, too much individual play."

What Wooden definitively *does* like is women's basketball. He has come to prefer it. "To me, the best pure basketball I see today is among the better women's teams," Wooden said in 2003, one of the numerous times he was quoted on the subject. "It's the game as I like to see it played."

That women's game, though, is changing. It has to in order to be taken more seriously, because it is not only power and thrust we admire but also competition with a nasty edge. No one wants to be accused of playing some kind of powder-puff game.

"Has the perception of your game by men changed?" a reporter asked Delisha Milton-Jones, of the Washington Mystics, at the WNBA's 2007 all-star weekend. "Definitely," she answered. "I can remember I used to hear men saying stuff like, 'Oh, I can take them.' But now people aren't saying that anymore because it's legitimate. What you see on the television is some hardcore basketball. You see some mean elbows, you see some dunks and nice passes and great shooting, so they know we can compete."

The best women's teams play better basketball, technically, than the men. They're good shooters, sophisticated passers, willing team players. To dunk and throw elbows is not to play the game better but to play it more like men. In 1998, the *New York Times* took note of Pat Summitt's Lady Vols of Tennessee, then at the top of the women's rankings: "Beyond the statistical dominance lies an aggressive, attacking style that has redefined the women's game."

The same trends are evident in the highest levels of women's soccer. Leslie Osborn, a member the U.S. team that competed in the 2007 World Cup, commented, "The men have always been more physical, but we can bring it."

The implication, always, is that a rougher style signifies progress, an evolution to a higher level of play. But physical play attacks skill. That's its point. If a player is fast and clever with the ball, you knock her off her stride. Bloody her nose. Intimidate her.

The star of the 2007 World Cup team was Abby Wambach, a 5-foot-11, 160-pound forward whose style was so aggressive that teammates and coaches kept having to to point out, correctly, that in addition to her size and strength and toughness, she had talent. In a preliminary-round game against England, Wambach elbowed an opponent and broke her nose. "I didn't do it on purpose. It was an accident. I apologized to her on the field," she said, adding that claims that her teammates celebrated while the British player lay on the field were "absurd."

But Wambach was quick to add, approvingly, "The game is different now. It's way more brutal. It's way more physical."

Interestingly, the one men's sport that has become notably less brutal—and more protective of skill—is football. In the NFL, the most important, and most skillful, player on the field, the quarterback, has been wrapped in a virtual bubble by the imposition of new rules. He can't be hit in the head, or below the waist if the hit comes from behind, and if a defender makes contact much more than an instant after he has let go of the ball, a penalty is called. The new rules make it nearly impossible to physically impede pass receivers as they run their routes. Some old-timers lament that the game has been turned into touch football, but it is more aesthetically pleasing than ever, and more popular.

The U.S. women's World Cup team got in so many knockdown, drag-out games in the 2007 tournament, contested in China, that it had to place an emergency order to a Shanghai hospital for surgical staplers in order to quickly stitch up players on the sideline and get them back on the field. But the Americans lost, 4–0, in the semifinal to a smaller, faster, and more offensively sophisticated team from Brazil, one that played the style made famous by that nation's male players and known to soccer aficionados as "the beautiful game."

The U.S. women had become more "athletic." They were bigger, stronger, and edgier. But they were not necessarily better, and they certainly weren't as successful as the famous 1999 World Cup champions.

• • •

Mary Jo Kane, the University of Minnesota sociologist, talks of how we "frame" notions of athleticism. "On the seventh day, God did not say, 'And let football be the most important measure of physical superiority,' " she says. "That's a notion that we have, and it is based on the physical advantages of men. What if the measure was doing a back flip on a balance beam? What if in basketball it was the ability to shoot free throws? We'd be saying, Why don't men measure up? Why aren't they as good as women?"

I attended the NCAA women's 2006 Final Four basketball championships in Boston. A young University of Maryland team, led by a marvelous freshman point guard, trailed nearly the whole game but tied the score at the end before prevailing in overtime. The action was fast, furious, and entertaining. But it was also ragged and rough, nothing like the style John Wooden admired.

As I sat at courtside on press row in Boston, I wondered, Are the women in the process of wrecking their elegant game? Where were the precision passes? The well-orchestrated offensive patterns? Sacrificed on the altar of "athleticism" and "progress." The women's game had been redefined to look more like the NBA. But beyond the hype, the money, and the highlight reel dunks, does any true basketball fan really think the quality of play in men's pro basketball is superior to what it was two decades ago? No—it has been scrubbed of its beauty. An artful style suggestive of improvisational jazz has been supplanted by a muscled-up ethos.

The other thing I could not help but notice was the lax officiating. Under the basket, women were beating on each other in a manner you wouldn't get away with even in the NBA. In the open court, defenders rode ball handlers from behind, with subtle and not-so-subtle pushes in the small of the back—obvious infractions that went uncalled. Among the writers, there were audible gasps, a rarity amid the usually jaded press corps. One woman columnist, a veteran of numerous Final Fours, kept turning to me with an incredulous look. Finally, in exasperation after yet another player was sent sprawling headlong onto the floor, she yelled, "Can you tell me how that's not a foul?"

I had my own question: Was there some misguided notion out there in the brave new world of women's sports that the athletes are so indestructible that even the enforcement of a safe game, the calling of reasonable fouls, would be like turning the clock back?

CHAPTER 5

PROVING GROUNDS

John Wilckens, a former Navy orthopedic surgeon, undertook a research project in the early 1990s when he was based at the U.S. Naval Academy in Annapolis, Maryland. His office afforded him a bird's-eye view of what was called the obstacle course at Hospital Point, a layout of twists, turns, and difficult climbs and jumps, including one eight-foot wall that was scaled by grabbing on to a cargo net. A handful of middies climbed and dismounted the high wall with care, but the competitive ones—which is nearly everyone at a military academy—went flying up it, executed a tight little flip at the top, then jumped down with abandon on to a gravel landing pit. They tried, literally, to hit the ground running.

All too frequently, Wilckens saw midshipmen taken straight from the course into his orthopedic clinic. They were almost always women. They were landing off balance and ripping their ACLs. It made no sense to him. Here was a test designed to measure military readiness, and it was having a countereffect, causing injuries and creating a state of unreadiness. He remembers telling a group of doctors at a conference, "This place is awfully hard on our women. They're 15 percent of our population but 40 percent of our surgeries."

He started talking about the issue with other officers at the Naval Academy but met resistance. "The military does not always like information," says Wilckens, who is now in private practice at Johns Hopkins Hospital, in Baltimore. "They see things as black and white. Their position was 'If there's a problem, John, fix it.' "

Wilckens looked more closely at injury rates and published a study of injuries at the Naval Academy between 1991 and 1997 that showed women running the obstacle course had a relative risk of rupturing an ACL, compared to men, of eleven to one. After the research became public, it was suggested to Wilckens that perhaps the Naval Academy was not attracting the best specimens among its female recruits—an absurdity since the extreme physical demands of the service academies are no secret. Very few candidates of either sex who are sedentary or soft bother to apply, let alone get admitted.

"Someone said to me, 'Maybe we're not getting the Title Nine girls, the real fit women. Maybe they're just daughters of officers and they want to be in the Navy,' " Wilckens said. "But that wasn't the case. They were all high school varsity athletes. That's who comes to the Naval Academy."

The academy brass finally got the point. Fixing the problem, though, required confronting a fiction—that men and women can do all the same physical things. The Naval Academy was (and still is) trying to fully integrate women, and there have been a series of ugly episodes of sexual harassment. Any research involving gender at any of the military academies is fraught, weighed down by history and heightened sensitivities, and therefore must be undertaken with care.

But the old obstacle course was bulldozed, although not without some griping that standards had been lowered. It was replaced by a new layout with a macho enough name—the Tarzan Course—but the walls were lower. And some allowances were made for women. They still ran a challenging course, but a modified one, with lower jumps. The injury rates plummeted.

THE U.S. military and its academies have been at the forefront of research into physical training, injuries, and gender. The subject matters to them because it directly relates to military readiness and money. When a trainee or soldier loses time or must leave the service with an injury, the government is out many thousands of dollars.

In 1917, during World War I, the United States government paid $200 an acre to a couple of hundred farmers on the western shore of the Chesapeake Bay in Maryland, and the land they vacated (along with their 12,000 horses, pigs, cows, and other livestock) became the Aberdeen Proving Grounds. The Army has used this vast expanse for an essential mission: to test how well its weapons blow things up, and how effective its own tanks, aircraft, and other vehicles *resist* being blown up. But the base has also long served as fertile ground for some of the Army's best thinkers and problem solvers. The Army Research Laboratory (smart munitions, robotics, survivability and lethality studies, battlefield weather) and its Chemical Biological Agency (defense against chemical and biological weapons) are just two indications of Aberdeen's intellectual firepower.

Colonel Bruce Jones, director of the Army's Injury Prevention Program, works on what is called the Edgewood side of the Aberdeen Proving Grounds, in a one-story brick building near the base's parched, forlorn-looking golf course. His office, at the midpoint of a long corridor, overflows with medical books, journals, and various reports.

At sixty, Jones has a full head of gray hair and the fit, trim look of a lifelong athlete. He excelled at distance running as a high schooler in Kansas, rarely losing, although he did come in second in a famous race: the meet at which Jim Ryun became the first high schooler to run the mile in under four minutes. Jones recalls seeing the finish from the other side of the track. He earned an undergraduate degree in history from Harvard University, then got an Army-financed medical degree at the University of Kansas. He figured he would serve out his military obligation and then quickly move into private practice, but he never made it. As a junior medical officer in Fort Jackson, South Carolina, in the early 1980s, Jones got "recruited into" one of the first research projects to look into injury rates in basic training, which the Army suspected was a problem but had not looked at in any systematic way. He found it fascinating, more so than the routine medical care he was providing.

Jones drifted into more research, "epidemiology by the seat of my pants," as he puts it, before the Army sent him back to Harvard for a master's degree in public health. "I took classes to learn what I was already doing, only better." He became an epidemiologist, a scientist who assembles statistics on illnesses and injuries and identifies patterns within the numbers. His subject was the impact of exercise—more precisely, the impact of the extreme, pushed-to-the-limits exertion of basic training. Who survives? Who breaks down? And why?

"In the civilian community, everyone is exercising at different levels and different intensities," he explains. "But in Army basic training, they are all doing the same thing. They are not driving cars, they're not playing basketball after hours. It's like a laboratory. So we're able to show things that the civilian community cannot do."

BASIC TRAINING, what the Army calls BCT (Basic Combat Training), consists of nine weeks of unrelenting activity, sixteen or more hours a day, for sixty-three days. Some of it is like schoolwork—studying first aid, reading manuals, practicing how to take apart and clean weapons—but about 25 percent is hard physical training. Soldiers run obstacle courses. They do lengthy road marches, some as long as fifteen miles. They run or march to meals, to hygiene, and to classroom sessions. They march in place and do calisthenics.

The research on injury rates in basic training has produced consistent results: more women than men suffer injuries. In Army studies, that was true before women and men began training in integrated groups—and from 1993 on, when they began training together. The vast majority of the injuries, for both men and women, are to the lower leg, caused by overuse: shin splints, Achilles tendonitis, plantar fasciitis, patellofemoral syndrome (knee pain), and, most seriously, stress fractures. Because trainees generally run and march in straight lines, they don't often tear their ACLs.

A mid-1990s study of Army basic trainees showed that 12 percent of female trainees suffered stress fractures, compared to 2 percent of male trainees. An older study, in 1984, when basic training lasted just eight weeks, showed that of a cohort of 140 women who began basic training, 34 of them—nearly one in four—suffered stress fractures.

Stress fractures, sometimes called *fatigue* fractures, are pure overuse injuries. They frequently do not show up on X-rays in their early stages, so soldiers (or athletes) continue to train. Ultimately, they are debilitating and usually require about eight weeks of rest to heal completely. Some recruits with the injury are "recycled," put into another basic training group after they have recovered, but more often they are discharged, which costs the Army a soldier and the loss of the tens of thousands of dollars it invested in his or her recruitment and training. The Army has estimated the cost as $34,000 per lost recruit, not counting health care for the treatment of the stress fractures.

In 2001, the Centers for Disease Control reviewed the Army's research on basic training injuries, as well as data from branches of the military, and concluded, "Sex has consistently been identified as a risk factor for injury in military BT [basic training]. In studies from the 1980s to 1997 that examined women and men at the same training site who performed essentially the same physical training, incidences of injuries for women were 1.7 to 2.2 times higher than those for men. In addition, rates of some specific injuries during military training are higher for women than men. In Army training, RR [relative risk] for stress fractures is two to ten times higher for women than men engaged in the same training regimen."

The link between females in military training and female athletes is obvious. Both groups are pushing themselves physically, to the point that deficiencies in conditioning, strength, and nutrition will emerge. A 1998 paper published in the *Journal of the American College of Nutrition* on stress fractures in the military explicitly made the connection between military and sports training: "The condition, however, is not confined only to military personnel. With increased emphasis on physical conditioning and participation in sports by the general population, it is quite possible that the incidence of stress fractures will increase in the future."

A study produced at Aberdeen showed yet another contrast between male and female trainees, an intriguing one: the women may be tougher. Yes, they get injured more often, but it appears to take a more serious injury to drive them out of the service.

Joseph Knapik, who works with Jones at the Army's Center for Health Promotion and Preventive Medicine, was the lead author of a 2001 article in the journal *Military Medicine* that uncovered what might be termed a toughness gap. Knapik and his fellow researchers reviewed the medical records of two cohorts of trainees, again at Fort Jackson, which trains the largest number of new recruits. Out of 756 men in the study, 102 were discharged for various reasons before completing basic training. Among 474 women, 108 were discharged. The authors wrote, "Only men were at higher risk of discharge with a less serious injury. This suggests that less serious injuries may be a larger factor in discharges for men than for women."

In the parlance of sports, women appeared to be more willing to play through pain. Certainly the fact that women must endure the rigors of childbirth suggests that they may have a naturally higher tolerance for pain, although the most recent scientific research does not bear that out. But particularly determined women who find themselves on what has traditionally been male turf—the military, the playing field—may endure more pain, often to their detriment, because they feel they have something to prove.

JONES AND his colleagues stratify the statistics they collect in various ways: by gender, race, age, education level, health risk behaviors (such as smoking), anatomy (flat feet, bowed legs), and levels of body fat. The category that is most meaningful to them is fitness level, as measured by tests administered at the start of basic training: times in the one-mile and two-mile runs and numbers of sit-ups and push-ups completed.

For both men and women, the most fit—as measured by running times—experience the fewest injuries. The differences, in almost all the studies, are stark. Jones showed me a study from Fort Leonard Wood, Missouri, of two-mile run times. Among those in the fastest quartile—with times between eleven and sixteen minutes—25 percent were treated for some injury during the course of their basic training. Of those in the slowest quartile—between twenty-one and thirty-two minutes—63 percent suffered injuries.

Just as striking was the gender breakdown in those quartiles. The men overwhelmingly were the faster runners. The top quartile consisted of sixty men and two women, and the bottom quartile, or slowest runners, fifty-two women and eleven men.

"Those guys are slugs," Jones said of the men in the slow group.

And the two women in the fast group? "They're probably cross-country runners," he said. "And probably some of them too," he added, referring to the women in the second-fastest quartile, which consisted of fifty-five men and eight women.

There were more men than women in the study—155 of the 250

total. But 85 of the 95 women—89 percent—placed in the slowest two quartiles. Overall, men in basic training average about sixteen minutes in the two-mile run and women about twenty-one minutes. The same trends exist in the mile run.

"Do the women we get come in with lower levels of physical fitness than what might reasonably be expected?" Jones said. "I wouldn't think so, but we have no way of knowing, because we don't know for sure what the relative level of fitness is in the general population."

The average man is 10 percent taller and 20 percent heavier than the average woman. The size difference is less pronounced than in other species. Male orangutans and gorillas are twice the size of females. But even with their higher weight, men have more lean muscle and a lower percentage of body fat than women.

I asked Jones if the term *fitness* was really appropriate to his research. Might he really be measuring physical *capability*—and doing so on a model scaled to men? After all, men who were just moderately fast, compared with other men, were faster than all but a handful of the women. And the women who ran in the fastest quartile were truly extraordinary.

For women who test out as fit as men, he answered, his research shows that they have similar injury risks. But his most fit quartiles, in all probability, consist of a handful of elite women—the cross-country runners, as he put it—along with plenty of men who are not as highly trained. Even the middle quartiles were likely filled with a mix of moderately fit men and some well-trained women who just do not run as fast.

Jones does not dwell on gender when he recommends modifications in training. He does not see the point. The Army trains women and men alongside each other, each performing the same physical tasks, and as long as that is the case, he will focus on his quartiles—the fit and the less fit. But the injury rates among men and women are so at odds that the differences cannot be ignored entirely. (An additional issue is that trainees undertake road marches while carrying about forty-five pounds of gear on their back—water, food, ammunition—which for most of the women is a greater percentage of their body weight.)

"Suppose we were going to hold all commanders accountable for their injury rates in basic training," Jones said. "Would it be fair for me to give a poor evaluation to the commander who just happened to get 50 percent women in his group, which would be an unusual occurrence, because he had more injuries than a commander with 25 percent women? No, it wouldn't be. He shouldn't get gigged because you would have to assume he is going to get more injuries."

Women account for 20 percent of the U.S. active duty military. They are one of every seven of our soldiers in Iraq. They pilot jets and helicopters, drive trucks, and guard prisoners. But on many levels, gender remains one of the military's most sensitive topics. And just as in sports, women's gains in the armed forces are recent enough to feel tenuous. There are no ladies' tees in the military, and most women would not want them.

Jones retired from the active military in 1998 and manages the Army's Injury Prevention Program as a civilian employee. He does not wear a uniform and cannot be deployed, but otherwise his job has not changed much. I asked if he felt in any way constrained by the political sensitivity of his research. "No," he said. "I mean, the facts are the facts. My job is to sort of describe, given the current situation, which is men and women training together, what the injury risks are."

IN ADDITION to looking at intrinsic risks of injury (gender, fitness level, age), the scientists at Aberdeen examine extrinsic factors, primarily the intensity and frequency of training. "There are thresholds above which injury rates go up and physical fitness does not," Jones says. "And, clearly, if you can find those thresholds, it doesn't make sense to train beyond them. It's true in sports. It's true here. The principles are exactly the same. The more you do beyond a certain point, the more injuries you get."

Soldiers in basic training still run long distances and go on road marches with full backpacks. "They need to be pushed to know they can make the distance," Jones says. "But as a commander, you have to be able to distinguish when you are pushing them so they can gain confidence and when you are doing it for physical fitness. If it's for fitness, you don't want to do it every day of the week."

Acting on the research from Aberdeen, some Army basic training now occurs in ability groups, with the less fit advancing at a pace they can handle rather than one that crushes them. Women tend to be in the lower ability groups, although the groups are not labeled as male and female. Injury rates have started to edge down. But Jones admits it is a tough sell down the chain of command and to the drill sergeants — still mostly men — who preside over basic training.

Sports culture borrows heavily from military culture. Jones says he is trying to change stubbornly held beliefs of military training, precisely the ideas that lead to so many injuries. As he rattles them off, he could just as well be talking about your daughter's travel soccer team: "More is always better. Faster is always better. No pain, no gain."

YOUNG WOMEN who suffer sports injuries are, by and large, the real go-getters. If you looked at a random collection of home videos, you would pick them right out. They're the ones who, as little girls in their first organized games, gravitate to the ball, seize it, and charge to the goal. They are the first ones picked for the travel teams, the future varsity players, the most aggressive, the most eager. And as a result, more is demanded of them. Too soon, they are called on to train and compete constantly and at maximum intensity, like soldiers sent on too many long road marches.

This is why the best of the women's teams, some pioneer pro-grams in the surge of sports participation and popularity, have been wracked by waves of injuries. And, cruelly, it is why the best and most passionate adolescent female athletes are at particular risk. They are pushed beyond their threshold, past the point of diminishing re-turns.

It is striking, the extent to which pain is accepted by young female athletes, from age twelve or so on up. They play through it. Live with it. Consider it an inevitable part of an athlete's experience. But they struggle to distinguish between normal soreness and actual injury. An extreme example is the tragic story of Arielle Newman, a seventeen-year-old cross-country runner in Staten Island, New York, who died in April 2007. The medical examiner ruled that she had accidentally poisoned herself by overusing methyl salicylate, the ingredient found in common sore muscle treatments such as Bengay, Icy Hot, and Tiger Balm. Her mother said she rubbed oint-ments on her sore legs constantly and also used adhesive pads con-taining the ingredient.

Athletes of both sexes are celebrated in the media for playing through serious injuries, women perhaps even more so than men. On the eve of the 2004 Summer Games in Athens, Kelli Anderson of *Sports Illustrated* wrote, "Although you would never wish them on anyone, hideous injuries can augur great things for gymnasts. Mary Lou Retton had knee surgery just six weeks before she became America's darling by winning the USA's first all-around gold medal at the 1984 Olympics in Los Angeles. Four months before the '92 Games in Barcelona, Shannon Miller dislocated and chipped an elbow and had to have it surgically repaired. She went on to win two silvers and a bronze that year as well as two golds in Atlanta in '96."

Says Steve Marshall, the UNC epidemiologist, "We're in love with the idea of the wounded warrior. The warrior girl who fell at the last hurdle or the one who goes on despite some awful injury." He cited the endlessly played videotape of U.S. Olympic gymnast Kerri

Strug "sticking the landing" of a vault at the 1996 Olympics in Athens, then wincing as she grabs her left ankle, which already had two torn ligaments.

These are extraordinary athletes, obviously, and well compensated. Whether they truly make informed choices about whether to compete while injured (the best female gymnasts tend to be in their teens) is open to question. The commentary about their choice to play on, if it is a choice, resonates through all levels of athletics, and the message could not be more clear: real athletes ignore pain. "That's a golden moment in U.S. Olympic history," Marshall says of Strug's final vault. "We enshrine injuries as part of the story. We should be preventing them. It's repulsive."

Rebecca Demorest, a sports doctor at Children's Hospital in Washington, said it is common for her to see young female athletes with a chain of injuries, from the feet up through the trunk. "They ache and they hurt and they use pain medicine and try to keep on playing," she said. "When they finally get to the point they can't play, they come in to see me."

Dr. Demorest, who has since moved to the Hospital for Special Surgery in New York, said girls come in "hurting all over. They have hip pain, knee pain, back pain. They have a series of nonspecific overuse injuries that comes down to being worn out. Don't get me wrong. There's a chain of events with boys too. But I see it more with the girls."

Demorest's most common prescription—rest—is a hard sell, for the kids and often their parents too. "I've had kids cry," she says. "Plenty of times. But I've had parents cry more than kids." With younger athletes, she says, it's a matter of convincing them to stay out of competition or practice long enough to heal. Demorest told me about a gymnast with a lower leg injury who came into her office. "She said, 'I can't walk, but what can I compete in tomorrow?' And I'm like, 'You can't walk, and you want to go out on a balance beam?' But when you tell one of these kids to take two weeks off, it's like you said two years. There's always some big tournament coming up that they can't afford to miss or some team they absolutely have to make. I have to bargain with them.

"I actually negotiate these huge contracts, right down to the minute of the day. I say, 'All right, you're going to take tomorrow off completely. The next day, you can go to the gym and ride the bike for fifteen minutes. And the next day, you can go to your practice, but only do half of it.' "

Demorest usually asks for their athletic schedules. She remembers a twelve-year-old girl who had soccer practices and games every day of the week—different teams and different venues in all directions. On weekends, she sometimes had a game and a practice on the same day on fields an hour apart. She looked at the girl's schedule in amazement, finally asking, "Do you have an assistant to keep track of this for you?"

CONSIDER AGAIN the concept of athletic "exposures," with each practice or game counting as one exposure. Think of a young woman's sports experience as a wheel of fortune—or misfortune. All good things have their limits. The more sports a person is involved in— games, practices, tournaments, camps, private sports tutoring—the more chances she has to be injured.

Stress fractures, shin splints, and chronically aching knees and ankles are commonly caused by overuse, as well as poor biomechanics—bad running form. Bones and joints become worn down over time. An athlete ignores minor pain, the first warning sign, until a minor injury becomes a major one.

But ACL tears and other acute injuries are what might best be called overexposure injuries—too many tickets put down on the wheel of misfortune. Girls play as much as boys. They compete on their school teams, club teams, travel teams, Olympic development teams, teams thrown together for long weekend tournaments. But because girls are more at risk, the mathematical equation for them, the possible consequence of playing year-round, is graver.

"They play constantly, year-round," says Bill Prentice, the long-time trainer of the women's soccer team at the University of North Carolina. "The ACL tears are overexposure injuries, not overuse. They give themselves too many opportunities to get hurt."

But there is not necessarily a clear line between an overuse and overexposure injury. Overuse can be a factor in acute injuries, because doctors assume that an athlete who is worn down is more vulnerable to suffering a major event like an ACL rupture.

The players a generation before Amy Steadman, players like Mia Hamm and her 1999 World Cup teammates, did not generally play the same kind of endless seasons. Some competed in other sports — basketball, softball, field hockey. This is virtually unheard of now, even though such versatility is widely considered to be protective as cross training. But no one wants to take away time from her main sport.

"They go from high school season to club season to tournament season," says Holly Silvers, a physical therapist and researcher in Santa Monica. "They have maybe two weeks off, then they go back to doing the same thing over and over again, repeating the same neural patterns. That's why we see overuse injuries we never saw fifteen years ago, and why we see some of the acute injuries."

Silvers is thirty-three, about the same age as many of the players on the 1999 World Cup team. She played high-level soccer as a girl in New Jersey, up to the Olympic development level. "We played seven months of soccer at most," she says. "We had the whole summer off. I played softball too. A lot of the girls played three sports. It's not possible now, the way things are set up."

Some members of that '99 World Cup team have suffered ACL injuries (Brandi Chastain had two of them), but not as many of them in adolescence. "That's why you've heard of them," Amy Steadman said to me. "They didn't get stopped by injuries. When they were in high school and there was a break, they rested or played something else. There weren't all these temptations to play all the time."

In 2005, Amy was one of three young women on the UNC team sidelined by knee surgery—three of the eleven projected starters. Ashlyn Harris, a goaltender, suffered ACL ruptures in two consecutive summers. By the time she got on the field for UNC, she was a twenty-one-year-old freshman (by NCAA eligibility standards). She helped lead the Tar Heels to an eighteenth national title in 2006. In a jubilant locker room after the game, Harris said, "My body feels old."

The University of Tennessee women's basketball team, the Lady Vols—winners of seven national championships—were in the grip of their own injury nightmare in 2005. Coach Pat Summitt had recruited six heralded high school players, dubbed by sportswriters as the Six Pack. The most promising of them was Candace Parker, an extraordinarily skilled athlete who at 6 foot 4 could play any position on the court, shoot with dead-eye accuracy, handle and pass the ball like a dream, and, most titillating of all, dunk—a rarity for a woman. As a seventeen-year-old high school senior, she won the slam dunk contest at the McDonald's High School All-American game in Oklahoma City against five male competitors, including two who were headed straight to the NBA.

But Parker already had a history of knee troubles. Between her junior and senior years of high school, she tore the ACL in her left knee. The next summer, she injured the same knee again, this time ripping cartilage. She had two more surgeries on her left knee and had to sit out what would have been her first season at Tennessee, as did two other of Pat Summitt's prize recruits with their own knee problems, putting half the Six Pack out of commission. In the course of that season and the next, eight Tennessee recruits—eight!—had knee surgery, most of them before ever setting foot on campus.

"We're seeing a pace at which the game has not been played before," Summitt, who began coaching at Tennessee in 1974, told me. "We're stronger, faster, and more aggressive. The women are playing year-round, which we didn't do in my day. It's progress, as far as I'm concerned, but it is related to the injury issue."

Summitt said she tries not to be, as she put it, "paranoid" about injuries (it's hard to coach and cringe at the same time), but the prospect of them does sometimes figure into her instruction. Candace Parker is explosive enough that she can rise up with defenders on her—in "traffic," as it's called—and dunk. No other woman has ever been able to do that. But the prospect of seeing her star player jostled in the air and landing awkwardly alarms Summitt.

The first time Parker dunked in a game, Summitt was the least excited person in the gym. "I was just relieved she didn't get hurt," she said. She then instructed Parker to confine her aerial act to the open court, when she is in front of the pack with no defenders nearby. "I haven't said, 'You can't dunk.' It's just, 'Be aware of the contact. Avoid contact. It's only two points, even when you dunk it.' I'm thinking, She's already had one ACL, I don't want her to have another."

Other coaches, though, have become fatalistic. In 2007, five point guards in the high-powered Pacific Ten Conference—five out of ten—tore their ACLs and were lost for the season. When Stanford guard JJ Hones went down in the first minute of a game against the University of California at Berkeley, her coach, Tara VanDerveer, told her team, "It's part of the game. The tournament isn't going to say, 'Let's wait for JJ to get healthy.'"

Focused on prepping her able-bodied players for the postseason, she resolutely did not want to talk about the syndrome of ACL injuries. "I'm numb to it," she said. "It's part of women's basketball."

The quote made it sound almost like these women, or their knees, were disposable. VanDerveer had a team to coach. She could not stop to tend to the injured and couldn't dwell on why the injuries were occurring or how they might be prevented.

ACL ruptures were, again, a big part of women's college basketball the following season.

In a span of one month during the 2007–08 season, two of the five starters on the University of Connecticut women's basketball team suffered ACL ruptures. The second one occurred to senior guard Mel Thomas, ending her college career. Typically, it didn't look like much. "I didn't even see what happened," her coach, Geno Auriemma, said afterward. "I don't know whether she stepped on her foot or jammed the knee or something. It just looked like she hit it and fell down. It just happened so quickly."

THE GIRLS' soccer team at St. Thomas Aquinas High School in Fort Lauderdale, Florida, travels widely—during the school season to Texas, California, or wherever else they can find worthy opponents, and in the summertime to tournaments in Europe. Less well known than Anson Dorrance's squad at the University of North Carolina or Pat Summitt's Lady Vols, they are no less a signature team. The Lady Raiders have captured ten Florida state championships and five national championships. St. Thomas Aquinas places a high value on attracting and developing outstanding athletes. It is the alma mater of tennis immortal Chris Evert, former Dallas Cowboy great Michael Irvin, and Olympic gold medal sprinter Sanya Richards.

In June of 2006, the team flew to Spain to play in the Donosti Cup, a tournament for teams in the under-nineteen age group, where they dominated several European clubs in the preliminary rounds, then claimed the first-place trophy with a triumph over a squad from San Diego. The high school's Web site hailed the achievement and the brave comeback performances of two of the star players: "In her first Raider appearance since an ACL surgery last year, Janelle Pierson led the Girls U19 division with a total of eleven goals in the tournament. Also coming back from an ACL surgery, Katie Collum scored the winning goal in the final match against FC Bratz."

I was struck by the matter-of-fact tone. It was like these two girls had missed a couple of games because they had head colds.

Janelle and Katie had plenty of company and support while rehabbing from their reconstructive surgeries: they were among *seven* team members who, in the year leading up to the tourney in Spain, suffered ruptured ACLs. Carlos Giron, the coach at St. Thomas Aquinas for twenty-five years, concluded that his girls were just playing too many games, leaving not enough time for rest and too many opportunities for injury. "They don't have an off-season," Giron told me. "They go from one tournament to the next and then the next. I put in a little more time off for them, but to tell you the truth, the way things are set up, it's not easy."

Giron set up his schedule the following season so that his team played fewer games, and the lighter load seemed to work. For the first time in memory, the Lady Raiders entered the state playoffs in the spring of 2007 injury-free, in stark contrast to their south Florida rivals. The girls from Spanish River were missing three starters, including standout scorer Katie Kadera, who tore an ACL for the second time in three years. Ten season-ending injuries left Wellington High School with just eleven available players. Boca Raton High was out its starting goaltender and four other starters.

The Florida injuries form a thread of a larger narrative, or nightmare, that plays out all across America: young athletic women injured at the very worst time, or returning from injury to play in the big game, or serially injured and finally sidelined permanently.

The injuries, even the serious ones, are reported as routine, part of the daily wrap-up, like goals scored. My local newspaper, the *Washington Post*, in May 2007, noted a playoff soccer victory by a Virginia high school despite losing two key players: "All-Met senior midfielder Morgan Benz suffered a season-ending tear to her right anterior cruciate ligament in last week's quarter-final win over Langley. Then All-Met freshman forward Jenna Richmond, the Wildcats leading scorer, was restricted from play after doctors informed her early yesterday of a stress fracture to her right leg."

Two days later, the same newspaper filed an account of the Virginia girls' lacrosse playoffs: "After spending her sophomore season as a disappointed spectator, Sarah Vinall is more than making up for lost time. The junior midfielder, who suffered a torn anterior cruciate ligament twelve days before last season started . . ."

The *Houston Chronicle* reported on a girls' high school basketball team that suffered six ACL injuries over two seasons: "Julie Kroll's knee injury changed her outlook on basketball. Suffering the same injury twice in six months changed her outlook on life. 'I really miss playing basketball,' Kroll, 18, said. 'But after I tried to come back a second time, I realized that I would like to be able to walk in 20 years.' "

In 2006 the *Washington Post* published a story about the trend of female distance runners' experiencing declines in their performance between their freshman and senior seasons: "Kay Comer sometimes felt stuck in a stranger's body. She looked in the mirror last summer and saw few remnants of the scrawny high school freshman whom cross-country coaches had once referred to as 'lungs with legs.' Comer's hips had expanded. Her shoulders had broadened. Her thighs had developed more muscle. Only a year earlier, Comer won a district championship at Colonial Forge High School in Stafford and earned a reputation as Virginia's up-and-coming distance runner. Now, even her shortest jogs ended in a hobbled limp. 'I went through a stage where running was hard and it hurt everywhere,' Comer said. 'I just didn't want to do it.' "

And on and on.

After Princeton squash player Jen Shingleton tore her ACL in her sophomore year, it seemed like everywhere she went on campus, another young woman approached her to share her own experience. "It is amazing—all of the female athletes that have had this same injury," she told the *Daily Princetonian*. "The week after it happened people would ask me what happened and would say, 'Oh, I did that last year.' I feel it is like a rite of passage for female athletes."

• • •

GIRLS ARE trained largely without regard for their changing bodies. Women can—and do—improve on their athletic performance into their twenties, thirties, and even beyond. The great American swimmer Dara Torres, who competed in her first Olympic Games in 1984, won the 100-meter freestyle at the U.S. national championships in 2007 at age forty. She was two hundredths of a second off her personal best time. The sum of the ages of the women who finished in second and third places, Dana Vollmer, nineteen, and Amanda Weir, twenty-one, equaled Torres's age.

But young women who overtrain or compete too frequently risk ending their athletic careers prematurely. Several Florida high school soccer players suffered injuries at the 2007 Orange Classic, a huge club tournament held over Christmas break that involved 357 teams—a "necessary evil," one of the high school coaches called it—in which girls play multiple games on the same day on fields lined with college coaches scouting for prospects. They are playing for their futures, or so they believe. The tourney is one of the many crucibles that a young woman must survive as she advances in competitive sports. Many do not survive—at least not in one piece.

Gregg Calhoon is the longtime athletic trainer for the women's soccer and basketball teams at the U.S. Naval Academy. "Between my two teams, we get an average of twelve new players a year—eight in soccer, four in basketball," he says. "On average, two of them enter here already having torn an ACL in high school. I've had them come in here with both knees already repaired. Seventeen years old, and they've done it twice. It's hard to believe."

Once they get to the Naval Academy, the ACL tears "come in waves." Some years are relatively healthy ones, others injury filled. For several years, the Navy women's soccer team averaged three or four ACL ruptures a year on a squad of about twenty-four players. The victims formed a club, a kind of sorority. They wore T-shirts that read, "ACL Special Ops," which they had received the night before surgery. "There's a perverse pride in being a member of that club,"

Calhoon says. (The UNC women's soccer team calls ACL injuries "the gift that keeps on giving" because so many of them go on to suffer the injury again.)

At Navy, women who tear their ACLs again do not get a new shirt, just an additional star put on their old one. The captain of the 2002 Navy women's soccer team, Erin Kelly, had three stars on hers by the time she graduated. (She also suffered a stress fracture to her hip.) "For some reason, it's the captains of the team that frequently have the multiple ACLs," Calhoon says. "They keep tearing it, rehabbing it, then getting back out on the field. They're focused, physically tough individuals."

Kelly's teammates wrote a tribute to her after her last injury: "Erin Kelly was not only our captain, she was a foundation that gave us all perspective on the idea of resiliency. She was a selfless leader who showed us exactly what it meant to *never quit,* and to always find hope despite the constant physical and emotional battering life handed her. Yes, selfless: though no doubt tears were had in the private, they were never shown to us; rather, she came to our aid, attended to our needs, and made the team the priority even after the fact she could never play again."

JANELLE PIERSON, of the St. Thomas Aquinas Lady Raiders, tore her ACL at a practice with her club team, during a simple two v. two drill. She slowed down to shoot, and when she planted her left leg, the knee buckled. To this day, she doesn't exactly know what happened because her mechanics felt no different from what she had executed thousands of times before, from the time she first started playing soccer at age five: Decelerate. Get the ball under control. Load up. Then kick. There were few things in her life she did with more ease or joy.

Her knee swelled, and she couldn't straighten it. She had an MRI the next day and soon learned that her sophomore season of high school soccer was gone. Her friends played on without her while she spent months—what seemed like forever—cheering from the sideline.

Janelle experienced moments of tears and frustration but not despair. She vowed to make it back stronger and better than ever, and she did. Her powerful performance at the Donosti Cup in Europe— eleven goals and a starring role against strong competition—was all the more remarkable for having occurred in her very first competitive game after her injury. The following high school season, she scored twenty-one goals and had thirteen assists for the Lady Raiders, and both the *Miami Herald* and *Fort Lauderdale Sun-Sentinel* named her first team, all–Broward County.

But she still had work to do: one more year of high school and more college soccer coaches to impress. In June 2007, she traveled with her club team to three out-of-town tournaments on successive weekends. The first one was across the state in Fort Meyers. Next came a tournament in New Jersey. The third was in Houston, the annual Texas Shootout, a massive event that attracted 300 teams and 360 college coaches as well as major corporate sponsorship: Adidas, Gatorade, and the Texas Sports Medicine Center. The shootout was mostly for rising high school juniors, but even though Janelle was a rising senior, she wanted more "exposure," as her mother, Maria, explained. One more chance to show her skills in a high-powered setting.

In the first game of the Texas Shootout, with about twenty minutes left to play, she ruptured the ACL in her right knee, the previously uninjured one. "This time I was pretty sure what it was," she said. "I was chasing after this girl, trying to cut to stop her. And it just went out on me."

She stayed down on the field, screaming. A trainer came out and tried to calm her, assuring her the pain would subside. But her screams came more from anger than pain. Anyone who suffers a second ACL injury almost can instantly project forward: another surgery, another long rehab, another season down the drain. It feels like a couple of hundred pages just got ripped out of your personal calendar. Janelle couldn't believe it.

The Lady Raiders were headed back to Europe in a few weeks, to Italy this time. Janelle and her family had already paid for the trip, so she went along as a spectator. In July 2007, she underwent reconstructive surgery. Her mother wondered about Janelle's future. Two major operations, and she hadn't even turned eighteen yet.

"I'm afraid for her, and for all these girls," Maria Pierson said. "What's it going to be like for them at forty years old? They're in so much pain now—knees and backs and hips—and they just keep on going. They've been going at this so hard for ten, eleven, twelve years and it's taking a toll. Are they going to look back and regret it?"

Janelle's mother took the surgeon aside and told him her concerns. Should her daughter keep playing? Absolutely, the doctor said. He had put her knee back together, and he expected that she would have a successful rehab and a full recovery. When Janelle found out about this conversation from the doctor, she got angry at her mother. How could she even ask such a thing? The college recruiters had not given up on her. If they stopped recruiting girls who had suffered ACL injuries, their pool of talent would dry up. Janelle was as determined as the last time. She had no intention of giving up soccer.

Eight other girls at the Texas Shootout suffered ACL tears. And by Janelle's count, the eighteen core players on her club team, the Weston Fury, had suffered a total of nine ACL tears over their high school years: her two, another girl with two, and five other girls who had done it once. They were an informal sorority, like the Naval Academy women. "It gets kind of tough," Janelle said. "But we talk each other through it."

Lisa Callahan, the codirector of the Women's Sports Medicine Center at the Hospital for Special Surgery in New York, told me, "A senior captain who tears her cruciate is the toughest thing in the world." Janelle had been a captain of her high school team as a junior, but in her senior season, she was not named captain because her coach could not be sure she was going to be able to play at all. She hoped maybe to be back for the Florida state playoffs in early 2008 but knew it was a long shot. More realistically, she would play for her club team in the summer of 2008 and then in college. Vassar and Lafayette, two excellent liberal arts colleges, were pursuing her; so was the Naval Academy.

Janelle pushed herself through rehabilitation. She knew the routine from eighteen months before: Ride the stationary bicycle. Walk the treadmill. Grimace and grunt and work through the pain of the leg lifts and leg thrusts and other exercises intended to rebuild muscle and flexibility in her injured leg.

But the hard part was the loneliness born of missing the game and her teammates. She knew what time they practiced. It was part of her internal clock, and she felt a longing when they were on the field. What were they doing? Who was showing well? What kinds of jokes were they cracking? "It's just hard emotionally," she said. "At night, all my friends are out on the field, and I'm just wishing so much I was there."

Her mother tried to have a more pointed conversation with her about whether she would continue playing. Maria could not bear the thought of Janelle's tearing an ACL for a third time and going through the surgery and rehab again. She said to Janelle: "I just want you to know, if you decide you don't want to play anymore, that's OK. It really is."

It was pointless. Janelle responded to her injury in the only way she knew how. "When I get down," she said, "I rehab harder so I can get back earlier."

CHAPTER 6

AMY: EIGHTEEN MINUTES

The human knee is a wondrous thing, at once the most athletic part of the musculoskeletal system—without its bend the muscles could not thrust for running and jumping—and often the most fragile. It is a jointed column, formed by the intersection of four bones. The femur, the large bone in the thigh, connects by ligaments to the tibia, the main bone in the lower leg.

Next to the tibia and running parallel to it is a smaller bone, the fibula. Between the femur and the tibia are the menisci and the articular cartilage. The menisci act as a natural shock absorption system, and the articular cartilage, which lines the end of the bones, is similar to a layer of ice providing a near frictionless surface during motion. The patella, what we commonly call the kneecap, rides on the joint as the knee bends. Running through, over, and around this mechanism is a network of muscles, ligaments and tendons.

The anterior cruciate ligament is one of two ligaments that form a cross (hence *cruciate*) in the joint, under the kneecap. The posterior cruciate ligament, or PCL, which tears very rarely, is in the back and the ACL is in the front of the knee.

Considering the size of the job it performs, which is to stabilize this large, important joint, and all the mischief its failure can cause, the ACL is tiny, about thirty millimeters long, smaller than a little finger and less than ten grams in weight. Its shape is rectangular, as if you took a section of a rubber band and stretched it against a flat surface. The ACL's main job, says William Garrett, is to "restrain abnormal motion. It keeps the lower leg, the tibia, from sliding forward, and to a lesser degree, prevents the tibia from rotating internally."

An ACL tear happens on the field of play in one of two ways: contact, which is the most frequent cause in football (a shoulder pad or a helmet crashes into the knee, buckling it), and noncontact, which is the predominant cause in other sports. In a noncontact injury, an athlete lands from a jump—a rebound, a headed ball—and then crumples to the ground. Or she is sprinting and suddenly folds to the ground just as she decelerates to turn.

The mythology is that athletes blow out their ACLs while cutting, but the injury usually occurs just before that, in the slowing-down phase. The leg in the direction of the turn, or the *plant* leg—the left leg when cutting to the left, the right when going right—is always the one that suffers the injury. It is usually painful, especially if there is other, collateral knee damage. But what an athlete is often most immediately cognizant of is a sudden sense of instability, a feeling that something—it's not clear what—has collapsed under her.

An ACL does not tear so much as it utterly disintegrates. It pulls away from the femur and turns into a viscous liquid. Researchers know the force required for this to occur: 2,000 newtons a newton being a unit of measurement. They could not learn this, of course, from volunteer medical subjects—you can't ask someone to tear an ACL to further medical knowledge—so they used cadaver knees.

They increased the force on these cadaver tibias to determine the level that causes ACLs to rupture.

But what actually causes that force of 2,000 newtons to settle in the ACL, rather than being more evenly absorbed in the lower leg and up the trunk—and why it happens sometimes but not most of the time—is a source of ongoing research and debate. Since its cause is not clear, an ACL tear is a perplexing injury, not easy to prevent. "I'm an injury epidemiologist, and I've been doing this for a while now," Steve Marshall, the lead researcher on a vast ACL research project funded by the National Institutes of Health, told me. "This is the first time I've studied something where I can't show you what did the damage. If we were reconstructing an incident where a child fell down a staircase, I could say, OK, he got a laceration here because that's where he hit the handrail. Or he rolled his ankle, or whatever. If it's a car crash, you say, OK, the road was slick, a crash occurred, and a loose object in the car came up and hit someone on the head. But here, you can look at a video of an injury all day long, and what you see is people in the air. People landing. People cutting. What we can't actually see is what tears the thing apart. No other acute injury is analogous, where you cannot clearly see the cause and effect."

Why are female athletes so much more likely to suffer the injury? There are suspicions, all of them under study: Women have wider *Q angles*, the measurement taken of the line between the middle of the kneecap and the center of the hip. It is more common for them to have knee valgus (knock-knees), meaning their knees collapse inward when they run. They are more upright when they run and cut. Some women have quadriceps muscles that are out of balance with their hamstrings: the quads are stronger and may "overfire" and rip the ACLs. There could be hormonal reasons or even causes related to shoe design. (Most women's athletic shoes are simply smaller versions of men's shoes, despite what is known about differences in anatomy, gait, and even the shape of the foot—and despite the intense efforts of Nike and other sporting goods companies to both celebrate the female athlete and capture her share of the market.) There could, as well, be a neurological component, a garbled message—an error in the motor program—that gets passed from the brain to the knee.

When the injury does occur, however, it is one of the easiest orthopedic events to diagnose. An MRI examination is generally just a formality. For starters, the injured athlete often hears a loud pop as the ACL blows, and if she doesn't hear it, others on the field often do, even amid the hurly-burly of an ongoing game. And almost any experienced athletic trainer can make the diagnosis as soon as he puts his hands on the injured joint. It feels mushy to the touch. When the athlete stands, the knee feels unstable under her, as if the injured leg were planted in a bowl of jelly.

An ACL cannot be stitched back together or otherwise repaired. Surgeons must graft a new ACL in its place, usually from the patient's own tissue, by taking a snippet of the patellar tendon or part of the hamstring tendon. Occasionally an ACL from a cadaver is used, especially if the patent has had multiple ACL tears and no more of her own tissue is available to harvest.

A knee, obviously, has no intelligence of its own. It cannot know what team it is playing for, or what coach. But it is sensitive to speed of play, intensity of play, and frequency of play. One of the cruelest things about the ACL injury is that it devastates the ranks of the best female athletes, those who compete with the most skill and passion.

Just kicking the ball around in a rec league with some semi-skilled, semifit players? An ACL tear is probably not an issue. You are probably moving too slowly and taking too much care to stay out of one another's way to be at a high risk. But playing on a go-go club team and seeing some kind of future for yourself in your sport—a spot on the high school varsity or maybe even a chance to play in college? Your odds are far worse.

• • •

Eighteen minutes.

That is how long Amy played in that first game in Vancouver, with the U.S. under-nineteen team, before the ACL in her right knee, the same one reconstructed ten months earlier, ruptured. It happened in the heat of battle, during one of her cherished one v. one challenges—a race for the ball she had to win. It came bouncing toward her, and she touched it and it rolled away a little too far. She and an opponent went racing after it and arrived at the same time. Amy got her foot on the ball first but, in trying to dodge her competitor, planted on her right leg and felt an explosion. It was a clear case of perturbation. The ball wasn't quite where she expected it and an opponent challenged her, causing Amy to adjust to what she believed would be a clear path to the ball.

In the moment after the injury, "I kind of hopped on my other leg, my good one, for a couple of seconds. But every time I tried to take a real step, my leg just collapsed on me. All the coaches thought I just rolled my ankle, so I tried to keep playing."

She kept repeating to herself, "I'm not hurt. I'm not hurt."

"I was sort of playing this whole game in my mind. I thought if I just kept saying it, I could make it be true. I've heard a pop when other girls tore theirs. Once I was in a tournament and I was on the bench and I heard a girl do it. It was that loud. But I didn't hear mine, so I was just kind of hoping that's not what it was."

She tried to keep playing for a moment, then hobbled to the sideline. She said to the doctor, "Just check it," still imagining that he might send her back on the field.

He put his hands on her knee and turned to her coach. "You've got to sub her out," he said. He took Amy back behind the bench and told her that he was certain she had torn her ACL. After the painful, solitary rehab in Brevard and the hundreds of hours spent in Chapel

Hill working to regain her soccer skills, she was right back where she started.

Ned and Carol Steadman were watching from the stands. "That's what I felt worst about," Amy recalls. "Other girls' parents had seen them play when we went to Europe, but with my parents' being teachers, they aren't very wealthy. They couldn't make it to these kinds of events. It was a really big deal for them to be there."

Amy recalls having "like a two-day emotional breakdown. It was just devastating not to be able to play, after what I had just gone through after the first ACL. All your teammates, everybody around you, wants to talk to you and make sure you're OK. They mean well, but of course you're not OK. You don't want to talk to anybody."

The tournament went on for nearly two more weeks. Another player, one of the two left behind in Chula Vista, was quickly flown into Vancouver to fill out the U.S. roster. Surgery for an ACL tear usually takes place a month or more after the injury to give time for the swelling to subside. With her knee wrapped, Amy sat in the stands and watched the rest of the games with her parents, right up to the American victory in the championship game.

"The girls were great. They included me in everything," she recalls. "And we were so good. It was so easy to be excited for us, but it was hard not to be playing the rest of the tournament. Everybody was saying to me, 'What's wrong?' All I could say was, 'Have fun. Celebrate. We'll have this discussion later.' It was great for my parents to be around everyone else's parents. I tried to get focus on that, but I wanted to be on the field so badly."

A GREAT many young women are told after having ACL surgery that they are as good as new. Do the rehab, get back on the field, and it probably won't happen to you again. They come to think of their injury as if they were hit by lightning. What are the odds of such bad luck hitting you twice?

It's a nice thought, but it's not true. The advances in the quality of the surgical fixes may actually have led to greater reinjury rates for young women. They go back out on the field, compete as intensely as ever, then rupture the ACL in the same or the opposite knee. Even as the exact cause of ACL injuries remains under study, most researchers assume that those who suffer the injury once are probably at greater risk of tearing an ACL in the future — not because the repair was inadequate, but because they have demonstrated a predisposition. It doesn't matter that the nature of the predisposition is not known for sure; whatever it is, they probably have it.

"Only an orthopedic surgeon would be vain enough to think he did a better job than God did," says Bill Garrett, Amy's orthopedic surgeon. "If we're honest, we have to say these young women who tore one ACL have a greater chance of doing it again. It looks like the risk is similar to the operated knee as it is to the nonoperated knee." (Some theorize that the other knee is more likely to suffer an ACL injury because an athlete, less confident of the repaired knee, may compensate by using the other knee for deceleration and other maneuvers that generate force.)

Two days after returning to Chapel Hill from Vancouver, Amy had her right knee reconstructed for the second time in a year, this time using tissue from her right hamstring tendon. She recalls her rehabilitation as saner, but she did not reset her goals. "I was still bound and determined. I was going to make it back. I was going to make the national team. I was going to be a star in college. It was kind of like I never got emotionally down. I never had that doubt in my mind. I just rehabbed and did all the normal things, but a little slower. This time, because I was so conscious of not losing weight, I actually gained about five pounds, which was probably better because it's easier to lose it than gain it."

She could not play for UNC that fall, but she made it back in time to qualify for the American under twenty-one team that traveled the following spring to a tournament in Brazil. She felt she was still on course for all her goals, including the biggest one: to one day make the "full U.S. national team," the one that plays in World Cups and in the Olympics.

Brazil, just like Vancouver, was "the coolest thing ever." But for the first time, she noticed a diminution in her abilities. "I played really well, but to be honest, there was still a little bit missing. I wasn't the same."

When she returned home, her college soccer season was still two months off, but she did not rest or take time to work on fitness and muscle strength in areas that might protect her knee. She went right back out on the field to rebuild her skills. In addition to playing pickup games with UNC teammates, she practiced with the Carolina Cougars, a women's professional team.

After one of the practices, the coach asked her to stay around to work out with a prospect he wanted to see play. "He was a really nice guy. He wanted a couple of us to play pickup with some girl who was trying to be on the team. There was some reason she wasn't allowed in the regular practice, but he wanted to see how legit this girl was. It was completely stupid of me."

Amy had been standing around for thirty minutes. She was tired and her muscles were cold. She went for a ball and felt a sudden excruciating pain in her right knee. This time, the initial diagnosis was a tear in the meniscus, or cartilage. The surgery for that is nowhere as complex as an ACL reconstruction. She thought she would be back playing in a few weeks.

But when she came out of surgery, Dr. Garrett told her that while cleaning up the meniscus he had discovered that "the ACL doesn't look good." Even in her drugged state, Amy was alarmed. "What do you mean?" she asked. "It's still there, right?"

Dr. Garrett said that it was not still there. It had exploded again during play or possibly just dissolved on its own. This was the third time in two years she was told her right ACL had ruptured.

"I was devastated," she says. "And my mom was in the room and had to be escorted out because she was in tears, so at that point I completely lost it and I just started hysterically balling."

Amy was told later that the ACL "hadn't been in there for a while. They thought maybe it just disintegrated. My body, for whatever reason, rejected it. It ate it up."

It had all happened so quickly—three ACL tears before she even turned twenty—that she never took stock or reassessed. Her youth and personality led her to respond to adversity with ever fiercer determination. So she just kept getting injured, rehabbing, going back out on the field, and getting hurt again.

A couple of days after her surgery, she went in to consult with Anson Dorrance. She was heading into her second season as a member the premier women's college soccer team in America, but she had not yet made it onto the field, and now it looked like she would again be watching from the sideline. "I said to Anson, 'What am I going to do? Get surgery again?' For so long, I hadn't been playing. I was like, 'I just want to play.' "

In MUCH of the published medical research, an initial ACL injury is shown to be not an isolated event but the starting point for a series of other problems—financial, physical, academic, emotional. "Rupture of the ACL is costly, with conservative estimates of surgery and rehabilitation at $17,000 to $25,000 per injury," Timothy Hewett, the Cincinnati researcher, wrote in a 2007 article in *The American Journal of Sports Medicine*. "This cost is in addition to potential loss of entire seasons of sports participation, loss of scholarship funding, lowered academic performance, long-term disability, and significantly greater risk of radiographically diagnosed osteoarthritis."

"Think of it like an ice pick going into a block of ice," says Holly Silvers, the physical therapist at Santa Monica Orthopaedics, explaining the long-term physical effects of an ACL injury. "You see the cracks on the surface of the ice, but below that are changes in the interior that aren't immediately apparent."

Dr. Bert Mandelbaum was the medical director for the women's World Cup soccer teams in 1999 and 2003 and is Silvers's research partner at Santa Monica Orthopaedics. "It's a cascade of events," he says. "First, the ACL, then the arthritis. That's what we're dealing with: the joint breaks down over time." Another of the Santa Monica researchers, Diane Watanabe, says, "Once you lay the scar tissue down, it doesn't go anywhere."

Some of the best research and most rigorous ACL prevention programs are conducted outside the U.S., in Norway, Sweden, Switzerland, and New Zealand. It is not coincidental that these are countries whose governments pay the cost of health care. "They see it as a public health issue," Mandelbaum says. "It's a line item that is too expensive on all kinds of levels, and they want to do something about it."

In 1998 to 2001, researchers from the Oslo Sports Trauma Research Center and the Norwegian University of Sport and Physical Education conducted a study of 2,647 women competing in professional team handball, a popular sport in Norway and one with high rates of ACL injuries. The fast-paced indoor game, something like a combination of basketball and soccer, includes a lot of sprinting, stopping, and quick cutting, and an estimated one in five elite-level female players suffer ACL ruptures. The study instituted an ACL prevention program in which women did "balance exercises focusing on neuromuscular control" and "planting-landing skills," and then followed the players to determine if injury levels were reduced.

The rates did come down, although not dramatically, the authors wrote, because researchers had difficulty convincing players of the importance of complying with the prevention program. They speculated that the injury had become so routine that athletes thought it was easily reversed by surgery and rehab. "It is tempting to speculate that players perceive the injuries as less serious than they may be in the long term, i.e., they believe that the only consequence is having to undergo surgery and six to nine months of missed participation. We may have to communicate even more clearly that although the ensuing instability after an ACL injury can be rectified surgically, future normal knee biomechanics and function usually cannot be ensured."

Previous studies of female team handball players in Norway showed that 82 percent of those who underwent ACL surgery returned to competition. That was the good news. "As many as half the injured players reported significant problems with [knee] instability, pain, and loss of range of motion when examined eight to ten years after their injury."

Even more alarming, the authors speculated that surgery may actually increase the risk of arthritis because players return to competition on a knee that is less structurally sound than they imagine. "It may be hypothesized," they wrote, "that an effective ACL reconstruction increases the risk of future osteoarthritis by enabling the athlete to return to high-performance pivoting sports: either through reinjury or due to the high demands put on the knee. In our follow-up study on team handball players, approximately 50 percent of the injured players had radiologic signs of osteoarthritis 8–10 years postinjury."

In the United States, Bert Mandelbaum and Holly Silvers at Santa Monica Orthopaedics have designed one of the most well-regarded ACL prevention programs. A dynamic warm-up meant to be done before each practice and game, it focuses on running and landing techniques that protect the knee from vulnerable positions. (Much more on this in a later chapter.) The program is in wide use in girls' soccer leagues in southern California, and initial research has shown it to be effective in reducing ACL injuries. But their program and others like it are not common elsewhere, not even in well-heeled communities with well-educated parents who are otherwise focused, sometimes to the point of obsession, on keeping their kids safe. Parents tend to defer to the experts in this realm—coaches—and most coaches do not like to waste precious practice time on injury prevention. Injury prevention programs are best sold as "performance enhancement," which, in fact, they also are.

What ACL injuries cost the U.S. health system is, at best, a guess. The NCAA numbers are based on a sampling of colleges that report injuries—a sampling that represents only about 12 percent of member schools each year. There is no routine reporting for ACL injuries at the high school or youth level. "How many kids tear their ACLs each year? That's a basic, fundamental question, and we don't have the answer," says Steve Marshall, the ACL researcher. "As a scientist, I'm embarrassed to have to say that. Sometimes I feel like I'm working in a dark room without a flashlight. There ought to be a registry, like there is a cancer registry, and every injury ought to be reported.

"You can say, OK, this isn't cancer. But the point is that cancer is still something that you mainly get when you are older, and this is something striking our nation's youth. And there's a huge loss involved. This is an injury that can lead to loss of physical mobility, and with loss of mobility comes other problems, including obesity and all kinds of obesity-related diseases."

What, then, should be done when a girl or young woman experiences her first ACL injury? Or multiple injuries? With each one, her chances for long-term consequences increase. At the Women's Sports Medicine Clinic at the Hospital for Special Surgery in New York City, Jo Hannafin and Lisa Callahan wrestle with this question frequently. "By the time someone injures their first one, they've had an acute injury but hopefully they have not done other damage to the structures within the knee," Dr. Hannafin says. "So I use that as an opportunity, if they have never done any prevention work, to inform them. Part of the rehab is education.

"But there are a percentage who go on to tear their opposite ACL, or they do the same knee again, despite all our best efforts. It is either fate or genetics. So now you have someone who is fourteen when they do the first one, fifteen when they do the other side, and maybe sixteen when they do a third one, and there is a point when as a physician you say, 'Yes, you've made it back onto the field, you've worked really hard and recovered, but are you going to be an Olympic soccer player or do you want to save your knees for other things in life?' Probably not enough of us have that discussion after the second injury, or certainly after the third, and that's a disservice."

Both doctors believe deeply in the benefits of sports. "We don't want girls not to play sports," Callahan says. "We're both athletes. We think it's so important for them—for their mental health, physical health, moral health, their development as humans. But not all sports are for all girls, especially if you've had one after another of these ACL injuries.

"It's not easy to give up a sport you love, and we understand that. But I suggest to them they find something else they can develop a passion for, because if you like to move and you love competition, there's always something you can do. You can bike. You can get in the pool. You can row. You can do speed skating, Pilates, weight training. There are a million things you can do."

BILL PRENTICE, the former longtime athletic trainer for the UNC women's soccer team, has treated a great many young women with ACL tears, including Amy Steadman and Leslie Gaston. "Will a lot of them have problems later on?" he says. "I'm sure they will. Very sure. My guess is that some of them, by the time they are forty or forty-five years old, will have to have a knee replacement."

Artificial knees do not last forever. A younger woman needing one, Prentice said, might need two, or in rare cases, even three knee replacements over the course of her lifetime.

ACL ruptures, particularly repeat ones in the same knee, damage articular cartilage, the tissue on the end of the bones that is critical in the movement of one bone against the other. "We're seeing this with a lot of them, these lesions, chunks the size of a pencil eraser or a dime in the cartilage. It's a form of osteoarthritis, and it's debilitating pain."

Prentice has often found himself in the role of counselor. (He stepped down as trainer of the women's soccer team in 2006 but remains on the UNC faculty as a professor in the Department of Exercise and Sport Science.) "It's more than one conversation. You say to them, 'Do you think it's time? Time to not be doing this anymore?' Usually, they don't think that. They're very young. It's their decision, but on occasion I say, 'Enough is enough.' "

Amy Steadman finally did get to play for North Carolina—without an ACL, and with a brace serving to stabilize the knee. The brace, in essence, *was* the ACL, serving to keep the knee from shifting forward or sideways in the course of competition. Others have done the same (including Leslie Gaston), although rarely with good results. But by the time Amy opted for the brace, the consensus was that she had already, unknowingly, been playing for several months without an ACL. She figured, How much worse could it be?

"They just gave me this big thing and said, 'Wear this. See if you can go out there and play.' And for a while I could. My knee didn't shift a lot. I was still fast, but I played timid, and I wasn't what I once was. I never used to get outrun, but now I did."

The brace had two big padded metal clamps on it to keep her knee from moving. Amy hated it. She told Dorrance, "I can't move with this thing on my knee. I'll get more surgery rather than keep this on." Dorrance told her, "That's your choice. It's up to you."

She competed for half a season, keeping the brace on, but decided she could not meet any of her goals in her condition. And running without the ACL was taking a toll off the field as well as on. Sometimes, when she stepped out of bed in the morning, her knee buckled and she would crumple to the floor. She stopped playing for the season and sought more surgery.

Dr. Garrett refused to perform a third reconstruction. He thought it was time for her to get off the field. As determined as ever, Amy moved from Garrett to another surgeon. Amy's father says, "Her strength more than anything is her willpower. She can will her way to things. The only thing she has not been able to will to happen is for her knee to get better."

She told the doctor she wanted another reconstruction so she could get her speed and mobility back. Those attributes felt like part of her. She was incomplete without them. "I had to have a really long conversation with the doctor, who really didn't want to do the surgery. He said the success rate is very low on a third one. I knew the statistics. I knew that every time you have surgery, scar tissue builds up and other things can happen. I tried to explain to the doctor, 'Look, I want to be on the national team. You have to do this.'"

Finally, the surgeon agreed. He wanted to take part of a patellar tendon from her left knee for the graft—the right one had already been snipped—but she talked him out of it. That knee was untouched, unlike her battle-scarred right knee, and she did not want a surgeon's knife cutting into it. She talked him into using a cadaver ACL. "Maybe I'm just different," she says, "but using the cadaver knee didn't freak me out that much."

After that third ACL reconstruction, she played the next year, in 2004, as the starting left back for the Tar Heels. It did not go well. "The season," she says, "was nothing but emotional turmoil." She showed glimpses of her old self and thought at moments she could still excel. But other times, she felt listless and slow, nothing like the whippet she once was. "If we played a Sunday game after a Friday game, my body would just shut down. I never got better. My speed never improved. My agility never improved."

Toward the end of the season came an indignity that she never could have imagined coming out of Brevard as a *Parade* All-American and as a sure bet for collegiate stardom. She lost her starting position at UNC. She had declined to the point that she was no longer one of the Tar Heels' best eleven players. "Anson decided to play somebody else at left back," she says. "It was very tough for me to deal with, because it was the final realization that I'm not going to be on the national team. I'm never going to be any type of star or stand-out again. It was unbelievably hard to admit that to myself and say, You know, that's OK. That's who I am now. Because I never expected to be in a situation like that."

She tried once more to play the following season. She ended up back in the operating room and back in recovery with a doctor telling her that her ACL was gone. It was then that she heard from the surgeon there was "nothing left to fix." Her third ACL reconstruction, the one with the cadaver graft, had ruptured during play, or just disintegrated. Her right knee, at this point, was shot. She had used her knee up. Left it on various soccer fields. The doctor said, "Come see me later in the week. We need to talk about your soccer career, what you're going to do."

She talked to her parents, to her boyfriend, and to Bill Prentice. Should she retire from the sport she loved more than anything?

Prentice recalls his conversation with Amy, "She said, 'What should I do?' She wasn't asking any longer what would give her the best chance to compete at an international level. She wanted to know how she could have a good life going forward. Amy has that angelic face and a quiet demeanor along with an inner intensity. She's boiling inside. But she's very intelligent and analytical. I told her it was time, but she already knew that."

Finally, she went to Anson Dorrance's office with her decision. She was nervous. "I'm on scholarship," she remembers thinking. "I didn't want him to think I was taking it for granted."

Leslie Gaston had also told me she feared losing her scholarship and being cast off by Dorrance and her teammates. None of those things were threatened or likely to happen, but it is significant that these young women feared they might. Somewhere in the course of their experience as elite female athletes, they came to equate injury with being shunned, with having done something wrong.

But how could Dorrance or anyone else possibly think she was shirking her responsibilities after all the physical and emotional trauma she had endured? "I didn't think he'd mind," Amy said. "That was kind of about me, not Anson. It's just the way I think. I want to see things through. I don't ever want to be a quitter."

As she sat that day with Dorrance, he told her she had made the right decision. It was time, finally, to step away. "This is crazy," he said to her, referring to her unrelenting injuries. "Maybe this is God's way of telling you that you shouldn't play this game anymore."

Even though that was what Amy wanted—permission to re-tire—a part of her wanted Dorrance to say something else. "Maybe I wasn't even sure at that moment," she says. "But I know now that it was the right thing. I just finally had to ask myself, Do I want to be able to walk when I'm thirty? Do I want to be able to play with my kids or even kick a soccer ball around with them if I want?"

CHAPTER 7

IN THE OR

"Do you want to watch a surgery?" Dr. Barry Boden asked me. Of course I did. I had talked to Amy Steadman, Janelle Pierson, Rachel Young—a couple of dozen young women in all who had undergone ACL reconstruction, some more than once. None of them had fully understood why it took them six months to regain strength and stability and a year or more to feel normal. They had not, after all, been awake for the procedure. They hadn't seen that it is complex, bloody, and—to use Boden's words—barbaric.

Boden is an orthopedic surgeon as well as one of the leading researchers into the cause of ACL injuries. I met him on a Monday morning, not at a hospital but at a surgery center on the penthouse level of an office building in Chevy Chase, Maryland. He pressed the code to let us into a locker room, where we changed out of our street clothes and pulled on pale blue scrubs along with face masks and plastic booties. In the OR, Boden's team was waiting for him: a surgical nurse, or "first assistant"; a technician who sterilized, organized, and handed him his surgical tools; and an anesthesia nurse.

The patient was a twenty-one-year-old woman who had torn her ACL in a most freakish way—play-fighting with a friend. She had simulated a karate kick and heard something pop in her right knee. Boden knew from her MRI that she had also partially torn her medial meniscus, the cartilage near the middle of the joint. She was not an active athlete, but it didn't matter—her surgery was the same, or similar, to what Amy Steadman and the others had experienced.

She was already sedated from the anesthesia when an attendant wheeled her into the room. A blanket covered everything but her right knee. Boden made a small incision on the outside of her knee and inserted an arthroscope, a miniature camera. He guided it around the inside of the joint, and we had an up-close visual tour that provided a much better view than he had seen in the MRI images.

He was already certain that her ACL was gone. A TV screen above the operating table, projecting pictures from the arthroscope, showed some remnants of it, tiny pieces of floating fiber that would have to be cleaned out. The arthoscopic image confirmed that the meniscus was torn but in a good way, cleanly enough so that it could be stitched back together rather than removed. "This is critical," he said as he started in on the job. "If I had to take it out, she'd have arthritis in five years."

Boden's technician handed him a small surgical tool that looked like a crochet hook, and he used it to expertly mend what he called a "bucket handle" tear of the meniscus, a flap that could be sewn back onto the main body of cartilage. It took him about fifteen minutes, and it was a gentle process compared to what would follow.

When he was done, he said to no one in particular, "All right, let's do the ACL." To his technician, he said, "Let me have a knife." He took the scalpel and made about a three-inch incision just below the kneecap. This was in preparation of harvesting the patient's own tissue from her patellar tendon—which connects the kneecap to the tibial tubercle (a bony prominence on the upper part of the shinbone)—in order to form a new ACL. This part of the procedure, the harvesting, was open surgery—the old-fashioned kind, not guided by an arthroscope. The incision needed to be big enough to allow him to work by sight.

After Boden made the cut, he parted the skin, reached inside the crevice with his right hand, and grabbed the patellar tendon so that I could get a look. It was thick and sturdy-looking, more like a cable than a thin fiber. Still gripping it, he said, "This is going to be our ACL."

With his scalpel, he cut a ten-millimeter-wide strip lengthwise, right out of the middle of the tendon. It came off, as he intended, with a chunk of bone at each end—a piece of the patella at the top and on the bottom, a chunk of the tibial tubercle. It looked like a scrap of meat. He handed the whole thing to his sugical nurse, who set it down on a flat surface at the foot of the operating table, atop a sanitary blue cloth that looked like a folded napkin. Her job was to measure it and prepare it for transplant.

She took a knife and carved off a silver of white matter, explaining, "That's just a little fat." She rounded and smoothed the bone to form "bone plugs." She then slid the sliver of tissue and bone through tubes to determine its width, which was 8.5 centimeters.

While his nurse worked, Boden, guided by the arthroscope, scraped and drilled inside the joint, in the notch where the transplanted ligament would go, between the femur and tibia. This part of the procedure is called a *notchplasty.* The goal is to carve the space into the precise size and shape of the graft so that the new ACL can be situated at the same angle as the original one.

What became obvious to me was that much of ACL surgery consists of trading body parts back and forth. Boden drilled little tunnels on each side of the knee. At one point he changed tools and switched to what looked like a surgical hammer and chisel. He formed the tunnels by drilling a hole in the femur and tibia at the sites where the ACL normally attaches to the bone.

In all the drilling and cutting, blood began to flow into a plastic bag set below the patient's knee and spilled onto the floor. Several times, an attendant bustled over to vacuum it up with a suction device. Boden finally pronounced himself satisfied with his shaping of the notch. "You have to be careful not to blow out the back side of the femur," he said. "You need that for the graft to attach to."

His nurse handed him the strip of patellar tendon, now fully prepared. With a small surgical tool, and using the arthroscope to guide him, he threaded it through an incision in the knee. The bone plugs on each end fit into the tunnels he had drilled in the tibia and femur. They would bind to the bone in the tunnels the same way a healing fracture does, which would help secure the graft in place. (The involvement of the bone is why this type of ACL reconstruction is sometimes called a bone–patella tendon–bone graft.)

Boden's last task inside the knee was pure carpentry. He took two titanium screws and, using a surgical screwdriver, secured the bone plugs into the femur and tibia. To do so, he braced his right leg on the floor (after the blood had been sunctioned again, so he would not slip) and strained almost to the point of grunting.

With the ACL graft complete, he turned back to the graft site, which was still open. "Remember where the bone came off?" he said to me. "We just can't leave those holes there." He then took the bone that came from the tibial tunnel and used it to plug the spaces where the bone portion of the graft had been harvested. Then the nurse sewed up the incision, and after about two and a half hours, the surgery was complete.

Boden estimates he has done about 450 ACL reconstructions in the last decade, including about 50 a year for the last six years. I was impressed by the skill required—forming the notch seemed more art than science—and by the seamless cooperation of his team. They had all worked together for years, and it showed.

My predominant impression, though, was of the complexity and scale of the surgery; it is called a reconstruction for good reason. Boden had worked inside the joint and below the joint. At one point he had inserted a long pin, the kind you might use to bind a turkey, and threaded it from the lower leg, up through the knee, and out the thigh in order to pull the graft into its proper position. The patient had lost as much as 100 ccs of blood. (Boden tries not to use a tourniquet because it creates more post surgical pain.)

"It's involved. It's complicated. It can be a little barbaric at times," Boden said as he was finishing up.

There are other types of ACL reconstructions. One involves taking part of the patient's hamstring tendon for the graft, which some tests show may produce a stronger ACL but may take longer to heal after surgery because there is no bone-to-bone connection. Quadriceps tendons are also sometimes used. These two methods, like the patellar tendon transplant, are called *autografts,* the taking of tissue from the patient's own body.

An *allograft,* taking tissue from a cadaver, is yet another option. Usually, a patellar tendon, a hamstring tendon, or an Achilles tendon is taken from a cadaver to serve as the graft. The surgery is less complicated, because there is no donor site, but it may involve a greater risk of infection or rejection, and the graft itself may not be as strong.

The type of surgery I observed is the most common and, along with the hamstring tendon procedure, is sometimes called *gold standard.* One study indicated that a transplanted ACL using a patellar tendon is 36 percent stronger than a natural ACL. (The tensile strength was measured to be 2,950 newtons to failure, versus 2,160 for an intact ACL.) But there are still disadvantages. The patellar tendon surgery results in more pain at the donor site than the other procedures, and many patients are left with a permanent loss of sensation in a small patch near the incision. The tendon itself usually regenerates over time, although patients may be at greater risk of

CHAPTER 8

A MEDICAL DETECTIVE STORY

ACL researchers are seeking to solve two related myster-ies. What forces—and from where—settle in the knee to rip the ACL apart? And why are women so much more susceptible than men? "Look, let's be honest, the predisposing risk factor here is the absence of testicles," Dr. William Garrett says. "But we can't leave it at that. There are other things we're looking at, and I believe we'll eventually find answers. We have to. Exercise has huge benefits, and they far outweigh the risks. But you don't want to get injured, and you sure don't want this particular injury, because it wreaks havoc."

What perplexes Garrett and other researchers is why a knee works properly for many years—game after game, practice after prac-tice, long season after long season, through tens of thousands of rep-ititions—and then without warning a tiny but crucial component of it suddenly malfunctions and disintegrates into useless mush.

When Garrett lectures to students on ACL injuries, he tells a riddle: "Why do planes crash?" he asks. He elicits a variety of answers: pilot error, weather problems, electronic and computer breakdowns, and so forth. Then he gives his own simple explanation. "The answer is gravity," he says. "The question is, why don't they crash more often?"

The ACL is like the plane that dives into a disastrous crash. Which is the greater wonder: that the ACL sometimes tears in the heat of battle, or that it does such a big job without malfunctioning at an even greater rate?

"That's the essence of the mystery," Garrett says. "It's not like it tears every time it gets in an awkward position. It just does it sometimes, with disastrous consequences. The knee does this thing it knows how to do, and then it forgets."

The knee, of course, does not operate independently from the rest of the body; it communicates with the entirety of the musculoskeletal system and with the brain, spinal cord, nerves and hormones. Males and females, in all these regards, are different—in some cases, *vastly* different. And somewhere in those differences lurks the answer to why girls and women are rupturing their ACLs at such comparatively high rates.

WE HUMAN beings are natural scorekeepers. Where we identify difference, we assign rank. One thing must be better, the other not as good; one superior, the other inferior. We do this on all kinds of levels, from ancient superstitions (right-handedness over left-handedness) to long-held cultural preferences for sons over daughters to banal magazine stories that rank everything from best rock-and-roll songs to best presidents to best places to raise a family. (What family? I suppose the kind that could discern the subtle distinctions between Sudbury, Massachusetts, and Manhasset, New York, the top two towns on one such recent list.)

Physical differences between males and females are essential to the survival of the species. They are not trivial and not as open to argument.

An expectant mother who chooses to have amniocentesis, a prenatal test to screen for certain birth defects, can learn the sex of her baby in utero. The answer is encoded in chromosome pair 23: two X's and the baby is a girl; an X and a Y and a boy is on the way. Or she may learn her baby's sex from an ultrasound: Penis or no penis? Ah, there it is, or isn't. But newborn girls and boys are, at that moment, as similar as they will ever be. One is no more likely to be bigger than the other or to have a significantly greater physical capability because, after all, neither can do very much.

The great divergence begins at the onset of puberty, usually anywhere between nine and fourteen for girls and ten and seventeen for boys. Over the course of a half dozen years or so, they part ways and go off on their separate journeys. Each in their own bodies, in their own ways, moves toward the same evolutionary imperative—the ability to reproduce. The changes are triggered by hormones, the body's so-called chemical messenger.

The gifted science writer Natalie Angier provides an elegant and succinct explanation of how hormones work in her book *Woman: An Intimate Geography*: "A hormone is a substance secreted by one tissue that travels through blood or another body fluid to another tissue, whereupon the hormone arouses the encountered tissue to a new state of activity."

The male hormone, in fact and in its outsized role in male mythology, is testosterone. But it's not exclusive to males. Women secrete smaller amounts of it in their ovaries and adrenal glands. Men manufacture it mainly in their testicles, and between the ages of twelve and fifty have on average ten times more testosterone coursing through their systems than women.

Testosterone's impact, on one level, is easy to understand. It's a strength enhancer. This is why various forms of synthesized testosterone have long been the performance drug of choice for weight lifters, sprinters, sluggers, shot-putters, and all other athletes—male or female—desirous of more strength and fast-firing muscle.

It is sometimes said—jokingly, unkindly, resignedly—that a man thinks with his penis, which, of course, cannot be the case. Nor is it correct to attribute a man's behavior, or a teenage boy's, to the properties of testosterone. But it is not entirely *incorrect* either.

Testosterone appears to influence thought patterns and even career paths. In studies, male athletes have been found to have above-average levels of testosterone, as have convicts, and the more violent the criminal, the higher the level of his testosterone. Blue-collar workers have higher levels than white-collar workers. A study in 1998 showed that trial lawyers, the pugilists of the legal system, have higher testosterone levels than lawyers who do not do battle in open court.

Men's testosterone levels are not static over the course of a lifetime or even a day. They rise and fall depending on the level of challenge, threat, or elation—going up before an athletic competition, and higher yet after a victory, but falling in the wake of defeat. One study even showed that testosterone levels of male fans watching a World Cup soccer match spiked or declined according to the fortunes of their team. If a man is about to parachute out of a plane, his testosterone level falls. It also falls if he is soon to become a father. (Apparently, impending fatherhood feels something like jumping out of a plane.)

The female hormone is estrogen. Like testosterone, it exists in the body in infinitesimal amounts but is powerful beyond its volume. "Keep in mind that regardless of whose hormones are under scrutiny, the concentrations are vanishingly small, measured in laboratory tests in nanograms or pictograms—billionths of trillionths of a gram," Angier writes. "To obtain one teaspoon of estradiol"—one of the three main estrogen hormones—"we would need to drain the blood of a quarter of a million premenopausal women. By contrast, the blood supply of any one of us contains at least a teaspoon of sugar and several tablespoons of salt."

Estrogen is not the opposite of testosterone, exactly, but it can seem that way. Testosterone tells the body to grow muscle; estrogen tells it to add fat. At birth, boys and girls have about 10 to 12 percent body fat, and prepuberty, both, on average, have somewhere around 16 percent. After puberty, the average man is about 15 percent body fat; the average woman 25 percent. (Estrogen circulates in the blood of men too, and as they get older, their levels rise at the same time their testosterone count falls.)

Fat, especially in this era of rampant obesity, needs better public relations. We can't do without a reasonable measure of it. It regulates body temperature and cushions our organs. It is part of every part of our body, from head to toe. The brain's white matter is largely composed of fat.

Fat is no less a physical necessity than muscle or blood. But in the narrow ways that we define athletics—running fast, throwing a football, hitting a baseball—it's not helpful. (A generous amount of fat does help those who swim long-distance races in cold water, a sport in which women outperform men, but not one that gets a lot of TV time.) Muscle is the work-producing fiber of the human body, the source of strength and propulsion, and men have more of it.

Robert Malina, a professor of kinesiology and the former director of the Institute for the Study of Youth Sport at Michigan State University, has written extensively on young athletes. His research consistently demonstrates that, on average, boys' gross motor skills in childhood, before puberty, as measured by performances in such standard tests as the long jump, vertical jump, and shuttle run, are superior to girls'—but only slightly so. Sex differences in athletic performance, he writes, are "relatively minor until the male adolescent spurt."

When I talked to Malina, he explained that the tests of motor ability measure something very specific—the ability, as he put it, "to move your body through space," which is exactly what our most popular sports demand. We pay high ticket prices to watch people run, jump, stop, and change directions. "The rare athletes you see who are fat, shot-putters for instance, are projecting an object, not themselves," Malina said. "If you watch baseball, sometimes you'll see a fat relief pitcher. It's the same principle. He just has to project the ball."

Girls who excel on America's athletic fields are rarely overweight. They look just as fit as the boys. But postpuberty, pound for pound and cell for cell, they are not as muscular. "The leanest elite female athletes may get their body fat down to 11 or 12 percent," Angier writes. "But that is nearly double the percentage of body fat found on the elite male athlete."

So, in the spirit of scorekeeping, which sex is physically superior? Which hormone, testosterone or estrogen, would you put Number 1 on your Top Ten list? It's ridiculous, of course, but for a moment, let's ponder it from this angle: every so often, some remote region of the world is reported to have a cluster of extraordinarily old people who are said to be living into their 130s, 140s, and even beyond. Writing in the journal *Gender Medicine,* Steven Austad, a biologist at the University of Texas, identified three of these regions as the Caucasus Mountains, between the Black and Caspian Seas; a remote area in the Ecuadoran Andes Mountains; and the Karakoram Mountains, spanning the borders between India, China, and Pakistan. But in every case, he wrote, researchers quickly concluded that the reports were untrue. "A telltale clue as to the falsehood of these claims was that the oldest people in all of these places were supposedly men," Austad wrote, "and anyone knowing anything about human biology knows that is absolutely impossible."

Women, obviously, are the stronger sex. They live longer, and that's a pretty important physical trait: survival.

In most of the industrialized world, life expectancy from birth for women is about six years greater than for men—80 to 74 in the United States, 84 to 78 in Japan, 81 to 74 in Germany. In Russia and much of Eastern Europe, the gap is closer to a dozen years. Of the 560 known "supercentenarians"—people at least 110 years old—in the world in 2006, 90 percent were women. Only in a few nations in Africa, where AIDS has devastated the female population, do men outlive women.

Part of the explanation for women's longer life spans may lie in estrogen's various anti-inflammatory qualities, including for the heart muscle; estrogen may be one possible reason why premenopausal women rarely suffer heart attacks. And women may also live longer because of their relative *lack* of testosterone. They don't act as impulsively, drive as recklessly, get into as many arguments that lead to shootings or stabbings—unless they are arguing with a man—and are not as prone to destructive habits like drug abuse and excessive drinking.

What is known definitively is that women survive longer and apparently always have. Austad writes, "Women have lived longer than men in virtually every place and at every time we can identify."

MEN HAVE long been the subjects of choice for most medical research while women, historically, have been an afterthought. Partly, the reason is cultural, a matter of orientation. The preponderance of leading researchers across all disciplines of science and medicine are still men, and it may not always occur to them that treatments that work for men will not always be equally effective for women.

But women are underrepresented in drug trials in part because experimentation can pose a danger for females of reproductive age. The bias for male subjects extends to animal research—to tests done on rats, mice, pigs, and dogs. Male subjects are often preferred because researchers do not want to grapple with how estrous cycles and related physiological changes might make results more difficult to calculate or present.

Research is like any other business, any workplace: those involved will often take the path of least resistance. And in fact, experimentation on a female rat, for example, who ovulates every four or five days, can be more complicated. Kathryn Sandberg, a professor of medicine and physiology at Georgetown University and director of its Center for the Study of Sex Differences, told me that researchers find male lab animals to be more expedient subjects. But the preference for them is likely one reason that women account for as much as 90 percent of adverse drug reactions. The drugs may seem to work fine for males (let's get through the FDA review process and out on the market!), but they've not been tested on females.

In the lab, researchers must sometimes be reminded to be what in other settings is called "inclusive." One protocol for psychological testing on rats that I came across stated, "Male animals are often the subject of choice in drug and other behavioral studies, because males are not subject to the complex hormonal cycling that has to be taken into account if females are used. Nevertheless, before behavioral generalizations are made, it is essential that parallel studies are carried out on female animals."

Sandberg sits on the National Institutes of Health review panels for federally funded research using lab animals. "I'm the person who raises her hand and says, 'And what were the results for the females?' And I get these sheepish looks and finally someone says, 'Oh, it's too complicated. Females have these cycles.' "

The sports medicine research looking into the ACL injuries is unusual in what might seem like an obvious way: it recognizes sex differences and looks at women as women. Stronger? Weaker? More or less vulnerable to certain injuries? It is agnostic on these points.

The research is the work of scientists who want to follow the data wherever it may lead. If it looks like girls and women are suffering more sports injuries, so be it. They want to know why and how to fix it. "A female athlete is a whole different entity. She is not a different model of the male athlete prototype," says Steve Marshall, of

UNC. "That has to be the starting point for what we're trying to learn."

Estrogen, to an extent, is a suspect in ACL injuries. This particular thread of research, it should be pointed out, sits right smack in the middle of a treacherous intersection, right where science and modern sensibilities meet. Sex hormones contributing to injuries in girls and women playing sports? Thirty-six years after the passage of Title IX, with each new landmark in the progress of women's sports still a cause for celebration, that is not something most people want to think about.

But estrogen, along with another hormone, relaxin, contributes to joint laxity and women's greater overall flexibility—a double-edged attribute for athletes. Too little flexibility and a person cannot excel at most athletic skills; too *much* flexibility and joints are unstable and vulnerable to structural breakdown. Think of a too flexible joint as a hinge that moves every which way—forward, back, side to side—and is not sufficiently buttressed to stay in place.

When Bruce Jones and his colleagues began testing recruits in basic training, they expected that those who were least flexible—women or men—would be the ones most often injured. What they found was that overflexibility was just as great a risk. What seemed to be protective was *moderate* flexibility. Their research concluded that stretching, for women or men, had no discernible positive impact on injury prevention.

After puberty, girls' scores in the sit-and-reach test (a measure of the flexibility of the lower back, hip, and upper thigh) increase; boys' steadily decrease as they grow stronger. Girls' flexibility is not always accompanied by an increase in strength and neuromuscular control. To compete at the intensity demanded in high school soccer, basketball, lacrosse, and other sports, girls generally need more strength. Good old-fashioned muscle wrapped around joints that may otherwise be too lax. One school of thought says that they are trying to do too much, and put too big a load, on a physique that will not with-stand it. "The huge difference in ACL injuries occurs right around ages fifteen to twenty, when girls are getting a much different body with a lot more size and not a lot more strength," Dr. William Garrett notes.

I saw this divergence when my own daughter was in her mid-teens and swimming competitively. Because male and female swim-mers usually train together, it was an interesting laboratory to observe body differences. In order to get faster, the girls had to train rigor-ously, rarely missing practice or giving less than full effort in work-outs. But even some who took that approach did not improve their times, or if they did, their gains were measured in just fractions of seconds. It was not unusual in this training group (or most others) for the female swimmers at seventeen years old to struggle to match times they swam at fourteen. The boys progressed on a different tra-jectory. Not surprisingly, those who trained the hardest usually got the best results, but even some of the less dedicated ones got faster, sometimes considerably so.

Training with the boys, the girls certainly took notice of the ineq-uity, and every now and then I'd hear one of them complain about a particular boy, pointing out how lazy he was but that his times still kept dropping. Just a few years earlier, the girls had been as fast or faster than some of these boys, but physically they were different people now. The boys continued to get taller and, sometimes without much effort of their own, stronger. The girls were mostly done grow-ing, and their gains in the pool came only with prodigious effort.

THE ACL itself has estrogen receptors. In addition to enhancing ligament laxity, which makes joints less stable, estrogen peaks are suspected to have a negative impact on neuromuscular control, co-ordination. At least one study has indicated that women taking oral contraceptives may be less prone to ACL tears, but the conclusion was based on a small sample.

Several studies have set out to determine if there is a particular time in a woman's menstrual cycle when she may be vulnerable to tearing her ACL, but they have come to contradictory conclusions. Women experience a rapid surge of estrogen just prior to ovulation, usually between days ten and fourteen of their cycle. But one challenge of the research is that the time of the month when a woman's estrogen level peaks may not exactly coincide with its impact on ligament laxity. "It looks like there may be a lag of a day or more, and it could be different from one woman to the next," says Sandra Shultz, the UNC Greensboro researcher. "The hormone environment is not the same in every female. It makes this difficult to study."

Researchers who have sought to learn on what day of the cycle women tore their ACLs have had to rely on self-reporting, which is notoriously unreliable. Timothy Hewett, one of the leading ACL researchers, looked at all the available published evidence on hormonal cycles and ACL injuries and more or less threw up his hands, labeling the whole of the research "confounding."

The research may also just be too charged to lead much of anywhere. "A lot of people do not want to hear that it has something to do with hormones," Shultz says. "They say, 'Well, what are you going to do about it?' If you know that hormones are having an impact on knee laxity on the twelfth day of the cycle, are we going to tell a woman not to play that day? Probably not. But I'd still want to know because maybe it will lead us to something else that is helpful."

Anatomy is another area of inquiry, in particular, a measurement known as the *Q angle*, the angle between a line drawn from the hip to the middle of the kneecap and a second line from the middle of the kneecap to the tibial tubercle (upper shinbone).

Typically women's hips are wider than men's, which gives them a greater average Q angle: 17 degrees in the typical adult woman, 14 degrees in men. If you scan an athletic field filled with adolescent girls, you will probably notice some who appear knock-kneed when they run; their knees seem to collapse inward. This is to some extent a by-product of wide hips. But knee valgus can also be a function of poor running mechanics and underdeveloped muscle.

The researchers are most intensely interested in variables that can be modified. To give one example, a trainer or physical therapist cannot change the width of an athlete's hips, but they can teach her to run differently. It is not inaccurate to say that the researchers have a bias—a bias toward finding causes for ACL injuries that can be addressed. It is easier to attract grant money for research that may lead to a cure, and more satisfying as well. "We're interested in motion science because we can change motion," says Steve Marshall, the UNC epidemiologist. "We can't change anatomy."

BARRY BODEN is among the cadre of surgeons who are not content just to operate on shredded ACLs; he wants to figure out why they keep occurring. One sunny spring day at his home in Chevy Chase, Maryland, he showed me his macabre collection of video clips of one athlete after another rupturing an ACL and then crumpling to the turf or floor in pain. The clips are labeled "Case No. 1," "Case No. 2," and so on. Some are grainy footage of obscure high school or college games. Boden acquired them over the course of a dozen years, from the athletes themselves, trainers, doctors, the NBA, and the WNBA.

"Watch this," he said, after we took seats in his study and he inserted a disk in his laptop. "This is a famous one." It was a clip of former NFL running back Barry Sanders juking defensive back Rod Woodson in the open field. The move, and Woodson's futile response, called to mind the old expression "being faked out of his jock." As Woodson tries to make the tackle but instead grasps at air, his cleats seem to grab on the turf before he goes down in a heap, his ACL ruptured.

"Here's another good one," Boden said. On the screen, a male college basketball player throws down a powerful dunk, swings on the rim, then lands off balance on his left leg. As his knee collapses, he falls in a heap and curls up into the fetal position.

The dunker is massive, perhaps 250 pounds, and he lands from a pretty good height. "You can sort of see how that would happen," Boden commented. "That was a lot of force."

Boden has watched these clips over and over again—at regular speed, in slow motion, and in superslow motion. We moved on to snippets of women suffering ACL tears. "You'll see that these look different," he said. In the next sequence, a WNBA player runs up the court at what seems like three-quarter speed, then suddenly falls to the floor as she turns to cut. "You see what I mean? She just decelerates. It was nothing! With the women, it doesn't look like it takes that much force."

From a soccer game: a blond ponytailed girl plants her left leg in preparation to shoot on goal, but can only get off a weak shot as she tumbles down. A basketball player, trailing a dribbler, loses her balance while changing directions and hits the floor. More basketball: a dribbler in the middle of a fast break slows to look for an open teammate, then crumples after she lets the pass go. The player who received the pass makes a shot, and the other nine players turn and run to the other end, oblivious to what has happened—a common scene in these snippets. The lead-up to an injury is so unremarkable that the other players often do not notice their fallen opponent or teammate. They huddle up to celebrate a goal or just turn and take off in the other direction. Only when the action sets itself do they realize that something is wrong. Where's Suzy? They turn to look. She's back at the other end, either trying to hobble to the sideline or still curled up on the ground.

Most of the young women we have watched are either slowing down to make subtle changes of direction or making seemingly routine landings from jumps. They fall so suddenly and bizarrely that if I didn't know better, I might guess they had been shot. Even in slow motion their movement patterns look normal—decelerations and landings that they have repeated thousands of times before—right up to the moment of injury.

Boden has painstakingly watched and analyzed the injury sequences. In addition to his personal research, he is affiliated with Steve Marshall's study at the military academies, a prospective study in which subjects are measured in a laboratory situation, then followed for the next four years. (I will provide much more detail on this research in the next chapter.) Boden's study of these video clips is *retrospective*, a look back at what happened and an effort to figure out why. "You try to put together everything you can get your hands on and see the problem from all sides," he says. "The one thing we can't do is have somebody volunteer to tear their ACL in a laboratory setting so that we can measure everything as it's happening."

WILLIAM GARRETT has viewed some of the videos collected by Boden, who trained with him. And he's seen other such injury compilations. "It's all the same picture," he says. "Someone is awkward in the air, comes down on an outstretched knee, and pop! It's not like looking at an ankle sprain, where you understand what you're seeing because you see the ankle roll. Here, you see it but you don't see it; you see the result but you don't clearly see the cause."

He picks up a model of a knee that he keeps on his desk and begins to manipulate it. The anterior cruciate ligament is situated at an angle in the front of the knee, more vertical to the ground than horizontal. Its critical role in holding the knee in place is why athletes who tear an ACL often sense a loss of stability before they feel pain.

"For as small as it is, it's probably also true that it's highly over-engineered, or it was until we invented sports like basketball and soccer," Garrett says. What he means is that you probably won't tear an ACL taking a cake out of the oven, walking to work, swimming, or

even taking a lusty swing at a baseball. You are unlikely to do it sprinting in a straight line. The ACL meets its test in high-intensity sports
that require stopping, cutting, and landing from jumps. Unless you
are involved in one of these, "you probably don't ever ring up twenty
percent of the force your ACL will withstand," he says. "You've got a
pretty big safety margin for normal activities."

Garrett believes that ACL ruptures occur because of a power
surge, almost like a spasm, in the quadriceps muscles above the knee.
This surge takes place during a straight-legged landing or deceleration, when an athlete lands with her leg extended in front of her
body—and most often when the landing occurs just a split second
after the athlete has expected it. (Biomechanically, a deceleration in
preparation to suddenly change direction is similar to landing from
a jump.) The knee is not flexed, and the hamstrings, which counterbalance the quads, are not activated. It is like stepping off a curb
awkwardly, but at full speed and force.

The split-second delay in the weight-bearing foot's hitting the
ground often occurs after perturbation—a slight jostling or an unan-
ticipated, quick-flash change in the action. You see it in Boden's
video: the young woman in the middle of the fast break, preparing to
pass to an open teammate, suddenly has to change her gait as a defender reaches for the ball. As she plants to make the play, her foot
does not hit the floor as she had planned. Instead, she lands with
one leg out in front of her and the knee locked—the at-risk position
for an ACL tear.

Women have stronger quadriceps in relation to their hamstrings
than men do—an imbalance suspected to be at the root of their
greater incidence of ACL tears. The difference is described in medical journal articles published by Garrett and others, and even in
some fairly technical language, the chain of events they describe is
not difficult to understand: women, in general, do not land as softly
as men. On poor landings, they do not have enough balanced muscle
strength to protect their knees. The quads take over, and not in a

good way. The thrust they should provide for running and jumping is instead concentrated in the knee joint, causing it to rip apart.

Garrett has a direct way of summing up dense research: "What tears the ACL is when you hit and land and the quads stop you from flexing your knee. Not everybody agrees with me, but I'm convinced of it. We took cadavers, and at twenty degrees"—20 degrees of knee flexion, meaning close to a straight knee—"we just pulled on the quads. And we tore the ACL on all of them."

Women have been found to have "lax hamstrings," leading to a "delay in hamstrings muscle activation" and an "absence of co-contraction between the quadriceps and hamstrings muscle groups for a period of time early in foot strike." (*Foot strike* is the instant when the foot makes contact with the ground, either when running or landing from a jump.) Compared to men, women demonstrate a lesser degree of *muscle synchrony* during landing—an interesting phrase. Much of this research can sound politically incorrect. I was told by one researcher that men appear to be more "elegant" runners and jumpers.

Some researchers believe that the tibia and femur actually slam together, creating a force that ruptures the ACL. This is referred to as a *crowbar* effect. "When playing sports, athletes generate both quadriceps and hamstring muscle contractions in anticipation of foot plant with changing directions or landing from a jump," Indianapolis surgeon and researcher K. Donald Shelbourne writes. "The quadriceps muscle has to generate greater forces than the hamstring muscles in order to absorb the landing forces and to keep the knee from being flexed too quickly. . . . These muscle contractions occur thousands of times during athletic practice or competition. When the timing of the foot plant is miscalculated and is a split second later than planned, the exaggerated [quad] muscle contractions cause the tibia to shift farther anterior [forward] than what would have occurred if the foot struck the ground at the correct time." He continues: "The impact of the femur on the posterior part of the tibia causes a fulcrum or 'crowbar' type effect on the tibia, pushing it far-ther anteriorly [forward] and medially, causing the stretched ACL to rupture."

Soccer in particular may make a young woman who is already "quad dominant" even more so, especially if she plays it exclusively from a young age. The repeated motion of kicking a soccer ball builds the quads; it does little for the hamstrings. "You create implicit mus-cle imbalances in your body by playing only one sport," explains Holly Silvers. "This is why we are such huge advocates of cross train-ing, especially in the younger athlete. Soccer players are quad and inner thigh dominant. This is the whole premise of prevention — fo-cus on the antagonistic muscle groups to create a more balanced athlete."

Silvers is echoed by nearly every medical professional with an expertise in youth sport, and the principle applies well beyond the narrow issue of ACL injuries. Parents who encourage or allow their children, especially their daughters, to specialize in a sport at an early age in the hopes that they will master it and become stars and perhaps earn college scholarships or become pro athletes are under-mining their own goal. Rather than nurturing achievement, they are more likely to increase injury risks and shorten their girls' athletic careers.

"LET'S SAY I'm about to pick up this magazine," says Dr. Anthony Beutler. He reaches for a medical journal on his desktop. "I'm mak-ing a plan. I'm saying to myself, 'This magazine weighs less than a pound, so I need to recruit these certain muscles with this degree of effort to pick it up smoothly.' If I'm fooled, and this magazine is made of lead, I'm going to have a jerk, what we call a perturbation, because my motor program is not adequate for the task."

Muscles are activated by the brain via electrical impulses sent through the spinal cord and nerves. Beutler's example parallels what he believes occurs in an ACL rupture. A perturbation causes a glitch in the information loop, and something goes haywire, probably at the point the foot does not contact the ground at the precise moment planned. As he puts it, "You get in a situation you didn't foresee, and your motor program goes to heck. Instead of a nice steady signal of nerve firing, this nice crescendo pattern, you get a big spike. That's what happens when your foot slips, or a tackler comes at you from an angle you don't expect, or your cleats give a little bit; suddenly you get a spike from somewhere. Did it come from your brain? From your spinal cord? We don't know. But as you try to shift to a compensatory motor program, suddenly the control is not there."

Major Beutler, in addition to teaching at the School of Medicine of the Uniformed Services University, in Bethesda, Maryland, has a clinical practice at two nearby military bases in family medicine ("kids and moms, obstetrics, you name it") with a specialty in sports medicine. He did clinical research with William Garrett while in medical school at Duke. Then in 2001–02, he worked as a medical fellow at the Naval Academy, where one of his jobs was to serve as team physician for the women's soccer team. Seven women on the team that season were lost to ACL injuries. Even with what he already knew from working with Garrett, he was stunned. "I thought to myself, What in the heck is going on here?"

In 2007, the women's soccer team suffered three ACL tears. "They thought that was great, a fortunate year," Beutler says. "Think about that. *Just three.* It's bizarre."

Beutler thinks fatigue has been a factor in the ACL injuries at the Naval Academy and probably at all the military academies, where athletes do not live like normal NCAA athletes. They rise at dawn for a day of demanding academics in addition to other responsibilities and are chronically weary and sleep-deprived. But plenty of young women playing high school sports live that same kind of life—classes all day, often in Advanced Placement or other college-level courses; homework at night; practices and games six or seven days a week; too little sleep and often poor nutrition. It is a difficult way to perform at a high level in sport. "If you're already fatigued when you take the field, your balance is not going to be as good," Beutler says. "You may not be as alert. If something happens that you are not prepared for, you may not respond as effectively."

The medical term for what laymen sometimes refer to as balance or coordination is *proprioception,* a person's sense of her body and limbs in space. "The unconscious perception of movement and spatial orientation arising from stimuli within the body itself" is the medical dictionary definition.

Beutler and Garrett are among those who have begun to think more deeply about the neurological component of ACL injuries—the possibility that short circuits in the message loop sometimes inhibit an athlete's ability to respond correctly. "We're pretty good once it gets to the muscles and bones, but we don't have a good enough idea what goes on up here," Beutler said, pointing to his head. "That's the black box for sports doctors, the brain and the nervous system."

Garrett is thinking in terms of what he calls "bailout strategies" or "saved programs"—practiced responses an athlete can default to if she senses she has ventured into a position vulnerable to an ACL injury. "I think what we need is not a training program for how you move all the time but strategies so that if you're in the air, out of balance, and can recognize that something bad can happen to you, you know how to lessen your chances by landing in a certain way. We know that from when a car spins: don't turn one way, turn the other. When you first start taking horseback riding lessons, you learn what to do when you fall off. They give you some sort of rudimentary instructions."

I asked Garrett if this was realistic. How do you create a program for avoiding catastrophic injury? From Boden's videos, it looked to me like athletes had little or no premonition of danger, nothing like the time a person might have if her car spins out or her horse begins to fall. But Garrett knows that it is some of the best athletes suffering this injury. "Look at the other things they can do," he said. "Just these remarkable athletic things. If we spent the time and figured out what exactly causes an ACL to rupture, couldn't we train somebody to avoid that?"

CHAPTER 9

AMONG THE PLEBES

S teve Marshall is among the doctors, physical therapists, athletic trainers, and other researchers trying to solve the mystery of ACL injuries. His passion does not allow him to be particularly measured in conversation. Even when he seems to want to be more temperate, words pour forth. Fragments of research. Thoughts. Observations. "Females jump funky," he says, by which he means some girls and women do not seem to land well. He can be as eloquent as he is snappy. "The human body is like a symphony," he observed in another of our interviews. "Some of us were written by Mozart or Beethoven, and some of us were written by committee. What we're hoping to find out is, Where are the discordant notes and what can we do about them?"

He did not want to imply by either of these statements that *all* women have biomechanical flaws that lead to injury or that all men move their bodies flawlessly through space. But whatever the glitches are that cause ACLs to rupture, women, statistically, are more prone to them. This is another inconvenient truth, like the high rate of stress fractures in military women or, on the male side, heart attacks and prostate cancer, which no one, by the way, equates with weakness; it is only female differences that are likely to be construed as deficiencies.

Marshall is leading the largest research study of ACL injuries, a $2.8 million project financed by the National Institutes of Health and involving 4,800 subjects enrolled at the nation's three main service academies: West Point, the U.S. Naval Academy, and the Air Force Academy. This is not a lavish amount of money by the standards of large medical studies, but the scope and cost are ambitious for athletics, which rarely loom as a big enough priority to attract much funding.

Marshall sort of stumbled into his life's work. He was a graduate student in his native New Zealand in the late 1980s, short on money and trying to figure out how best to make a career out of his facility for numbers and computers. "Somebody suggested, 'Go down the hallway. There's a guy down there who might have a half-time job for you,'" he recalls. "Things are a lot less formal in New Zealand. I just went down there and he took me on to help out in his research."

The professor offering the job was an epidemiologist, a field of study that until that moment Marshall had never heard of. But he was quickly attracted to it, sensing that it offered him an opportunity to apply his skills to work that included "a human element." He met his future wife, an American, moved to the United States, and earned his PhD at the University of North Carolina's School of Public Health.

Marshall explains what he does in terms that are almost ghoulish. "As an epidemiologist, what I'm looking for are large, willing groups of subjects, and then I want to follow them until they have interesting events happen to them—bad things, to be honest about it. The numbers can be an end in and of themselves. But early on, I was told by someone I admired that our subject is people, not numbers. It's the most important thing I ever learned."

Marshall feels a sense of urgency because he believes the syndrome of ACL tears will only get worse in coming years unless it is better understood. "We're studying an elite population at the service academies, but the big concern for me is the girl down the street who wants to play soccer on the rec team or the travel team. They're ripping their knees up, and they shouldn't be. There's got to be a way to prevent it. And we're really on the up curve of this, because it's still relatively recent that girls played sports in these large numbers. Participation has exploded in the numbers of girls playing and how much they're playing, five and six times a week, all year around. So if you think we have a problem now, ten years from now we'll have a much bigger problem."

Incoming students to the United States Naval Academy do not experience the typical fun-filled, post-high-school summer. They have scant opportunity for weekend parties, long good-byes, or serial shopping excursions to find just the right dorm room accoutrements. They report to campus in late June (as do freshmen at the other service academies) for an intense seven-week regimen of dawn-to-dark physical and mental rigor, all of it designed to begin the molding of military officers who will think clearly and lead under the most stressful conditions.

The newcomers are commonly called *plebes*, short for *plebeian*, and the Naval Academy still labels its seven-week indoctrination Plebe Summer. But Marshall does not find the term respectful enough. He refers to the students as "new middies." "No one is required to participate in our study," he says. "They're asked if they want to volunteer, and this is a population that when you ask something of them, they say, 'Yes, sir.' They're terrific, and I'm just very grateful to them."

In the summer of 2007, I spent a day with Marshall as new middies streamed into a cramped space in the campus orthopedic clinic to undergo a series of measurements and physiological tests—a "baseline assessment protocol," in the terminology of his research study. They came in about six at a time, as big a group as the space could accommodate, and were greeted by Marshall and his team from UNC's Sports Medicine Research Laboratory. Their work would take most of the summer; they had arrived about the same time the students did and were living together in a rental property within walking distance of the academy. Two other research teams were in place at the U.S. Military Academy at West Point and the Air Force Academy in Colorado Springs. Marshall would travel between the three sites.

The middies had changed out of their uniforms, their "summer whites," and into athletic shorts and T-shirts. Some wore their new military-issue eyeglasses, awful-looking things with big black frames that they call BCGs (birth control goggles). A big bowl of animal crackers sat on a desk in front of them. "There is no compensation except for these cookies," Joella Schiepan, a graduate student at UNC's School of Public Health, announced to one group. Several hands immediately shot into the bowl, and some of the young men shoveled so many cookies into their mouths that they looked like they were working on a wad of chewing tobacco. Schiepan added, "And you'll never hear from us again unless you have an ACL injury."

The official name of the study is JUMP-ACL (Joint Undertaking to Monitor and Prevent ACL Injury), and it is the largest sports medicine study ever funded by NIH. It actually originated with Beutler among others in a group who were seeking money from an NIH panel convened in Orlando to fund ACL research. He suggested to Garrett, who was at the meeting with Marshall, that they combine forces, telling him, "You guys have the think tank, and we"—the military—"have the people." It was in Orlando that Beutler first met Marshall, who he thought of as "the guy with the funny accent."

One reason the military was eager to participate is that ACL tears cause the most lost duty time of any neuromuscular injury in the armed services. At the academies, where future officers undergo a mix of intellectual and physical training, they are a particular source of concern. Any delay in producing a commissionable officer is expensive. "Time is the coin of the realm there, and it's limited," Beutler says. "You have to have a stable knee. If you lose six months, it's significant."

JUMP-ACL began testing students at the academies in 2005, and when it completes enrollment, it will have a cohort of 2,250 women and 2,550 men. Its three stated goals are to determine the association between neuromuscular risk factors, including poor jump-landing technique, and the rate of ACL injury; to determine the roles played by gender, anatomical factors, and hormones; and to quantify differences in risk factors between men and women.

An overview of the study published by its principal investigators says, "We hypothesize that the etiology of ACL injury is multifactorial in nature, with neuromuscular risk factors playing a crucial role. . . . This hypothesis is suggested by biomechanical studies indicating that the increased risk in women may be largely due to neuromuscular risk factors, such as gender differences in muscle strength and human movement. Unlike anatomical and hormonal risk factors, neuromuscular risk factors are readily modifiable and amenable to intervention."

More succinctly, Marshall and colleagues want to assemble a big group and test them in various ways. From that larger group, an "injury group" will emerge—midshipmen, cadets, and airmen who at some point in their four years of schooling suffer ACL injuries, some during military training but the majority probably in intercollegiate and intramural sports. The researchers will look back on that group and try to identify commonalities. What traits did they share that seem to portend ACL ruptures and which of those traits are modifiable?

The middies moved from station to station as the UNC team put them through a series of measurements. Using a device called a dynamometer, Will Rondeau, an athletic trainer, gauged the strength of various muscle groups—hamstrings, quadriceps, hip adductors. At other stations, their Q angles were measured with a goniometer, a strange-looking thing that looked like a stick with a protractor on each end, and a different instrument measured foot pronation, the extent to which the arch collapses upon bearing weight.

Next, the middies moved to a more elaborate station where a jumping platform, about thirty centimeters high, stood next to a landing pad, or *force plate*, that would measure the impact of their landing. This element of the study had been constructed with the most thought and had the potential to produce the most useful information.

The middies spent much of Plebe Summer not allowed to talk except when addressed by an officer, to smile, or in some cases even to make eye contact. But here, they were "at ease." "Have you played basketball?" Michelle Boling, a graduate student in UNC's School of Public Health, asked one middie as the student prepared to take a practice jump off the platform. She said she had, that she'd been on her high school team. "OK, then just pretend you're going for a rebound and land on that pad."

Each subject took one practice jump. Then Lindsay Strickland, another UNC graduate student, quickly attached sensors to the inside of their shins, the thighs, and the small of the back. On their next jump, the sensors produced a set of measures, most of them showing body positions through the jump and through impact after landing.

A knee that was bent at a 30-degree angle or greater at landing received a score of zero; a knee bent less than that got a one. (The higher scores were indicative of the suspected at-risk positions.) The sensors took note of fourteen different postural characteristics, among them hip and trunk flexion; the angle of the feet and ankles at impact; knee valgus at landing. Each one got a score. An overall grade based on the total of the scores was assigned to each subject— excellent, average, or poor. In addition, the sensors produced a digitized, animated image of the jump and the landing, something that looked like a skeleton moving through the air. "We're looking basically from the big toe all the way up to the ribs," Beutler explained. "Any muscle, any joint that moves or twists."

Even without seeing readouts from the sensors or the digitized image, some of the landings were visibly good or bad. And it was not strictly on a male-female basis. One young man jumped with his legs splayed and landed with a thud. If he had ever played a sport, it wasn't evident. As one female middie landed, her knees caved in so dramatically, they looked like they might crash into each other. After both jumps, Boling, who was monitoring the laptop as it took data from the sensors, glanced at me with a look of alarm.

The JUMP-ACL project is an effort to go beyond observation and supposition and to try, systematically, to learn what characteristics predict the injury. Would the jumpers who scored poorly, who looked so ungainly on the digital animation, be the ones to end up with ACL tears? Or was there something else going on, not as obvious through visual observation, that the data would reveal?

THE ACL puzzle invites a multitude of theorists and theories, some of them complementary, others utterly opposed to one another. It's not surprising. Just as in any other medical or scientific conundrum, it is difficult to entirely discount any one hypothesis until another is proved right.

Many of the prominent ACL researchers are orthopedic surgeons whose numbers, overall, are dominated by men, often former athletes. The stereotype of the orthopedic surgeon is the former football player who goes to medical school and gravitates back toward what he knows and loves: sports. They are rarely regarded as the intellectuals of the medical world; they're the brutish mechanics, the so-called bone crackers.

But the men I spent time with were thoughtful and dedicated to finding a cause and a cure for something they just as easily could continue to be handsomely paid for fixing in the OR. Several were conducting research on their own time and with their own money. Where they did not depart from stereotype was in the realm of ego. They tended to believe strongly in their theories and were eager to be proved right.

I waited in the office of Bert Mandelbaum, the Santa Monica orthopedic surgeon, talking with two of his colleagues, when he blew in fresh from the operating room and still in his surgical scrubs. "Let's talk about evolution," he said.

He moved through the Pliocene, Pleistocene, and Miocene eras in a few rapid-fire sentences, then on to *Homo erectus, Homo sapiens*, Neanderthal men, and hunter-gatherers. He zoomed forward to the ancient Greek Olympics and then to the modern Olympic Games, which began in 1896, detoured back to Neanderthals, and sped forward right up to Title IX. "Why is this all going on?" he said. "Go back in history to the ancient Greeks, to the Olympiad in 776 BC. Women didn't participate. Why? Let's go back to the Neanderthals. The women stayed close to the cave. They held babies. The men hunted. They were active. Men were on the battlefield; women were never on it."

Mandelbaum's point was twofold. As males and females developed, the work of men was athletic: hunting for food, engaging in warfare. They needed to be fast and springy—butts down, on the balls of their feet, ready to pounce. Women moved with an erect posture because that's the only way to carry a baby, and it is the way a woman *must* move when she is pregnant, to balance the weight load in her abdomen.

As a baby in utero grows in size and weight, an expectant mother leans back to counterbalance her protruding belly, and her pelvis tilts forward. What enables this, anthropologists have learned, is a female spine that is curvier than a male spine. That greater flexibility, however, probably has an impact on the hip and knee joints, and it can be a detriment to women during the long stretch of their life span when they are not pregnant. Evolution, with its ruthless focus on getting genes into the next generation, is unimpressed with Title IX's misson to level the field of play.

When sports were invented, the former hunters and warriors moved from the battlefield to the sports arena, where women were no more welcome than they had been in war. The modern Games did not include women in significant numbers until the mid twentieth century.

But what could this history possibly have to do with girls bounc- ing out of minivans and onto playing fields on Saturday mornings? What could it have to do with their tearing their knees up? Mandel- baum believes he sees the legacy even now—men running and cut- ting in a posture that is protective of their knees, while women move with a more upright and straight-legged gait.

If you truly look at the entirety of history, he says, "Women are new to this. We conveniently forget about that because we just see the here and now, but it's relevant."

Mandelbaum was the chief medical officer for the women's World Cup soccer team in 1999 and 2003. He is a proponent of women's athletics. He just doesn't believe that Title IX trumps all other forces.

Like Mandelbaum, Barry Boden believes he has an original theory, the key that opens the door and sheds light on the whole mystery. For six months in 2006 and 2007, in the evenings after saying good night to his kids, he would sit back down in front of his laptop and analyze the joint angles on his ACL video clips. His wife gave him looks of concern, which he understood.

When I visited him at his house a second time, I asked if he thought he had seen each of the clips hundreds of times. "It feels like thousands," he said.

Boden decided that he would make a frame-by-frame series of what he considered the critical moment in each injury—the instant when the foot below the injured knee struck the ground. Did the athlete land on her toes? On the balls of her foot? Flat-footed or on her heel?

He assembled an injury group thirty athletes on video tearing their ACLs, as well as a control group, thirty-two athletes landing or decelerating, performing similar-looking movements but ones that did not result in injury. Both groups were a mix of males and females. He determined that almost all of the injured athletes were performing what he called "highly competitive athletic maneuvers" at the time of injury. They had an opposing player in close proximity, and most were playing offense and had control of the ball. The scenarios "may have placed additional stress on the neuromuscular system that could cause an alteration in the normal landing patterns."

Using specially designed software, he also compared the angle of the hips, knees and ankles at foot strike. Boden's findings gave a hint of his extreme focus. "The portion of the foot (hind foot, midfoot, forefoot, or combination) touching the ground was . . . calculated for each frame by drawing a line on the plantar portion of the shoe touching the ground and dividing by a line drawn along the entire plantar portion of the shoe," he wrote. "The joint angles were assessed at the first point where the entire foot was flat on the ground, and the number of frames until the foot was 100 percent flat on the ground was calculated."

Unlike Garrett, Boden postulated that the ACL tears did not result from an "overfiring" of the quadriceps—a force from above. He belived the culprit was "faulty dissipation of ground force"—energy created at the moment the foot contacts the ground.

"When an athlete lands after jumping in the air the body must somehow absorb five to ten times the body weight on impact," he explained. "The force of impact can easily exceed 5,000 newtons"—well beyond the 2,000 newtons at which an ACL tears.

Boden's videos did not amount to a big sample and were by no means an ideal one. Camera angles were similar, but they could not be identical. He could not tell at what speed players were moving, or any number of other variables, including the conditions of the playing surface. Nonetheless, he believes he made some important discoveries.

In each case, those who tore their ACLs landed with their injured leg extended, and they landed in a flat-footed position. In contrast, all the control subjects landed on the balls of their feet.

Boden broke the video clips down into thirty frames per second. For the injured athletes, it took an average of 1.67 frames once the foot hit for it to come to a flat position. Those who were not injured averaged 2.93 frames. The injured athletes landed or decelerated with a sort of thud on a flat foot. Those who were not injured came down on the balls of their feet, and their heels fell more gradually. "We're talking about split seconds," he says. "But it was statistically significant."

In a normal high impact landing, the calf muscles absorb a large portion of the ground reaction force. In the injured athletes, Boden concluded, the flat-footed landings transmitted the ground force straight up to the knee, overwhelming the ACL.

"Make a small jump in the air and land flat-footed with your knees straight," he said. "It's uncomfortable. Now imagine landing after a dunk with your leg in that position."

From his data, Boden developed a theory at odds with Garrett's. He did not accept that the quadriceps had much to do with ACL tears or that it made any sense that any force above the knee was causing the problem.

The ACL sits in the knee at an angle across the front, but it is aligned more vertically than horizontally. The force that causes it to rupture, Boden says, is *axial*—exerting pressure from both tips. "Think of a twig," he says. "It can be snapped by a blow to the middle. Or it can be snapped by an axial force—pressure applied to each tip causing it to bend and then snap at its weakest point. That's what's happening to the ACL. It's the weakest point in the kinetic chain where these two forces come crashing together.

"It's well known that on an MRI after an ACL rupture, you'll see a bone bruise. The femur and tibia are both bruised. That's another sign that something has gone wrong in the kinetic chain: the energy is absorbed too much in the knee, and those two bones slam together with the knee in a position that causes the tibia to shift forward instead of the knee normally flexing or bending. In that collision, there is some rotation, and the ACL is torn."

Boden believes that women have higher rates of injury than men for two reasons: women more commonly land or decelerate with a straight leg, and their greater knee valgus, from their wider hips and greater Q angles, places a higher axial force on the outside portion of the knee. The tibia shifts forward, and the ACL ruptures.

Boden came to his theory in consultation with Joseph Torg, a Philadelphia orthopedist, now in his seventies, who was one of the first to call attention to the dangers of helmet-on-helmet hits in football, so-called *spearing.* Spearing creates an axial force, and it can cause a neck to snap like a twig.

"This isn't any different," Boden says. "I don't buy the overactive quadriceps stuff. It's ground force, not something from above snapping the ACLs."

. Boden's conclusions mark a departure from the Garrett think tank. He considers his journal article an ode to Torg. "He has insight like nobody I've ever known," Boden says. "He's a genius."

He professes confidence in the theory he was able to draw from his videos. "I am not arrogant and I don't want to sound cocky, but I really think what we're doing right now is going to explain a critical component of the ACL puzzle. I believe that within three to five years, this will be accepted."

STEVE MARSHALL does not exude such self-assurance. It is not his nature, and additionally, he does not have the luxury of selecting his own data, as Boden did with his pictures. Marshall presides over a large, longitudinal study, which is something like outlining a novel and creating the characters but then having them act in ways you do not control. It's nerve-wracking stuff. Only a fool would be over-confident.

Marshall's first concern was that the volunteer subjects at the military academies would go on to suffer enough ACL ruptures to constitute a large enough injury group. ("The best way to prevent something is to try to measure it," says Garrett. "It's the same as when you take the car into the mechanic and it won't make the noise you've been hearing.") And when injuries did accrue, Marshall had to hope they correlated in ways that would form a coherent narrative, a deeper understanding of how ACL tears occur and what characteristics predict them.

Marshall, Michele Boling, and I gathered in a conference room one day in Chapel Hill to review the data on some of the first subjects in the study who had torn their ACLs. One young woman we looked at had torn an ACL in her freshman year as a result of a non-contact sport injury. Because of confidentiality reasons, I was not permitted to specify which of the service academies she attends. Boling, sitting at a laptop, called up the woman's statistics from the JUMP-ACL study. On her jump, she had landed with 10 degrees of knee flexion. "That's not a lot," Boling said. "It's one of the things that could be a problem."

Boling, an athletic trainer and doctoral student in human movement studies, then projected the digitized animation of this young woman's jump onto a big screen, commenting on it almost as if she were telecasting a gymnastics or diving competition. "She looks OK there," Boling said at the start of her jump. "But she's not getting real flexed. And her butt could be lower."

We moved on to an animation of another jumper. "Watch her knees collapse," Boling said. When the young woman hit the landing pad, her knees caved in dramatically. "My guess is that's not uncomfortable for her," Boling said. "It's a way of generating control, but one that may put her ACL at risk."

Marshall added, "Obviously, it looks bad. We can see that. But is it the thing that causes her ACL to tear? Maybe it's a symptom rather than a cause. Maybe she needs to strengthen her hip muscles, or maybe her hip muscles need to fire in a slightly different way. We don't know yet."

Boling replayed the jump so that she and Marshall could take a closer look. "She's sort of asymmetric, isn't she?" Marshall commented. "Is one leg longer?"

"No, I think it has to do with how flexed her foot is," Boling said. "She's flexing her left foot as she lands, but not the other. That's why she has that hard landing on her left foot."

The force plate measures ground force. It gives one indication of how protectively subjects jump and land—whether they come down softly, with knees bent and on the balls of their feet, or straight-legged and flat-footed. If ground force is causing ACL tears, as Boden and others suspect, it may be that those suffering ACL tears are creating more of it. The last subject we looked at created, on landing, a force equal to more than three times her body weight. "That's a lot," Marshall said. "She came down hard. It didn't look like she bent her knees until she hit the ground."

The JUMP-ACL study has its critics. It is a big target, with its multimillion-dollar budget and some prominent figures, including

Garrett, involved. But some of the criticisms are substantive. The main one is whether the key component of the study—the jump from the platform onto the force plate—is a close enough simulation of what causes ACL tears to yield meaningful data.

ACL injuries occur on a large field of play and in conditions ripe for various kinds of perturbations—surprises that can cause an athlete to quickly stop and change direction. The lab setting of JUMP-ACL is quite different. The subjects jump on command in a controlled setting. "If it was realistic enough to be useful, you'd have some people tearing their ACLs during the test," says Donald Shelbourne, the Indianapolis surgeon. "But that is not going to happen."

Shelbourne has a simplified theory of ACL tears. He believes that those who suffer them—women or men—have ACLs that are too small to do the job. In his surgeries, he shaves enough away from the notch where the ACL fits to leave room for what amounts to an enhanced ligament. His grafts are ten millimeters wide and five millimeters thick, bigger on average than the natural ACL of most women or men. (The ACL is rectangularly shaped and usually somewhere around thirty millimeters long. Some studies indicate that women have smaller ACLs than men, even when adjusted for their average lower body weights.)

I asked Shelbourne how he would advise a young woman who wanted to prevent or at least lessen her chances of suffering an ACL injury. "I'd say to her, 'Good luck. I hope you make the team. If you get hurt, we'll take care of you.' I'm focusing on how to fix ACL tears and how to give someone a good knee."

When I repeated this to Barry Boden, he responded, "What are we going to do, take out everybody's ACL and replace it with a steel cable? Are small ACLs a risk factor? Maybe. But it's not something we can do anything about."

Marshall was similarly incredulous. As a public health professional, he believes in exploring causes that are modifiable. But he was not dismissive of the questions regarding the design of his study.

The doubts raise the nightmare scenario for any researcher. Has he set up his project correctly?

I began to approach these questions delicately, but Marshall got right to the point. "I think what you're asking is, 'Do we have the right test?' He turned to Boling. "How many nights sleep do you think I have lost over that question?"

He explained how they had settled on the design of the test. "We do see injuries that happen under these circumstances. People tear their ACLs landing from jumps. And this was something we can do in this location. Logistically, it's possible. The criticism is that this is low velocity, but even with that, we are seeing differences between how men and women land. So we have that part right. Obviously, we can't injure people, but I think this is a reasonable proxy. We're looking at more than a hundred variables per jump. I think that will produce something useful.

"The thing Dr. Garrett would have liked would have been to introduce some neurological challenges—if we would get them to run, and someone would say, 'Go left, go right.' But we would have to get them to hit that force plate at the right time, and that is difficult to do."

Marshall's injury group has built more slowly than he projected. A likely reason is that the service academies attract a physically active, sports-playing population of young women, many of whom enter as first-year students already having torn an ACL in high school. By the design of the study, they are excluded from the sample, which focuses on first-time ACL tears.

Marshall, though, has been following the recurrent ACL tears, sort of as a sideline. His data show that of all those who enter the academies with a history of one or more ACL tears, women are five times more likely than men to suffer another at some time during the next four years. The finding troubles him because it seems so ominous. "I don't want anyone to think they're doomed," he said. "I don't know if the injuries indicate a bad [surgical] fix or that they have movement patterns that predispose them. We just don't know."

He has been encouraged by information taken from the sensors attached to his subjects as they jump from the platform. "It's just amazing to me how different the men and women are in so many different aspects of how they move. It shouldn't be that surprising to me, but it's astonishing when you look at our results. Women tend to be more erect and upright when they land, and they land harder. They bend less through the knees and hips and the rest of their bodies, and they don't absorb the impact of the landing in the same way that males do."

Marshall is cheered by the results because he and many others believe strongly that movement patterns can be modified. "These things are eminently retrainable," he said. "I don't want to sound horrible about it, but we can make a woman athlete run and jump more like a man."

The funding for JUMP-ACL runs out in 2010, although the grant could be extended. The project may produce no definitive results until then. "The Holy Grail would be that we are able to identify a high-risk movement pattern or set of movements and say, 'This is what is causing the injury.' And then that we can reach in and change these movements. And we know that we *can* change movement, especially in some of these very good athletes who are hurting themselves. That's why they're elite. They can be trained.

"It may be something so simple as saying, 'Land softly.' Those two words, and the retraining, could have a profound effect."

CHAPTER 10

THE ACL WITCH

Holly Silvers has a pretty good idea of how males and females move on a soccer field, or in any athletic setting, because she has observed them from numerous perspectives. She was a fine soccer player herself at the high school and club levels. As a physical therapist, she has worked with teams at the highest levels of soccer, including the U.S. women's national team and the men's team Chivas USA of Major League Soccer. (She also happens to be the sister-in-law of Tony Meola, a longtime pro and the former goalkeeper for the U.S. men's national team.) Silvers is, as well, a scientist—a key figure, along with Bert Mandelbaum and Diane Watanabe, in the research that takes place at the Santa Monica Orthopaedic and Sports Medicine Research Foundation.

She has on occasion heard herself referred to as the "ACL lady" by people who recognize her but can't recall her name. They likely attended one of her many lectures on ACL injury prevention or were part of a team when she was helping a coach install a prevention program. I came to think of her as the ACL witch, because she believes she can sense misfortune before it occurs.

Steve Marshall and his JUMP-ACL team have their sensors, cameras, and digitized images; Silvers believes she sees much the same thing, but in real time. She surveys the field and, as she puts it, "red flags" certain players, identifying them as at high risk for ACL injuries—not necessarily at that moment, of course, but somewhere down the line.

"Look at the girl on the left back with the ponytail," she said as we stood on the sideline of a game at the Home Depot Center, a vast complex of fields in Carson, California. "She really concerns me."

At first I couldn't pick out who she meant; there were lots of ponytails out there. "Number eight," she clarified, and I fixed my attention on a tall, stiff-legged girl whose upper and lower body seemed not to be in communication. She ran bolt upright, with very little bend in her trunk. Her knees seemed not to flex. When she came to a stop or slowed to change directions, she landed flat-footed. "She's got really poor form," Silvers said. "She won't hold up running like that."

The players on the field were thirteen-and-unders, the teams from the west side of Los Angeles and Palos Verdes. They had risen to the highest level of their age group, surpassing hundreds of their peers. At the very least, they were future stars of their high school teams, and some would likely progress beyond that. But their soccer skills and competitiveness masked athletic deficiencies and biomechanical flaws.

Many of them moved in ways not likely to help them hold up under the extraordinary demands of year-round involvement in a cutting, pivoting, and jumping sport like soccer. They could make themselves more injury-resistant, but would have to work on it— probably harder than most boys would.

That morning, Silvers had been contacted by the mother of a girl on a team in this same league who said she knew of two teams that had already suffered a combined five ACL injuries. I asked Silvers when the season had started. "Three weeks ago," she said. "Astounding, isn't it?"

We were standing amid a few dozen parents and could overhear their conversations. "In a couple of weeks, they'll let her run in a straight line," one of the mothers said. "But she's not going to be allowed to run side to side for a while."

Silvers whispered to me, "I'm sure that's an ACL."

A few minutes later, the injured girl herself came onto the sideline. She was wearing her team jacket and jeans and walked with a slight limp. She exchanged greetings with a couple of teammates, but they did not seem to interact much, and she watched the rest of the game with her mother. It is hard for injured athletes, males or females, to still feel a part of a team, no matter how hard everyone tries. And sometimes they are subconsciously shunned, as if what happened to them is contagious and it is best to keep a distance. ACL injuries are endemic, but not contagious.

We turned our attention back to the field just as a player went down with some kind of knee injury. Neither of us saw exactly what happened, but she lay for a moment on the grass, grimacing. The referee called to the sideline to ask the coach if she was staying in the game. Two of her teammates shouted to the coach, both of them yelling that the injured player was "fine."

"Did you hear that?" Silvers said. "Her teammates said she's fine. How do they know that?" The girl got up and kept playing but left the game about ten minutes later.

Silvers directed my attention to another player, one who was clearly among the best on either team. From the midfield, she was forcing the action, rushing the ball up the field under her own control, then either finding teammates with penetrating passes or pressing all the way into the scoring zone and getting off shots herself. She was adept with either foot and had good speed and an obvious toughness about her. "This girl concerns me a lot too," Silvers said. "It's really amazing she can get all that done."

She was not as upright as the other girl, but I could see she moved without bend. She had a plastic brace on her right ankle showing above her soccer shoe. "A sore ankle is often a sign something else is going on," Silvers said. "She's very skilled, but she doesn't really have control. That's probably why she has an ankle problem."

By that, Silvers meant that she did not have the core muscle strength, balance, or overall coordination to protect herself. Her movement patterns put her knees—and probably her ankles, back, and hips—at risk for a range of overuse and acute injuries. I asked Silvers if any elite male players moved like that. "Yes," she said, "some do, but you don't see it nearly as much. Boys play lower to the ground. They have stronger cores and stronger hamstrings. It's protective."

Silvers is not as boisterous as her colleague Bert Mandelbaum. She does not blow into a room and make pronouncements, but in her own way, she is as confident.

A new player came into the game. She was knock-kneed, and her left leg turned inward when she ran. Silvers does not approach girls on an individual basis and seek to intervene and retrain them—she works with clients who come into her office—but I wondered what she could do, given an opportunity, with this completely out-of-whack-looking athlete. Could she fix her?

"Yes, I could," she said. "In four to six weeks I could improve her a lot. In three months, I could get the job done. I would work on her antagonistic muscles. I would educate the muscles, educate the nerves. She could build strength and change her patterns. It's possible for any of these girls. They're determined, and they're coachable, which is how they got to this level. Somebody just has to work with them."

Silvers pointed out one more player, a girl who seemed light on her feet—quick and springy. When she changed direction, she stayed in what generations of gym teachers called the "athletic position"—knees bent, butt low to the ground. Even when walking casually during stoppages in play, she seemed more lithe than the other girls.

"She moves more like a boy," Silvers said, echoing Steve Marshall. "Believe me, that's a good thing."

THE KNEE, sometimes said to be part of a *kinetic chain,* is a particularly vulnerable link in the complex interaction of bones, muscles, ligaments, tendons, and nerves that influence our movements. Throw hormones into the mix too. "The way we move may not be a fixed concept," Marshall says. "It may have a hormonal variation. As researchers, we need to pin down our own contributions, but at the end of the day, these are not discrete bits and pieces. How do these other things—hormones, anatomy, whatever else—influence our biomechanics? That's where we need to go with this."

In the meantime, though, injuries are mounting, and the top ACL researchers—among them Marshall and his colleagues at UNC; and Silvers, Mandelbaum, and the team at Santa Monica Orthopaedics—are using preliminary data and their best educated guesses to construct prevention programs intended to decrease the numbers of young women being wheeled into the nation's operating rooms to have their knees pieced back together.

Preliminary data from nascent ACL injury prevention programs have been highly encouraging. In Southern California, the Santa Monica Orthopaedic and Sports Medicine Research Foundation studied about 6,000 high-school-aged girls playing on high-level club teams in the vast Coast Soccer League. Teams in the control group did their usual warm-ups before practices and games, usually light running and some stretching, if that. The others were enrolled in Santa Monica's PEP program, a customized warm-up of stretching, strengthening, and balancing exercises.

An entire soccer team can complete the nineteen exercises in less than thirty minutes, and no special equipment is required. There is nothing complicated about the program. And nothing really exciting about it, either—which, as in all such preventative routines, is its greatest challenge. It can feel repetitive and boring, and therefore difficult to keep to.

The PEP (Prevent Injury and Enhance Performance) program includes light jogging, side-to-side shuttle running, backward running, walking lunges, and a series of stretches. The key drills are the *plyometrics*—forward, backward, and lateral hops, or short jumps over a cone, with soft landings and neuromuscular control emphasized.

The step-by-step instructions, in printed form or on the DVD put out by Santa Monica Orthopaedics, take a team through the routine from start to finish. For the lateral hop: "Stand with a cone to your left. Hop to the left over the cone, softly landing on the balls of your feet and bending at the knee. Repeat this exercise, hopping to the right."

The toe raise: "This exercise stengthens the calf muscle and increases balance. Stand up with your arms at your side. Bend the left knee up and maintain your balance. *Slowly* rise up on your right toes with good balance. You may hold your arms out ahead of you in order to help. Slowly repeat 30 times and switch to the other side. As you get stronger, you may need to add additional repetitions to this exercise to continue the strengthening effect."

Walking lunges: "Lunge forward leading with your right leg. Push off with your right leg and lunge forward with your left leg. Drop the back knee straight down. Make sure that you keep your front knee over your ankle. Control the motion and try to keep your front knee from caving inward. If you can't see your toes on your landing leg, you are doing the exercise incorrectly."

The overarching instructions are as follows: "This prevention program consists of a warm-up, stretching, strengthening, plyometrics, and short specific agilities to address potential deficits in the strength and coordination of the stabilizing muscles around the knee joint. It is important to use proper technique during all of the exercises. The coaches and trainers need to emphasize correct posture, straight up and down jumps without excessive side-to-side movement, and reinforce soft landings."

As simple as it is to execute, the PEP program is ambitious in its goal: take girls who may have biomechanical patterns that leave them at risk for ACL injuries and reprogram the way they move. The hope is that the modifications may leave them less vulnerable to other injuries as well—in the feet, ankles, knees, hips, and back.

Mandelbaum and his group published the results of their trial in *The American Journal of Sports Medicine.* Their research was nonrandomized and therefore not to the highest scientific standard (The coaches of teams doing the exercises made a choice to participate; the control group consisted of those who declined.) Nevertheless, the results were attention-grabbing.

The subjects were all between fourteen and eighteen years old. In the 2000 soccer season, researchers calculated 37,476 athletic exposures for the group doing the PEP program (the "trained" players) and 65,550 for the ("untrained") control group, those who did not do the PEP warm-up.

Two girls in the trained group suffered ACL ruptures that season, a rate of 0.05 per 1,000 exposures. Thirty-two girls in the control group suffered the injury—a rate of 0.47 per 1,000 exposures. That was almost twice the rate for women playing NCAA soccer, another indication that younger female athletes are at higher risk for ACL injuries. "These results indicated an 88 percent overall reduction of ACL injury per individual athlete compared to skill-and-age-matched control athletes," the authors wrote.

Santa Monica Orthopaedics compiled numbers in the same league for the following season and came up with similar results—a 74 percent reduction in ACL tears among girls doing the PEP exercises (four injuries in the intervention group, thirty-five in a control group that was about twice as large.)

Mandelbaum's group conducted a similar research trial of their PEP program with sixty-one NCAA women's soccer teams in 2002. This one was randomized; the intervention and control teams were not self-selecting. The overall ACL injury rate among the athletes on the twenty-five teams that did the PEP warm-ups was 41 percent lower than the control group, and 71 percent lower when the injury sample was limited to noncontact injuries. The data also indicated that the PEP program may be particularly effective for players who have already shown a predisposition to the injury. "This program," the authors wrote, "reduces the risk of ACL injuries in collegeiate female soccer players, especially those with a history of ACL injury."

Mandelbaum finds it disturbing that so many girls who suffer ACL injuries return to play without exposure to any ACL prevention program. "We take these warriors and put them back on the battle-field without retraining them. So they have no protection against it happening again—and it does happen again."

IF AN athlete who is stronger, faster, more balanced, and more coordinated will be a more effective player, why wouldn't every coach of a girls' youth team, every parent, and every young player insist on being part of this or some other ACL injury prevention program? Some may not know that such programs exist, although any coach involved at a high level of girls' or women's athletics, in any game that requires running and changes of direction—soccer, basketball, lacrosse, volleyball, and field hockey—absolutely *should* have such knowledge.

But if ignorance of such programs is one reason more girls are not doing ACL prevention, the second part of the program's name—Prevent Injury and *Enhance Performance*—gives a clue to another. Plenty of coaches cannot be bothered with devoting time to anything that they do not feel relates directly to goals scored, goals prevented, and victories accumulated. The original PEP program was designed specifically for soccer; a newer version was tailored for basketball.

"The coaches have to see a performance boost," says Diane Watanabe, head athletic trainer for the 1999 U.S. women's World Cup team and part of the Santa Monica research group. "Otherwise they won't do it. That's the only way we can sell them on this program."

I heard the same thing from some parents—that it is difficult to engage coaches about injuries. In every sport and for every coach, practice time is finite. But if a player gets hurt, the supply of good, skilled replacements can seem infinite. "Most coaches don't think it's part of their job to think about injuries," Lynne Foltz, a soccer mom who is also a physical therapist, told me. "They care if a kid gets hurt, but it never occurs to them they could have had a role preventing it. I've made it a cause to get them to pay attention, but I don't know how effective I've been. The message you get as a parent is, Stay off the field."

Foltz, whose daughter, Victoria Gersh, plays on high school and club soccer teams in Maryland, attended an all-day workshop in January 2007 in Baltimore for coaches, parents, and players sponsored by the Maryland State Youth Soccer Association. She estimates that thirty or more coaches attended. The coaches filed into sessions on skills and tactics and browsed the booths where equipment, instructional videos, soccer camps, and other products were being sold.

Foltz and her husband, a pediatrician, took in a one-hour Power-Point presentation by an orthopedic surgeon on soccer injuries and their treatment. They were the entire audience, until three other parents wandered in part of the way through. Not one coach was there.

It is possible, perhaps, for youth and high school coaches not to be exposed to information on ACL injury prevention. But collegiate coaches have no excuse. They are, after all, part of academic communities, which at many larger universities include extensive sports medicine components. Certified athletic trainers are attached to their teams, a rarity among even the best high school and club teams. So even if the coach has not educated himself, the trainer certainly has come across that information and should have passed it along.

The rates of women's ACL injuries in the NCAA have stayed constant. In 2005, researchers published an article in the *American Journal of Sports Medicine* that reviewed thirteen years of ACL injuries at a sampling of NCAA institutions. It was a follow-up of the study from a decade earlier that pointed out a wide disparity in the rates of ACL injuries between male and female soccer and basketball players. The 2005 article showed that not only had the gap not closed, but in soccer it had grown, because the men's rates of ACL injuries had significantly decreased while the women's had stayed the same.

The authors expressed frustration at both the continuation of the injury pattern and their inability to find a reason for it. They expected or at least hoped that greater public concern, education, and improved training methods would have made some dent.

They wrote, "If the theory that lack of experience for the female athlete is a reason for ACL injury had validity, one would expect with the existence of Title IX that some decrease in ACL injury to female athletes would be evident. If the theories of poor mechanics or neuromuscular control were to have validity, one would expect to see some evidence of change in the rate of injury over the years of study. Although we cannot identify the training regimens the schools in this study followed, one could assume that one would see some change in some aspect of the injury rates."

But there is no comprehensive ACL prevention program in place at NCAA schools. Participants in the PEP collegiate study represented a small fraction of NCAA women playing one sport—soccer. Different trainers put varying degrees of thought and effort behind preventing ACL ruptures. Many, like Gregg Calhoon at the U.S. Naval Academy, are knowledgeable and rigorous and construct their own programs by adopting from PEP and other programs. But trainers get a range of cooperation from their coaches. Some of them may still not be able to get coaches to take injuries and prevention seriously.

And even when religiously applied, the prevention programs may just not be as effective in colleges as they are with younger girls. College-age women have well-established movement patterns, reinforced during a dozen or more years of training and competition. The PEP trial indicated that it is possible to make changes in their biomechanics, but the bigger payoff is likely to come from starting with girls in their early teens.

"Once something is learned neurally, it is never unlearned," Holly Silvers explained. "It never leaves you. That's mostly good. It's why motor skills are retained even after serious injuries. But ways of moving are also ingrained, which makes retraining more difficult with the older athletes. The younger girls are more like blank slates. They're easier to work with."

THE PEP program is one of several ACL prevention regimens. Another of the more prominent ones, Sportsmetrics, grew out of the research of Frank Noyes, an orthopedic surgeon, and Timothy Hewett, the human movement researcher. It was created in Cincinnati and has since branched out across the nation.

Sportsmetrics differs from PEP in that it is an intensive, six-week training course rather than an ongoing routine that takes place before practices.

Elsewhere, certified trainers—and even some club and high school coaches—have fashioned their own programs, taking the best of PEP, Sportsmetrics, and the others. ACL prevention programs are also available at dozens or even hundreds of for-profit training centers.

Almost all of them are varations on the same themes. They start with an acknowledgment that female athletes do not run, jump, decelerate, and land in the same way men do. "When I was a team physician at the University of Cincinnati, I would see women jump, and when they landed, their knees would do what I call the wiggle-wobble," Noyes, the Cincinnati surgeon and researcher, said in a 2006 interview. "They were like accidents waiting to happen."

The ACL prevention programs address a range of related issues. The literature in the medical journals can be dense, but the underlying theories are not. Anyone who has ever been to a physical therapist knows that they always seem to point to some place on your body other than where you're hurting. The commentary is usually some version of: Well, *here* is where your problem is actually coming from. A strength deficiency in one area causes a breakdown or pain in another.

Weak abdominal and hip muscles are prime suspects in the case of knee injuries for women and the related issue of knee valgus — the inability to keep knees from collapsing inward. "Increased ability to decelerate from landing and control dynamic valgus might be related to hip muscle strength and recruitment," Timothy Hewett writes.

The solution: build balanced strength in the hips, buttocks, abdomen, and lower back in order to enable greater stability in the knees. The PEP program's hip muscle exercises are uncomplicated, like the rest of the regimen. For example, the "bounding run," across the width of a soccer field: "Starting on the near sideline, run to the far side with knees up toward chest. Bring your knees up high. Land on the ball of your foot with a slight bend at the knee and a straight hip. Increase the distance as this exercise gets easier."

And another, called "bridging with alternating hip flexion": "Lie on the ground with your knee bent with feet on the ground. Raise your buttocks off the ground and squeeze. Now, lift your right foot off the ground and make sure that your right hip does not dip down. Lower your right foot and now lift your left foot making sure your left hip does not dip down. Repeat 30 times on each side."

What thwarts the success of these kinds of programs is the

time they take—many coaches feel it's wasted—and the boredom they engender. It's far more fun to be kicking the ball around or playing a game. ACL prevention probably ought to be marketed like programs on safe driving that show graphic examples of traffic accidents; in this case, they would show ACL injuries along with videos of the brutal surgery and painful rehab. That would get everyone's attention—coaches, parents, players.

GENERATIONS OF coaches and gym teachers have harped on playing sports in the "athletic position"—head up, shoulders squared to the action, knees bent, butt down. This is the position an infielder takes as the pitch is delivered, and the one a rebounder assumes before jumping. It is the approximate position an athlete should be in when landing from a jump or when decelerating from a sprint.

Just this one thing—training young women to play lower to the ground, in the athletic position—would prevent injuries. Consider field hockey, which when played well is a fast-moving game of full-out sprints and quick changes of direction. But the ACL injury rates in college field hockey are relatively low—0.07 per 1,000 exposures, a quarter the rate of women's basketball and soccer.

Why? No one knows for sure, but it is probably significant that in the heat of battle—contesting for a ball, shooting, preparing to shoot—girls have their sticks on the ground. In order to get the stick in that position, they must bend their knees and lower their butts. Just running with the stick may cause field hockey players to set themselves lower.

The last, most complicated, and probably most important part of ACL injury prevention is *proprioception*—awareness of body position and spatial orientation. When Holly Silvers talks about "educating the nerves," she is referring to proprioception. It is not the same as balance, coordination, or strength but is related to all three.

Proprioception is the body *knowing* what to do in certain physical settings, or being trained to do so. It is specific to different realms and activities and often does not transfer from one to the other. The best swimmers are said to have a "feel for the water," which is a form of proprioception; it means they know how to move their muscles and position their bodies to efficiently knife through the pool. Michael Phelps, the world's top swimmer, has advanced proprioception in the water that utterly abandons him on land. While researching a magazine profile of Phelps a couple of years back, I learned that his coach would not let him engage in any other sport, not even bowling, for fear he would injure himself. Recently, he broke his wrist after he stumbled getting out of his car.

Similarly, a teenage boy may be a portrait of grace on a basketball court, capable of midair ballet and quick stops, starts, and changes of direction. But put him in a crowded party and he bumps into tables and endangers china. In one realm, he is aware of his body in space, but not in another.

A young woman who plays basketball or soccer may display exquisite control of her body and posture in all kinds of settings. She has terrific balance on her mountain bike. She's a great dancer. She just took up golf and plays like a natural. Waiting tables on weekends, she just glides through the restaurant.

She is physically gifted in almost all ways, including in her sport, where she's a star. But if when landing from a jump or slowing down from a sprint she cannot really feel her legs under her—if her nerves do not tell her hamstrings to engage at just the right moment; if her quadriceps fire before her foot hits the ground; if one leg extends too far forward, putting her knee in an exposed, vulnerable position— she has a problem. She is not fully fit for the thing she wants to do.

The ACL prevention programs are far from perfect, and they have their critics. The skeptics ask, How can you attempt to solve a problem before you are even confident of its cause?

Donald Shelbourne, the Indianapolis orthopedic surgeon and

researcher, is perhaps the most vehement critic of the ACL prevention programs. "It's like me taking antioxidants," he said. "I don't
have cancer yet, so it's working, right? These retraining programs
play on emotions without data. They're unproven. Jumping and
landing is something that everyone knows how to do, and now we've
got people saying, We can teach you to do it better. I don't buy it.
There's no basis for it."

Shelbourne is a forceful man, highly respected in his field. No
one would disagree with him that there is a cart-before-the-horse
element to the ACL prevention programs. But what's the other option? To wait? And besides, it is not unusual in medicine for the
search for a cause and a cure to run along parallel tracks.

Those involved in designing and implementing ACL prevention
strategies disagree with Shelbourne that everyone knows how to run
and land. Some athletes do so in more protective ways. And those
who do not, they believe, can be taught. Such training, Hewett wrote,
"allows female athletes to adopt muscular recruitment strategies that
decrease joint motion and protect the ACL from high-impulse loading during performance."

All the ACL prevention programs include a series of short jumps
with soft, bent knee landings emphasized. Athletes are reminded to
"keep their feet under their hips." Again, nothing complicated. The
idea is to practice the jumps and landings repeatedly so that old habits are extinguished and better ones ingrained.

Ultimately, the goal is to avoid vulnerable positions—ones in
which the leg is extended, the foot strikes the ground flat, and a bolt
of energy surges into the knee.

Silver Spring United, an under-sixteen girls' team in Maryland, assembled for the last practice of the 2007 fall season at their usual site,
a lumpy, dry-as-a-bone playing field adjacent to a YMCA. It was late

November and a little chilly, and their coach, Karen Giacopuzzi, made sure to tell her players that she had put a box of tissues on the sideline in case anyone needed one.

Anthony Beutler has been working with the team and thirteen others in a pilot ACL prevention program funded by the School of Medicine of the Uniformed Services University. The project is an extension of his work with JUMP-ACL, an attempt to take its elaborate testing regimen—the multiple testing stations, the video and computer analysis setup—and pare it down for a community setting.

A couple of medical students under Beutler's supervision videotaped the players jumping from a short platform at the beginning of the season. One of them, Becky Slogic, had a personal connection to the research, having torn an ACL playing college soccer. The girls then ran through a warm-up before each of their practices, similar to the PEP program—strengthening drills, walking lunges, jumps with flexed-knee landings.

On this last day, they were being videotaped again to see if their form had improved. Instead of the $80,000 in equipment in use at each JUMP-ACL site, Beutler noted that the girls' jumps were being recorded on video cameras "that anyone could buy for a couple of hundred bucks at Radio Shack." Diagrams of the exercises fit on two sides of a laminated 8-by-11-inch sheet of paper.

The program was a small experiment in whether ACL prevention could be seeded in the community as a public health initiative. Would the model work? Was it really possible to tell, just by observation of a player jumping and landing from a short platform—rather than through computer analysis—whether her form predisposes her to a knee injury?

The other question centered on the issue of compliance. Can you get coaches and league organizers to be concerned enough about injury prevention to invest time in the effort?

Beutler had seen Giacopuzzi putting the tissues out at the beginning of practice and wanted to make sure I noticed. "You see that?" he said. "It's a small thing, but you can tell she cares about them."

Beutler did not want any recreational-level teams in his trial because they are poor candidates for injury studies; they move so slowly and create so little force that they don't stand much chance of hurting themselves. Silver Spring United is a mix of middle-of-the-road varsity high school players, some junior varsity performers, and a couple of middle schoolers. They are not an elite team. Nevertheless, the previous season they had suffered two knee injuries, both of them meniscus tears that required surgery.

Giacopuzzi has been coaching the team for several years. "I saw a need [for injury prevention], and I went looking for something," she told me. She learned that Beutler was seeking teams in the Washington DC area and volunteered.

"I find it amazing more teams do not do something like this and that more parents don't demand it," Beutler said. "This is a competitive area. Parents are smart and highly involved in their children's lives." He estimated that among highly competitive girls' club teams in the Washington area, "one in four do some form of this training, something that could be construed as involving injury and ACL prevention. Half of those—one in eight—do it to some level of competence, meaning they have some professional, a trainer, physical therapist, someone knowledgeable about exercise science, who can institute it."

I watched the Silver Spring United players go through the exercises, which took about fifteen minutes. Afterward, I asked some of the girls what they noticed after doing the routine all season. Beutler too was curious and followed along.

Three of the girls volunteered that they felt they had better balance. "I used to feel more wobbly," Becca Arbacher, one of the team's eighth graders, said. "I would fall down, like a couple of times a game, and I don't think that happens as much now."

Michelle Morris, fifteen, caught Beutler's attention. He thought she looked like the best athlete of the bunch. She moved with a low center of gravity and a springiness—the opposite of the stiff, upright gait that draws the attention of Holly Silvers. When we asked her if the exercises had made a difference, she said, "I think my balance is way better now. I never learned how to land properly. I fell down a lot—but now, not at all."

Their responses were interesting because Hewett, among others, has identified poor balance as a predictor of ACL ruptures. In one of his studies, he had college athletes, men and women, sit on devices that mechanically twisted under them. The women who had the most trouble stabilizing their bodies later suffered higher rates of knee injuries. (Not so the men.) His supposition was that when they lost balance, they twisted their bodies at "inopportune times," like when one leg was planted on a soccer field, causing ACL and other knee injuries.

The Silver Spring United girls took their ACL prevention seriously. Their captains led the exercises, with Giacopuzzi standing off to the side. It became part of their routine. No one has suffered knee injuries since they began doing the exercises. "This is the wave of the future, where we can bring prevention to this level, out of the laboratory and onto a field," Beutler said. "I think we are getting to the point where we can look in real time and say, with 95 percent certainty, 'You are at low risk. You're at moderate risk. And you're at high risk.' And we can design programs for each of those athletes."

Steve Marshall has his own pilot prevention program, nearly identical to Beutler's in Maryland. It began at the urging of the father of an injured soccer player.

Doug Bell's daughter Jamie experienced her first ACL tear in January of her junior year and missed her high school soccer season, which in North Carolina takes place in the spring. She had surgery and rehabbed and was back playing club soccer by the next September. She was the third girl of the fifteen on her U-19 club team to have ACL surgery. The next spring, competing for her high school, she ruptured the ACL in her other knee.

"She was depressed the whole time," Bell told me. "My wife was depressed about it. It was just despair. We couldn't understand how she went through that long rehab—and then did the other one."

The Bells' younger daughter, Emily, is still playing. His wife goes to the games to be supportive, but she can barely watch. Bell did not like feeling powerless—as if he were just waiting for the same fate to befall his other daughter or anyone else on the field. (The Bells' son also has torn an ACL and has since quit soccer.)

Bell is a scientist as well as a soccer dad, a principal investigator with the NIH's Institute of Environmental Health Sciences who studies the role of genetic variation in human toxicological responses. He is not daunted by complexity; his official bio includes such phrases as "genetic basis for several phenotypes in carcinogen metabolism," and "gene-environment interaction component of disease." The repeated incidences of adolescent girls and young women tearing and retearing the same small ligament in their knees did not seem like something that ought to be beyond the scope of scientific understanding—or that should just be accepted as an inevitability.

At Bell's urging, personnel from UNC's Sports Medicine Research Laboratory—Marshall, along with Darin Padua, a professor at the lab and another key figure in JUMP-ACL—began working with both boys' and girls' teams in the Triangle United Soccer League in the Raleigh-Durham area of North Carolina.

"If parents were aware of it, I don't think they'd tolerate it," Bell said of the prevalence of ACL injuries. "In selling this program to parents, I pushed the guilt thing. I said, 'Look, we're willing to spend $150 on shoes. How can't we do this for them?' "

For Marshall, the program has been an opportunity to test his laboratory theories on the playing field. His staff has been filming jumps at the beginning of seasons and at the end of seasons and compiling results on the Landing Error Scoring System designed by Padua.

The system calls for observations of various elements of the jump and landing, including the degree of knee, hip, and trunk flexion at initial contact with the ground, as well as angles of the feet and ankles at ground contact. There are seventeen categories in all. In fourteen of them, males and females fell into different ranges at the beginning of the season, before they began doing the exercises.

Some players who scored as having particularly poor form were given customized exercises beyond the fifteen-minute warm-up. "We could improve the girls' landings more readily than the boys'," Marshall said. "You might argue that's because they've got a longer way to go. It's easier to move them along."

His on-the-ground experience with the Triangle League players has made Marshall, like Silvers, even more convinced of the importance of intervening with younger girls, before their movement patterns are ingrained. "The critical period is not the college years or the high school years, but the middle-school years, before the carnage sets in," he said. "You want to be ahead of the wave of the epidemic."

OR MAYBE it would be best to begin with grade school girls.

Hannah Coy, of Boca Raton, Florida, played for a team that was ranked as high as fifth in the nation—that is, among all teams of ten-and-under girls. On May 7, 2006, Hannah, then in fouth grade, was named Elementary School Athlete of the Year in Palm Beach County.

A local radio station, ESPN 790, presented her with a plaque and a laptop computer at a gala dinner at the PGA National Resort and Spa in Palm Beach Gardens. Her coach on the Boca United Football Club said she was the best player her age in all of Florida. The director of the club, Erich Eichmann, a former United States World Cup player who calls her "Beckenbauer," for the former German star Franz Beckenbauer, offered even more lavish praise. "In all my years of coaching, I have never worked with an athlete that was capable of playing so well and so consistently in training and games," he said. "This is a rare quality even among professional athletes, and she is only nine years old."

A few months later, I stood along the sideline of a beautifully groomed field in Sunrise, Florida, and watched Hannah compete. It was an under-eleven game, so she was "playing up" with older girls, including her sister Sarah, who is fourteen months older and also an excellent player. From the start of the game, Hannah struggled to find open space, and when she did get the ball, she could not do much with it. "You see that. They've scouted her," her father, Lenny, commented. "They're marking her."

He wasn't imagining this. Everywhere Hannah went, at least one player followed. When she touched the ball, several more defenders quickly closed on her.

Hannah is solidly built, with a low center of gravity, similar to her father, an agent for the Drug Enforcement Agency and a former high school and college lacrosse star. Her sister Sarah is wispier, like her mother, Danielle, who played high school soccer in upstate New York.

Hannah likes to set up teammates for scoring opportunities, but because her understanding of the game surpasses that of her teammates, they are not always in the right place to receive her passes. Sarah has a powerful right leg and more of a scoring mentality. "Sarah is even more of a target because she's a scorer," Danielle said. "I have seen her literally picked up and taken down and no foul called. In the twenty years since I played, the game is twice as aggressive. What you see, even among girls this age, would not have been allowed in my high school games."

The local soccer culture in South Florida is, in its own way, also rough and tumble. Players compete for a team one season, then jump to some new opportunity the next, like big-leaguers who have played out their contracts. Eichmann "discovered" Sarah first, as Danielle puts it. Both girls had been playing on a Nike-affiliated club. "But this particular club is an Adidas club," her father said.

Sarah and Hannah compete in full Adidas regalia—cleats, uniforms, shin guards. They play organized soccer ten months a year, usually five times a week—two practices, two games, and one shooting lesson with a private coach. In their two months off, they may go to a soccer camp, but their parents strictly enforce several weeks when they are not allowed to touch a soccer ball.

With a mother and father who were both athletes, the Coy sisters have parents who may be a little savvier than average—and also, perhaps, warier. Danielle has been around soccer most of her life. Her sister suffered two torn ACLs as a teenager. Lenny coaches high school lacrosse, so he is well aware of the wave of injuries that befall young women.

Danielle said that she knows that in the coming years, the demands on her daughters will grow. "I pray every time before every game that they won't get injured," she said. "It's a huge fear of mine, and I know it only gets worse when they get older."

ONE-TRICK PONIES

The science and medicine of young women and sports
injuries is far from settled. Biomechanics, anatomy,
and hormones all likely play a role, but in what measures we cannot
yet be sure. But the injuries have an external cause too, an unambig-
uous one: our youth sports culture. Year-round play. Early specialization. And the trend toward sport as aspiration, a means to some
perceived end.

The culture produces injuries, especially to girls, who accept
pain as a routine part of competing because it is all they have known.
Too many of them are wrecking themselves, and we, the adults—the
parents—are abetting them.

To understand how this is so, it helps to broaden the context beyond sports, and beyond just girls, and to consider notions of childhood and parenting. Start with the concept of unstructured or free
time. Growing up in the 1960s and 1970s, I had loads of it—hours and

hours after school and vast expanses of it on weekends—and so did nearly every other kid I knew.

Perhaps this was the heyday of free time. Living in suburbia, we had no farm chores. We generally had no shops or small businesses nearby in which we might be expected to stock shelves or sweep floors. A few unlucky souls among us, or so they seemed to me at the time, had paper routes, which they carried out in predawn darkness on empty streets. We had homework, but I don't recall it amounting to much.

Living in neighborhoods presumed to be safe, we roamed widely, and our after-school and weekend hours unfolded largely out of the sight of our parents. We played football at the school yard or in the street, and ice hockey on lakes that were not always fully frozen. We coasted around on bicycles (without helmets) while our friends or younger siblings rode along on the back or on the handlebars. We hitchhiked to the local mall and sometimes all the way into the city.

I did play organized sports, from age seven, when I started Little League, all the way through varsity high school teams, but like most children of my generation, I spent many more hours engaged in *unorganized* sports: burst out of the house, pick a game, choose sides, play till dark. If we had only five to a side for baseball, we closed right field, and any batter who did not hit the ball to the left of the pitcher was called out. (Left-handed hitters got the courtesy of having left field closed.) We played basketball outdoors in the winter, even if we had to bring snow shovels to clear the court and play in gloves.

We had girls who joined the games. Tomboys. Even pre–Title IX, they had high school teams—field hockey, basketball, softball, track and field—but the seasons were short and, by today's standards, undemanding. But that was as true for the boys as the girls.

Our sports seasons had something that no longer exists: a definitive end. In late August or early September, we threw our baseball or softball mitts back into the closet and pulled on our football or soccer gear, or just sat out a few months and knocked around.

Come winter, we moved on to basketball, wrestling, swimming, gymnastics. Left on our own, we were natural cross trainers, not that we would have ever called it that. But by playing each sport in its own season—as well as bicycling year-round, climbing trees, wading in streams—we used different muscle groups. We didn't get burned out on any one activity.

I recount all this not to bask in some idyllic or idealized time but to show how dramatically children's play has changed in just one generation. Our parents never expected that all our discretionary time would be filled up with organized, supervised, adult-approved activity. Much of the time, they had no idea of our precise whereabouts other than that we were outside somewhere, down the block, at the school yard, or in the woods—the pre-deer-tick, pre-Lyme-disease woods.

The current generation of parents, my generation—raised by moms and dads who sometimes seemed to be barely paying attention—keeps a much closer watch. It is a paradox of modern child rearing. We had a degree of sovereignty over our time, but we do not grant it to our own children. Our kids are more likely to be in the house or, when they are not, to be participating in a scheduled activity.

Sociologists Sandra Hofferth and John Sandberg published a study in 2000 titled "How American Children Spend Their Time." Making use of time diaries kept by a cross section of families, they estimated that for American children between six and twelve, the average time spent outdoors in unstructured play, *per week*, was just thirty minutes. That study, and a follow-up six years later, found that fewer than one in five children spent *any unstructured time at all* playing outdoors.

No doubt this is due in part to the Internet and cable TV making the indoors a vastly more interesting place for children than it once was and the outdoors, by contrast, more boring. But parental caution and wariness play a role as well—fear of accidents that might occur on heavily trafficked streets, of bullies, sexual predators, peers who might lure children into drug use. The equivalent of unstructured exploration now occurs on the Internet, and there is plenty of worry about that too.

The threats are real enough, but the dread often exaggerated. Pollsters consistently find that fear of violent crime scores high on the list of Americans' concerns, even among those who live in communities virtually untouched by it. Hofferth, a professor in the Department of Family Studies at the University of Maryland, said that fewer parents let their children walk to school, even if they live nearby. "Some of it may be convenience," she said. "They drop them off on the way to work. But there's been this concern since the seventies about child snatching, even though it's rare and almost always done by an estranged parent or some other relative."

Novelist Dana Spiotta, in a 2007 essay, recalled her parents allowing her to go off on a loosely supervised bicycling trip to Greece when she was fourteen. She camped on beaches, stayed up till dawn, drank her first cocktail. This was in the mid-1980s, only two decades ago, but Spiotta, a mother now, senses more caution among her parenting set. "These days, my parents' willingness to send me off almost seems careless. American child rearing has tipped away from curiosity and toward fear."

The fear extends to unstructured time itself. We don't trust it. In what ways will our kids fill it up? How might they abuse it? Even if they're engaged in nothing particularly bad, we wonder, Are they doing something productive? And if not, might they be falling behind other kids who are filling their hours with goal-directed activities?

Our own relationship to time has changed. In an era of two-career couples and long commutes, it feels ever more precious, a perishable resource. Perhaps the sight of children engaged in nothing in particular—goofing off, inventing games—looks wasteful, like leaving the lights on or the refrigerator door open.

Developmental psychologists cite the value of unstructured play, sometimes saying that a young child's "work" is play. This is not exactly privileged information. It's the kind of thing that many educated parents have probably come across in the popular press—in magazine stories or stories in the so-called "soft" sections of newspapers (read more by women than men) that lament our "overscheduled" children. The features usually play off academic studies, like a 2001 report in the journal *Pediatrics* titled "Organized Sports for Children and Pre-Adolescents," a collaboration of American Academy of Pediatrics committee on sports medicine and its panel on school health.

"The involvement of preadolescents in organized sports is a relatively recent phenomenon," the authors wrote. "In the early twentieth century, physical activity was a more regular part of life for the average child. Sports and play provided an additional outlet for physical activity and were characterized by play that was generally spontaneous, unstructured, and without adult involvement. Participation in such sports and games allowed for development of motor skills, social interaction, creativity, and enjoyment for participants. During the latter part of the twentieth century, "free play" or unstructured games primarily gave way to organized sports. The starting age for organized sports programs has also evolved to the point that infant and preschool training programs are now available for many sports. Organization of sports has potential benefits of coaching, supervision, safety rules, and proper equipment but can also create demands and expectations that exceed the readiness and capabilities of young participants. Organization can also shift the focus to goals that are not necessarily child oriented."

Few other activities attack idle time like organized sports, which swallow up hours of a child's life in practices, games, and carpools. And the higher a child rises, the less time there is for anything else. Parents may complain—one joke is that AYSO (American Youth Soccer Association) actually stands for All Your Saturdays Are Over—

but in fact, the time-eating qualities of organized sports are part of the attraction.

Sports serve as a seductive escape, a wholesome firewall against all the unsafe and unsavory activities we fear that our children might otherwise take up. And they throw off tangible measurements and rewards—wins and losses, statistics, trophies, promotions to higher-level teams—that signify children are establishing a trail of achievement.

Janelle Pierson, the St. Thomas Aquinas star who suffered two ACL injuries, lives deep within a gated community in Coral Springs, Florida, in a big house alongside a golf course. Her parents are sick about her injuries. But in adding up the pluses and minuses of her sports involvment, her mother, Maria, says, "The one payoff is that it kept her out of trouble. There was less time to go out on the weekends. She knew she couldn't drink or do drugs, because you can't do that and be in shape for your sport."

As ORGANIZED sports fill up more of a child's time and take on an ever more central and unassailable place in American households, the whole enterprise has become professionalized, an industry. From top to bottom—from high school athletes who operate as near pros to twelve-year-olds who attend expensive sports academies to fourth graders with private pitching coaches—it is saturated in money as never before.

Money confers import. It buys expertise. And it raises the stakes, causing people to expect a return on investment (yes, even from their children) and to suspend their better judgment.

Consider some examples of what I will call Extreme Youth Sport—not daredevil feats of athleticism but extreme spending, extreme expectations, extreme focus on children's games. Much in this realm may seem, at first, easy to dismiss, far from your own reality. The kids are too athletically gifted. Or their parents are too wealthy, not to mention insane. Perhaps. But Extreme Youth Sport mirrors mainstream youth sport at the community level—and inside typical households—all across America. It exhibits all the same trends, just in more grandiose form.

Let's begin with an old standby, Little League Baseball, the traditional starter sport for tens of millions of American boys. Founded in 1939, it has long been a vehicle for certain types of out-of-control sports parents, usually fathers, to make fools of themselves and victims of their kids by pushing them too hard, verbally abusing them at games, and yelling at coaches, umpires, and anyone else in the general vicinity. Hence the term *Little League parent.* Psychologists even gave the behavior a name, Little League Parent Syndrome, or LLPS, sometimes said to be related to Achievement By Proxy Distorted Behavior—vicariously living through your children.

In a perverse way, Little League became a pretty good place for adults to learn to curb their worst instincts and to understand that their kids' sports, after all, are not that big a deal. The Little League parent is an object lesson, a buffoon, someone who any person with a modicum of self-reflection does not want to be.

But more recently, Little League itself has become the Little League parent, a pioneer in a new form of Extreme Youth Sport: enlisting children as unpaid content in the multibillion-dollar sports-marketing-entertainment complex.

The Little League World Series was for years a modest affair in Williamsport, Pennsylvania. Only the championship game was televised, as a sort of novelty—little boys playing baseball on a national stage. You got to see that once a year. Now the tournament gets blanket coverage—all thirty-two games on ESPN and its affiliates, each of them counted on for ratings during a low ebb in the sports calendar before baseball's pennant races heat up and college and pro football begin.

The announcement touting a new contract signed in 2007— $32 million to be paid by ESPN for eight years of games—makes clear how Little League Inc. and its young players serve the ever-expanding media universe: "The multi-media agreement includes coverage across 15 ESPN platforms—ESPN on ABC, ESPN, ESPN2, ESPN HD and ESPN2 HD, ESPN Classic, Spanish-language ESPN Deportes, ESPNEWS, ESPNU, ESPN International, ESPN Radio, ESPN.com, ESPN360 (the company's growing interactive and customizable broadband service), Mobile ESPN Publishing (ESPN's wireless content licensing business) and other ESPN-branded services (i.e., iPod, video-on-demand, etc.)."

Got all that? The tournament, contested by eleven- and twelve-year-olds, is to be maximized for profit, like a butchered cow whose usable parts are sold off in every direction and to every possible market. If you want to watch the games on your cell phone, in Spanish, it will be possible.

To be fair, the games are great reality TV. The boys make amazing plays. They screw up dramatically. The camera catches them crying and exalting, then pans to their parents in the stands, who are always a nervous wreck. Only one winner is left at the end. But in this deal, as in others like it, the innocence and small scale of youth sport is venerated at the same time it is exploited. "Little League captures the heart of sport—a balance of competitiveness, sportsmanship, and passion for the game," John Skipper, ESPN executive vice president for content, said. "This new deal will allow fans to enjoy—any way they choose—these moments that touch so many."

High school football is the latest youth sports product to be embraced by the marketplace. Over the Labor Day weekend in 2007, eleven high school football teams from Ohio squared off against the nation's best—the "Ohio vs. USA Challenge"—with games televised by ESPN and streamed online by the NFL network, which charged $7.95 per game, or $17.95 for a four-game package.

Russ Klein, the spokesman for the event's lead sponsor, Burger King, explained that what attracted the fast-food giant was high school football's straightforward, small-town aura, the image of boys battling it out on the gridiron in a pure competition. "We like the fit with our customer," he told the *Washington Post*. "We like what the sport stands for. We like the every-town authenticity and appeal that high school football represents. We think it's an underdeveloped and untapped segment, and we're going to be aggressive about building it on the national stage."

Left unspoken is the certainty that tapping this particular "segment" will strip it of its virtue. The only question is how quickly and how completely. Just as money has poisoned college sports, it will leach into high school sports and youth sports, or at least that segment of them it designated as "big time" enough to be on TV.

Money makes sports feel bigger and more thrilling. It buys brighter lights, snazzier uniforms, better equipment. It validates success, in the same way Nike endorsement contracts do for the women of the WNBA, but it also redefines it. Have you had a successful season if you do not make it onto TV? If Nike, Reebok, or Adidas does not grace your school with free shoes and apparel?

And money, inevitably, leaches some of the joy and sense of play out of sports by weighing it with significance and inviting cheating and corruption. It makes it difficult, if not impossible, to keep childhood sport in perspective when the games themselves generate content and profit for big corporations.

Each of the teams in the Ohio football extravaganza that traveled in from outside the area received seventy-five plane tickets, free hotel rooms, and a $5,000 cash payment to their schools. "I don't see how anybody who is offered a trip like that can turn it down," Bill McGregor, a coach of one of the teams, commented.

MONEY INFLUENCES childhood sport in another way, from the bottom up, in what families are willing to pay for their children's success. This is sports as consumerism, guided by the same ethos: if you want it badly enough, you can buy it.

The mecca for this particular faith is the IMG Academies, a 180-acre facility in Bradenton, Florida. About 600 girls and boys, most of high school age but some much younger, specialize in tennis, golf, basketball, soccer, or baseball. They practice their sport four or more hours a day, at least five days a week, from early September through May, longer than most professional seasons. They participate in physical conditioning at what IMG calls its International Performance Institute and undergo weekly "mental conditioning," or sports psychology sessions. One-on-one sports psychology sessions are also available, at extra cost, for youngsters who "want to take their mentality to the next level." Including tuition, room and board, private lessons, and fees for other add-ons such as media training (to prepare the IMG children for when they become stars and must face the press after games), total costs can approach $100,000 per year.

Wimbledon tennis champion Maria Sharapova spent much of her childhood at IMG, and the academy usually has a handful of prodigies on campus. But the vast majority of the kids are good but not great at their sports—earnest strivers, some of them candidates for college athletic scholarships if they keep improving and others just marginal high school players. The threshold for admission to IMG is money, not talent.

In 2004, I spent some time at IMG, mostly with the baseball players, because the idea that not just tennis players, golfers, or gymnasts but also team-sport athletes could be trained in such a hothouse environment was new. One day I watched as a baseball enthusiast named Tommy Winegardner, who was fourteen, practiced on one of the academy's lush, manicured diamonds. On the other side of a dirt road, a long line of golfers hit balls on a range, and on other nearby fields, several dozen soccer players had just started their practice.

The temperature was in the mid-nineties, and stifling humidity had brought out a thick swarm of gnats. But Tommy looked happy, and I could well understand why. His classes at Pendleton School, on IMG's campus, which had begun at 7:30 a.m., ended at noon, at least two hours short of a typical high school day. Some IMG students attend other private schools in the area, but after IMG opened Pendleton—"added an academic ingredient on the compound," as one administrator put it—most students enrolled there. "The thing about Pendleton," Tommy said, "is they respect your sport."

As he stretched and played catch along with about thirty other boys, Tommy's mother, Lisa, sat on a lawn chair in a shaded area, watching practice, as she did every day. She was living with Tommy and his sister, a college student, in a $310,000 condominium on IMG's campus that the family had purchased. Her husband, Chuck Winegardner, had stayed home on the Eastern Shore of Maryland to tend to his car dealerships, but he visited frequently for long weekends. Lisa called after every practice. "I need to give my husband full reports," she said. "What they're working on, how he looks, is he paying attention."

I asked Tommy, who is a devoted ballplayer, if he had ever wanted to play so badly that he just rounded up friends in his old neighborhood for an impromptu game. He didn't think he ever had. Every time he played, it was part of an organized practice or game, or with his father, who had built a batting cage on their property. His friend and IMG classmate, Tyler Pastronicky, said he had never played pickup baseball either. "Even if you wanted to," he said, "you couldn't get anybody else to play. They wouldn't do it."

I believed him. Kids rarely play on their own, away from a scheduled practice or game. Take a ride around your area on some pleasant summer afternoon, past the local athletic fields. Most of them will be empty, and if you spot one where kids are playing, look a little closer and odds are you will see a coach in charge.

The gateway to sports is now *organized* sports. Several years ago, I began coaching a recreational-league basketball team of fourth grade girls. They had great fun—*I* had fun—and we stayed together as a team for several years. But I never quite got over that our first practice was the first time—the first!—that several of these girls had ever held a basketball in their hands. The clarion call to play was the notice that an official team was forming. Once forms were filled out and checks written, they got uniforms, an official schedule of games, and a warm gym to play in with officials and an electronic scoreboard.

Like other IMG parents I talked with, the Winegardners seemed to believe their son's passion and talent compelled them to enroll him—that if they had not, a moment and an opportunity would have passed. His zeal had to be matched by their money and maximum commitment. "He's sort of like a natural," Lisa Winegardner said. "I'm his mother, so I would feel that way, but that's what coaches have said ever since he picked up a ball. We just felt like he needed this to get to the next level. If you have talent and it's overlooked, you're not doing your kid justice."

The staff at IMG—many of whom are successful former pro, college, or high school coaches—is first-rate. Some of them consult to pro athletes who travel to IMG to train in their off-seasons. I doubt a kid can get better instruction anywhere. But what struck me was how little these coaches really believed in the IMG model—children playing one sport to excess.

David Donatucci, who was director of the academy's International Performance Institute, lamented that the typical incoming student to IMG is a surprisingly poor athletic specimen. He or she comes from the first generation of indoor children and exerts himself or herself only on command, and in well-worn patterns, like a lab animal in the maze. By specializing in a single sport just about from the cradle, Donatucci said, most kids had missed out on "important neural parts of athleticism."

"We've got tennis kids who can't hop, skip, or jump. We've got golfers who if you threw them a ball, they'd duck; basketball players who can't swing a baseball bat. We've got some kids who are really good at their sports, but if you looked closer, you'd be surprised at how unathletic they really are."

Donatucci also believes that this makes the kids particularly susceptible to injury. The first thing he sets out to do is to try to remake them—to give them better balance, strength, and well-rounded coordination. The IMG soccer coach, Tom Durkin, told me about one high school girl on campus, a national-level player whom he referred to as "broken." She had a series of knee and other injuries. "She's very good, but in constant pain," he said. "All her injuries are from overuse. She was playing on club, state, regional, and national teams. She might still have something to offer, but first we have to rebuild her."

The concept of the "self-made" athlete is one of the most persistent myths in sports. Strictly speaking, it doesn't exist. Elite athletes all come from the same genetically gifted pool, those with the particular traits their sports demand: Hand-eye coordination for softball and baseball. Speed, balance, and agility for soccer. Height for basketball or, if lacking in that, extraordinary quickness and jumping ability. An athlete can sometimes bump herself up one level through hard work and dedication—a bench player may crack the starting lineup; a pretty good varsity player can work extra hard and become the team's star. But in sports, perhaps more so than in most realms, DNA is destiny. Athletic talent can be flagrantly squandered, but the extent to which it can be acquired is limited.

Donatucci did not expect that most of the kids passing through IMG would have a future in professional or even high-level sports. "What we've got here are kids with parents who were not athletes who say, 'I couldn't do this, so I'm going to give you what you need so you can do it,' " Donatucci said. "Isn't that America? You want something better for them, right?"

Ken Bolek, the baseball coach at IMG, said it was a rarity for one of his players to get drafted into professional baseball—despite the years they devoted and the hundreds of thousands of dollars their parents may have spent. (Tommy Winegardner will begin playing in 2008 for the baseball team at Coastal Carolina University.) "Creating professional players is not the standard I set for success, and it's never been suggested to me by the administration that it should be," he said. "Every now and then, you get a kid with great genetics, a real quick kid or a big, exceptionally strong kid. But those are the exceptions. We take what we're given here and work with it."

Trevor Moawad, a sports psychologist at IMG, told me, "We're not here to burst anybody's bubble. But let's be honest. DNA plays a role. Maria Sharapova came here"—at eight years old—"already a champion. We just refined it. Whatever it is, she had it."

THE THIRD rail of television sports commentary, the thing that years ago got the late Jimmy "the Greek" Snyder fired, is any suggestion that black athletes may be more genetically gifted than whites—that they are faster runners and better jumpers and therefore better suited for certain sports. I'll leave that for others to trip over. I have another thought: what if, in the less prosperous communities that many of our most vaunted pro athletes spring from, athletes are less hovered over, less coached, less smothered—and more left on their own to discover the individual genius that all great athletes possess?

A component of athletic success is physical creativity. Modern childhood does not encourage it. A recent *New York Times* editorial took note of two best-selling books, *The Dangerous Book for Boys* and *The Daring Book for Girls,* which advise children how to do such things as form a snowball ("Scoop up enough snow to fill your hands") and throw a ball ("Start with the ball in your right hand, stretching your arm straight out behind you"). The headline on the *New York Times* editorial was "Childhood for Dummies," but "Parenthood for Dummies" would have been more fair, since it's not the kids' fault the way adults structure their time.

Creativity in athletics comes from noodling around for hours with a ball in the backyard or school yard, from inventing moves and playing out fantasies either alone or in pickup games away from the censorious eyes of coaches. Like any other kind of creativity, it can be either nurtured or deadened.

Consider the soccer culture here in America, and the failure to produce men's teams that can compete with the world's best. Why is that? We are a populous nation, with athletes of every conceivable shape and size. We have good nutrition, excellent training facilities, well-organized sports committees. But relative to much-smaller soccer-playing nations like Ecuador, the Netherlands, and Ghana—to say nothing of traditional powers like Brazil, Argentina, England, France, and Italy—we are not very good. (The U.S. women were dominant when the women's game was not as popular around the world, but other nations are now quickly catching up.)

The best male soccer prospect the United States has produced in the last decade, and perhaps ever, is Freddy Adu, who made his professional soccer debut at age fourteen and is now playing for a pro team in Portugal. Adu emigrated to the United States from his native Ghana at age eight. Ben McGrath, profiling Adu in the *New Yorker*, theorized that his genius emerged in a way that it would not have if he'd spent his early childhood in the United States. "Broadly speaking, American soccer is known for being obsessively structured, conservative, and focused on conditioning; in other countries, by contrast, individual creativity and flair tend to be more encouraged," he wrote. "Adu's style of play, having emerged in the unstructured environment of Ghanaian pickup games, more resembled that of the Brazilians or the French, with their traditionally strong sense of touch. He was a gifted trickster and ball juggler, so deft that he could appear, at times, as though he were dancing."

Durkin, a former college coach and director of IMG's soccer

academy for both boys and girls, spent much of his childhood in Brazil, where, as he put it, "they play soccer in every form—on grass, cement, dirt, in the street. Our society is one of constant supervision—it doesn't allow for that." The consequence, he said, is that even some of his best players come to him technically proficient but lacking spontaneity and daring on the field. They are robotic, able to do specifically what they have been taught.

Durkin recalled a weekend morning that he and his college players were to give a clinic to about fifty children in North Jersey. He arrived at the field early and threw some balls out on the field, then walked back out to the parking lot to finish his coffee and wait for his team to arrive. His college players were a little late (he suspected they were out too late the night before and perhaps hung over), but he didn't fret about it. He left the soccer balls out on the field and figured the children would be kicking them around, loosening up while his boys straggled in.

When he walked out to the field with his team, the balls were right where he put them and the kids were lined up, waiting to be told what to do. "It's one of the by-products of an affluent society," Durkin said. "Kids have things done for them, and they can't do for themselves."

An estimated $5 billion a year is spent on private sports instruction for U.S. children, although a precise number is hard to come by, since instruction at the lowest end—for example, high school or college athletes charging by the hour to tutor younger players—occurs off the books. Personal trainers, fitness centers, and "performance centers"—facilities promising to enhance athletes' speed and strength—eagerly seek out children as consumers.

"Let a handful of kids and teens increase your profit margins," advised a 2006 article in *IDEA*, a publication for those in the fitness business. "What do a seven-year-old uncoordinated kid, a slightly overweight thirteen-year-old, and a star high school soccer player have in common? Each one could be your next client."

The article quoted the director of youth programs at a fitness club in Valencia, California, north of Los Angeles, about how to make fitness fun for teens. She had designed successful camps based on the reality TV shows *Survivor* and *Fear Factor*. Rather than have them eat bugs, she made the campers eat vegetables.

Brendan Sullivan, a former minor-league baseball player who founded Headfirst Baseball, a league and instructional program for both boys and girls in Washington DC and its suburbs, has made a career out of sports instruction. But like Durkin, he has a sense of being at the center of a transformed and bizarre culture. "I got all the way up to Triple A ball," he said. "That made me, what, one of the fifteen hundred best baseball players in the world? But my whole professional career, I never saw video of myself. Maybe I should have; it probably would have helped. Now I'm videotaping ten-year-olds. I had a kid who had this off-balance, bailing-out swing. His parents said to me, 'Can we get video analysis of that?' I had to tell them, 'We can sort of see what's going on here without resorting to that.' "

Sullivan grew up in Washington and graduated from prestigious St. Albans School, and then Stanford University. His father, Brendan V. Sullivan Jr., is a prominent lawyer who has represented, among others, Oliver North. "I know this world. I came from it. These are high-end kids under pressure, even on the field. Everything they do is with excellence in mind. They're not allowed to get anything but an A. I have to tell them, 'It's OK to go oh for four.' Baseball's a hard game; it doesn't care how hard you're trying. Sometimes you're not going to do well."

Sullivan's league runs ten months a year. He operates a large summer camp and provides year-round private instruction in baseball, soccer, and tennis as well as all-around physical training for boys and girls as young as four years old. He has expanded into academic mentoring and college guidance for high school students.

He is counted on to impart sophisticated coaching yet sometimes finds himself trying to teach children how to be kids. For a change of pace, he will encourage them to organize their own games, or he'll show them stickball or some other derivative form of baseball. But they are so burdened by expectations and so unused to playing on their own that his efforts are rarely successful. "They can't do it very well," he said. "And they don't like it. They're like: 'If I'm going to play baseball, I want Sully around. I want to be in uniform and I want an umpire.' "

Sullivan, like Donatucci and Durkin at IMG, has also noticed the consequences of early specialization—athletes who can perform the mechanics of their particular sport but too often in a repetitive, almost metronomic way. "I see it all the time. I look at some kids, and they look good with the bat in their hands. They're perfect. And then they go out on the field, and I say, 'My God, this kid is a horrible athlete. He can't run. He can't move. He's spent all his time in the batting cage.' So many of these kids have played no other sport. They're one-trick ponies."

CHAPTER 12

"ARE YOU ASKING ME WHY I'M DOING SOMETHING I KNOW IS BAD FOR KIDS?"

The youth sports culture, at the community level, is designed to serve an athlete I think of by an acronym, CDA—competitive, devoted, ambitious. The CDA has some talent, enough to experience success in her sport, but her physical gifts are not as defining as her other attributes. She plays hard, is willing to play all the time, and—this is key—believes that she will stay with her sport as far into the future as she can see. If she is a high school athlete, she plans to play in college. If she's younger, she has her eye on the next level up and the one after that, all the way to the high school varsity and beyond.

Her sport is her identity, her calling card, and it has been as far back as kindergarten or first grade, when the teacher asked for a self-portrait and she made a crayon drawing of herself in uniform—in soccer gear, complete with cleats and shin pads; with a softball glove on her hand; or in a swim cap, with goggles pulled down over her eyes.

This is a new identity for girls, and in most regards, a good one. For these girls, sports offer a joyous sense of play as well as a place to test strength and determination—and to learn to rally from defeat and disappointment. Sports can be protective for them, in just some of the ways parents hope. An athlete who does not want to engage in some unsavory activity always has an out: I've got a game tomorrow. Or a practice. I can't let my teammates down.

Without exception, the girls I interviewed for this book had winning personalities. They were confident but humble, and attractive in their utter lack of fussiness, the types who roll out of bed in the morning, wash their face, pull up their hair, and go off to school. "Ten minutes. That's all I need," Janelle Pierson told me. "That's from the time I get up until I'm in the car."

Various studies have looked at whether playing sports helps women achieve leadership positions. In a 1988 survey, 86 percent of women holding key positions in *Fortune* 500 companies said they participated in sports as children, and 80 percent said they would have been described as tomboys. In a 2002 survey of female executives, 82 percent said they had played team sports.

None of the research is considered definitive. Women looking back at their childhoods may have different ideas of what constitutes involvement in athletics, and the relationship between sports and leadership may be casual—other childhood pursuits could have been as influential in making them leaders. But intuitively, the connection seems correct. No one gets ahead in business without knowing how to compete and how to bounce back from disappointment. And no other pursuit teaches that as well as sports.

Among American children six to eighteen years old, as many as 45 million play some form of organized sports, roughly half of them girls. How many are CDAs? Millions, for sure, although it's impossible to fix a precise number. But if you have one, you know it, because she has been seized upon for her talent and enthusiasm. The emergence of a competitive, devoted, ambitious young athlete is like a new free agent on the market, a magnet for adults immersed in the local youth sports scene. They invite her in more deeply, flatter and even pressure her.

The CDAs get an intensified sports experience, a higher dose than any previous generation. Girls form deep bonds with their sport, their coaches, and their teammates. For most, it comes naturally. They are drawn to relationships and the idea of community. Sports may not be political for them, as it was for past generations, but they like the idea of being a part of something larger than themselves, a team. Putting themselves on the line, even at personal risk, becomes a core value. They don't want to let anyone down.

I met Ariana Cook, a quintessential CDA, at the end of her senior season of high school soccer. A bright young woman with an especially keen memory, she remembers the moment she knew her soccer talent had been recognized. She was in fourth grade and had been playing at the low-key rec-league level for about three years. A coach she didn't know approached her after a game. "He said to me, 'Do you want to take it to another level?' I remember the words because they sounded so strange. I was kind of shocked. I knew he was complimenting me and wanted to put me on a different kind of team, but I didn't know what it entailed."

Ariana was a fast runner and a naturally aggressive player. Other girls held back; like Amy Steadman, she went for it. As she advanced, she played defense; if any attacker was going to score a goal against her, that opponent would first have to win a hell of a battle.

The coach who approached her that day led a select-level team of ten-and-under girls. Ariana agreed to join, skipping what for many players was the next step, the premier level. The team was packed with good players. It wasn't easy to find teams who could give them a competitive game, so they often played against boys' teams.

The world Ariana entered was entirely different from what existed a generation ago, when kids' sports were the province of moms and dads who organized the local teams—and of gym teachers and other athletically inclined educators who made a few extra bucks coaching the school teams. Now many large, multiteam soccer clubs are run by paid directors, and their best teams are coached by professionals. This is especially true in the affluent neighborhoods of America's cities and in the middle- and upper-middle-class suburbs, where parents are accustomed to paying for expert tutoring for their children across all fields.

In some communities, the whole youth soccer industry has been taken over by paid coaches, in almost all cases men. Many come from nations with deep soccer cultures in Europe, Africa, South and Central America—places where soccer also remains a predominantly male sport.

In other sports, as well—basketball, baseball, softball, field hockey, lacrosse, volleyball—a serious youth player is likely to affiliate with a private club team, even after reaching the high school varsity level. The clubs offer what the schools do not: year-round play. This represents a radical change, because up until about two decades ago, only athletes in individual sports—golf, tennis, gymnastics, swimming, and diving—typically trained and played privately. School districts still have strict rules on when sports seasons begin and end, as well as limitations on the numbers of allowable games and practices. But the limits are meaningless, because the kids go off and play elsewhere, often concurrently with their school seasons.

An athlete's paramount relationship is typically with the club team, not the school team. Annual fees and travel to tournaments often run into the thousands of dollars. Parents also pay for camps and private sports tutors. The guiding principle is that childhood sport is too important to be left to volunteers and amateurs. The coaching, in terms of skills and tactics, is probably better than in past generations, but it is also narrower.

Rather than being coached by educators who see them during the school day, teach them in a class, and have some holistic sense of them as children, young athletes are now mentored by coaches who cultivate one aspect of them—the athletic side. A coach of a go-go club team is expected to produce victories, invitations to prestigious tournaments, and teams good enough to attract the eyes of college scouts.

At what age should a young athlete begin traveling to out-of-town tournaments? How many days a week should she be playing? How many months a year? When should she give up her other sports and devote herself fully to one? The professional coach is usually not trained or educated to know what's best, but he wields tremendous influence, sometimes by threat. He makes the schedules and sets the rules, and a child who does not go along risks losing her place on the team.

Parents sometimes employ sports psychologists, but their mission is rarely to sort through these questions or to help a child cope with the demands of the culture. Sports psychologists are most often hired to enhance performance—to help a child set goals and sharpen focus. They are personal trainers for the mind.

A star player can sometimes say she wants to sit out, say, the fall season of soccer and perhaps try another sport, or just rest and then return in the spring. But most kids risk being replaced if they balk. They're told: The train is leaving with or without you. Are you on board or not? Because there are dozens of other girls who want your spot.

U.S. Youth Soccer, the governing body of state soccer associations, recommends that children under the age of twelve should not be encouraged to play one sport exclusively. In its coaching courses, it emphasizes that soccer is a "late specialization sport" in which players often do not peak until they are in their mid twenties. The guidance is just flatly ignored.

Even many high school coaches have given up on the idea of

multisport athletes and prefer the polished specialists who emerge from club play. Kids who play more than one high school sport have become a rarity. Ned Steadman, Amy's father, has noticed the change over the course of his high school teaching career. "The football teams used to practice a couple of hours after school, then go home. The boys played other sports in the winter and spring. Now I see them on the field until seven p.m. some nights, and it's just about all year-round. I don't know how many coaches they have—as many as a college team, from the way it looks."

Rob Kurtz, the coach of the girls' soccer team at Bethesda–Chevy Chase in Maryland, was a three-sport athlete himself—"soccer, basketball, and baseball, and I loved all three"—but now advises against it. "I don't think it's possible anymore. You're doing yourself a disservice. You might make two varsity teams, but you probably won't be a contributor to either one of them. That's what I tell the parents. I wish it wasn't true, but it is."

But it is only true because we have made it extremely difficult to pursue more than one sport. A child who wants to must fight against a system that discourages her every step of the way—and to repeatedly fight that system, year after year, as she is pressed to give up all but her "best" sport.

Athletes who specialize in one sport may become impressively fluent in it and more adept at, say, performing long-familiar practice drills. But from a purely physical standpoint, there is no reason why a good all-around high school athlete could not excel in soccer, then join the basketball team, and after that play shortstop for the softball squad. It doesn't happen because we do not allow it.

To play multiple sports is, in the best sense, childlike. It's fun. You move on from one good thing to the next. But to specialize in one conveys a seriousness of purpose. It seems to be *leading* somewhere—even if, in fact, the real destination is burnout or injury.

Colleen Hacker, the team psychologist for the U.S. women's soccer team, has worked with everyone from preadolescent athletes up through competitors in the college, Olympic, and professional ranks. "The big misconception is thinking that there is a linear connection between the development of a young athlete and the time spent being coached, attending organized practices, and playing organized games. There's no support for that. There may be belief and a hope, but not evidence."

Hacker said that few youth coaches are "well-versed in developmental realities" and that the biological age of prepubescent children can range plus or minus four years. The early bloomers, she said, "are put in central positions. They get more touches of the ball, more coaching, more acclaim. The rich get richer." But their success comes at a price. "They're the ones who get overuse injuries. They're the ones who burn out. They pay dearly for those early expectations."

One of Hacker's clients, an all-star big-league baseball player, was a gifted soccer player as a kid. Tim Duncan, a perennial all-star on the San Antonio Spurs and among the top handful of players in the NBA, was a champion youth swimmer who only got out of the pool when a hurricane wrecked the only training facility in his native St. Croix. One study showed that, on average, U.S. Olympic athletes played three sports through adolescence.

"This message is not getting across," Hacker said. "We need to encourage parents, coaches, sports leagues, the culture itself to go back to multiple sports participation. And there needs to be real off-seasons with unstructured play. No adults. No rules. No leagues. No registration cards. One of the best sentences a parent can utter is 'Go outside and play.' One of the worst is, 'It's nine a.m. Get in the car, we're going to practice.'"

A few years ago, Hacker served as a guest instructor at a school in Bolivia, where soccer is a means of economic and class mobility. Even so, there were periods of the year when even the best young players were not allowed to play. "It's a very poor country, but they had the wisdom of *no ball*. They took it away. The ball becomes precious, the game becomes more precious. There's motivation around that, but also rest, recovery, and rejuvenation."

In 2007, the American Academy of Pediatrics took another stab at trying to inject sanity into the youth sports culture by issuing a series of recommendations in its journal, *Pediatrics*. Among them: "Encourage the athlete to take at least two to three months away from a specific sport during the year." "Encourage the athlete to participate on only one team during a season." "Encourage athletes to strive to have at least one to two days off per week from competitive athletics, sport-specific training, and competitive practice to allow them to recover both physically and psychologically." More broadly, it stated, "Young athletes who participate in a variety of sports have fewer injuries and play sports longer than those who specialize before puberty."

But parents are easily convinced that early specialization and year-round play is the only course for children who hope to master a game, because it is the only model they see. Children who show athletic promise are stampeded as if they were being rushed by a fraternity or sorority. A cohort of serious players forms—kids who stay at their sport twelve months a year. They are the cream of the crop, the ones headed to the next level, and the one after that, at whatever price.

Up until she was nine, Ariana Cook was still playing on a basketball team and dabbling in swimming and tennis, but after being invited into select-level soccer she dropped those sports. "I knew I had to choose one sport, because of the demands," she said.

By the time she was fourteen, she was part of three soccer teams: high school, club, and Maryland's Olympic Development Program (ODP) squad. To be invited into ODP is prestigious and hard to turn down—it's *Olympic development*—but every state has one, so the nationwide program involves a couple of thousand girls at any one time, most of whom will never get anywhere near an Olympic team.

Ariana's ODP practices were one to two hours away, depending on traffic, twice a week. She was part of a carpool; the girls tried to do their homework while crammed together in the backseat. Some of the games involved even longer trips. At times in the spring and fall, she rarely had a day off, even while trying to keep up with demanding academics. "I think it was spring of my sophomore year that I was playing like seven days a week somewhere," she recalled. "It was ridiculous."

Her parents had doubts about the crushing schedule, but it was what Arianna wanted to do, and there did not appear to be alternatives. The level of play she had reached seemed to demand the extraordinary time commitment.

Finally, in the fall of 2007, Ariana took her first real time away from soccer in a dozen years—an entirely unplanned leave. As we talked in her living room, she reclined on a couch, her right leg extended and in a big brace. She had torn the ACL in her right knee, and two days earlier had undergone reconstructive surgery.

The injury occurred in a preseason high school game on a field at St. Mary's College, in rural southern Maryland. "We got there like eleven a.m. and took at our of the school," Ariana said. "It was a really hot day. Everybody was exhausted. We watched the JV game. Our game wasn't until like five o'clock. Nobody really wanted to play. Our warm-up was terrible. We did some running, a little bit of stretching. It was all halfhearted."

About ten minutes into the contest, Ariana got tangled up with an opposing player as they both went for a ball. "My knee popped. I knew it wasn't good." An MRI confirmed what she feared, that she had ruptured her ACL and lost the final season of high school soccer. "I found out during school," she said. "I started crying and basically I cried for a week and a half. Emotionally, I was just a mess. But it's such a long recovery period that you have to come to terms with it. You can't cry the whole time until you get back on the field."

Injuries usually cannot be diagrammed like traffic accidents, with precise lines connecting cause and effect. Ariana's indifferent warm-up could have been a factor, leaving her body unprepared to react to imminent danger. Physical or mental fatigue might have worn her down and made her more susceptible to injury. Or it could just be that her number finally came up and she fell victim to what Bill Prentice of UNC calls an "overexposure injury"—after all the thousands of games and practices, she finally ran into misfortune. Between high school and club play, Ariana, on the day of her injury, was competing in her fifth game in seven days. If she had not been hurt, it would have become nine games in ten days, because she was about to start a club tournament the next day.

After Ariana learned the severity of the injury, one of her first thoughts was that college coaches who had expressed interest in her would stop calling. "I felt like, what if I'm damaged goods? I was afraid I might not be wanted by anyone anymore. Basically, the last year or so it's all been about trying to get seen by college coaches. It's definitely not the reason I play, but I was at a place where it's like all my efforts were paying off. It was all coming together."

Several people advised Ariana that she was under no obligation to share medical information with prospective coaches and that she should keep the injury a secret. "They were like, it's self-preservation. Do what's best for you. Don't tell them. But I talked to my high school coach, and he said he would be really angry if someone did that to him. And my Dad said it would be morally reprehensible. So I did tell them, and the coaches were supportive and really great about it. They kept saying, 'We've seen you play. We know how you play. We're here for you, even if you have to take the first year off.'"

What Ariana did not realize was that if college coaches shunned girls with a history of serious knee injuries, they would struggle to put quality teams together. The percentage of top high school girls who have already blown out their ACLs is too high.

In the period between her injury and the surgery, Ariana visited Amherst College (where she will enroll in the fall of 2008) for a "recruiting weekend," when coaches bring prospects onto campus. Another recruit on the same trip was in a similar limbo, awaiting ACL surgery, and so was one of Amherst's best players, who had torn her ACL days before. "We all commiserated," Ariana recalled. "We were going through the same emotions, having this realization that we were going to be out so long and not be able to do this thing that's been such a huge part of your life. Soccer is what I've done, basically, for the last fourteen years."

The enforced layoff gave Ariana time to ruminate, to think about her sport in a way she never had. It was clarifying. "The injury has made me ask myself, Why do I play? Do I really enjoy this? Is it worth it for me?' It was like a test of my faith in soccer. And I decided I really do love it. I love the whole thing, just the game itself. It's nothing specific I can pinpoint. But it's so different from school. It lets me relieve a lot of my stress."

In the wake of the injury, though, Ariana and her parents questioned aspects of her last dozen years of soccer. Between high school and her other teams, she had played fifty or sixty games most years, double the number most college teams play in a season. "I looked up the college schedules," her father, Jacques, an international trade lawyer, said. "I was nonplussed. She'll play less in college. There's a disconnect there."

Ariana had never been exposed to anything she would construe as an ACL injury prevention program with any of her teams, and she wondered why. "We've done agility training," she said. "Speed training. But not specifically ACL prevention. With us playing so many games, and with so many girls getting this injury, you'd think they would be all over that."

• • •

I TRAVELED back down to North Carolina in 2007 to watch Anson Dorrance put his famed women's soccer team through preseason workouts. This was a high level of soccer, obviously, but even Dorrance's players, when they are not competing for him, parcel out their time to different teams—to their clubs, to various levels of U.S. national teams, or for some of them, to the national teams of their home nations. They're still CDAs—just at the most elite echelon.

In the mid-August heat, the players competed in a series of what he calls *bogies,* drills that take place right in front of the goal and involve two attackers, two defenders, and a goalkeeper. Bogies are like basketball games contested on a driveway hoop—elemental and rough. Dorrance uses them to remind his team of the point of the game, which is to close the deal and shoot the ball past the goalie and into the net. "Every year," he told his team, "there's a direct relationship between the high scorers in bogies and the high scorers in the full field game."

The losers in bogies had to, as Dorrance put it, "bend over." They trudged into the goal area, turned their backs to the field, and put their hands on their ankles as teammates kicked soccer balls as hard as they could into their backsides. I remember that we sometimes imposed the same consequence on the losers of our playground basketball games. We called it "asses up."

I was shocked to see these college women doing the same thing. It seemed demeaning for them to have to "bend over" at the behest of their coach. But they seemed to find it amusing.

Toward the end of the practice, I stood on the sideline with Nicole Fava, the UNC athletic trainer, as the team took part in a full eleven-on-eleven scrimmage. I asked her how many of the players we were watching had torn their ACLs in the past. She scanned the field and counted. "Just six. But three of them have done it twice, so nine tears among the twenty-two" she said, adding, "We're doing pretty good. It's been worse, but we've graduated some."

While their teammates scrimmaged, a half-dozen players sat on the side with Ace bandages, braces, and big bags of ice attached to various parts of their bodies. They had all reported back to school already hurt, which Dorrance said occurs every year. Their injuries included an ACL tear (suffered by a player competing for England's national team), a foot fracture, a pulled hamstring, and a severe ankle sprain.

"My kids are in great demand," Dorrance said. "I've got them for nine months, and it's very rare for the catastrophic things to happen while they're here. But then they leave for three months, and when they come back, they're shattered. They've been back in this environment where they all came from, where everybody wants a piece of them and they're caught between everyone's agenda. Very few of them can say, 'No, I've got to rest,' because they fear, and with good reason, that they're going to be excoriated and whoever is offering them this great opportunity won't ask again."

Like all college coaches, Dorrance has a bird's-eye view of youth sports culture. It's where he gets his players. He explained some background about the development of girls' soccer and the rise of big, multigame tournaments: When the sport was just starting to become popular a couple of decades back, good teams were widely spaced geographically. To find competition, they had to travel. Coaches, understandably, wanted to make the trip worthwhile by packing in a lot of games.

"You would play three, four, or five games over the course of a weekend," Dorrance said. "It was a lot, but that might be your only trip for the year. So that became the template for tournaments, and it was based on a legitimate angle on player development, that players have to play a certain number of quality matches against quality competition.

"But now everybody's got a tournament. There's the Raleigh

Shootout, the Surf Cup in Southern California, and ding, ding, ding, they're everywhere, for players of every age and ability level. Say you're a soccer promoter in Houston, Texas, or Kansas, or wherever, and you want in on the action. You put one of these things together, and it becomes another must-attend event on the calendar. But we still have the same template, because if somebody's going to fly to you, they don't want to play just one match."

Dorrance was animated, his words coming out in torrents. "So now girls are going somewhere every two or three months and playing this inordinate number of matches. And you know what? They're playing to survive. And the survivial is not just the five games in three days. It's the two or three weeks following. They've got a niggling this and niggling that—sprained ankles, swollen knees, aching backs. They were overplayed, and they never rested. But part of what's developing is this question of who's tough enough, who can play through it?

"Then, before you know it, the coach is telling them, 'Let's get ready for the next event, because you know what, I think we can develop into one of the top ten club teams in America.' So now our ambition is to win this event, this tournament, this championship, and everyone better damn well be aboard. You have this subtle pressure, not applied overtly, about how committed are you, how successful do you want to be? The result is that they end up shattered, and for no good reason."

For all his love of aggressive play and risk taking, Dorrance is a fierce critic of overplay. He sees a senselessness in the way the industry of youth sports chews up players.

There are hundreds of tournaments nationwide, from the Blues City Blowout in Memphis to the Holiday Festival in Las Vegas to the early-spring Dust Off the Rust Classic in Middletown, Ohio. In the marketing for these tournaments, bigger is always better, more is more. Here is the pitch for the Disney Showcases in Orlando, from the event's homepage: "The Disney Showcase Soccer Series has grown from one 80-team tournament to a series of three top-level national events with more than 600 teams. If your team has something to prove, then Disney's Showcase Series, presented by the Chelsea Football Club, has an event for you. Make it a goal in 2007 to take your team to the next level. Then watch them rise to the challenge at Disney's Wide World of Sports Complex—The Proving Ground."

Playing too many tournaments and too many games is just another version of Extreme Youth Sport. And like overcoaching, overplay has the opposite of its intended effect. Rather than enhancing players, it stunts them.

"In a ninety-minute match, the average player handles the ball for three minutes. That's not going to develop you into an elite player," Dorrance said. "What develops players are training blocks. Blocks when you are building your speed and your agility. Blocks when you're resting. Blocks when you're doing all these different things with the ball, touching it and having fun, but not playing full-field games. All these games are the worst possible thing for a player in terms of both development and injuries, but we keep on doing it."

TOURNAMENTS, OR "classics," "showcases," or "cups," as they are also sometimes called, are as much about commerce as athletics. Elaborate undertakings involving hundreds of teams and thousands of players, they fill up hotel rooms in the host communities and pack local restaurants.

The 2007 Adidas Potomac Memorial Tournament, contested over the Memorial Day weekend at the 160-acre SoccerPlex in Boyds, Maryland, about thirty miles north of Washington, attracted three hundred teams—both boys and girls, from U-10 squads to U-19's—drawn mainly from the Middle Atlantic states, the Carolinas, and New England, but with some traveling in from as far as Texas and Arizona. It was by no means the biggest tournament in the nation, but the Potomac tourney still felt like a bustling trade show, with no single focal point but activity in every direction.

The walkways between fields were crowded with players, coaches, parents, and little siblings walking to and from games. Lots of people seemed to be peering at maps, trying to figure out where to find their next game among the nineteen fields or on the ones off-site, miles away, because the tourney had overflowed its venue. Golf carts zipped by hauling big orange water jugs, desperately needed since the late-spring weather felt more like August—hot and oppressively humid.

I attended the tournament with Gayron Berman, an avid, skillful player who was just finishing her sophomore year of high school. The previous season, she had expected to compete for a spot on her high school team's varsity. But in the summer between eighth and ninth grade, she tore her ACL during the championship game of a club tournament. She was playing on artificial turf for the first time, and her cleats grabbed and her knee buckled. At fourteen, she was on the young end for when girls start suffering ACL ruptures.

She went through reconstructive surgery and rehab and recovered well enough to become a star for the junior varsity squad as a sophomore. But her cohort had gotten out ahead of her, and her soccer career assumed a form she did not anticipate. She was desperate to make the varsity as a junior, but had to stay healthy.

On day one of the Potomac Memorial, Gayron played two games for the Potomac Flamengo, her longtime club team—one at 10:00 a.m., the other at 4:00 p.m., each of them eighty minutes long. They won the first, lost the second. After the second game, Gayron collapsed into her parents' minivan, ate a quick pasta dinner when she got home, and was in bed and asleep by 8:30 p.m.

At eleven the next morning, she was back at the SoccerPlex, in heat and humidity even more intense than the previous day. Because the Flamengo had split their first two games, a victory would have qualified them to play another game in the afternoon—and possibly another the next morning. Five in three days. A loss and Gayron and her teammates would be done for the weekend. Normally the type of athlete who hates to lose, Gayron said, "I don't even know if I'd want to win."

The Flamengo team began their warm-up that morning with a light jog that lasted all of ninety seconds, then did some stretching in the only open area available, a sloped grass embankment between their field and a parking lot. With games packed in one right after the other, they could not warm up on the field because the previous match was not yet over. When it ended, they kicked the ball around for a few minutes and took some shots on goal.

Gayron's parents are highly educated, as are many of the Flamengo parents. But before their daughter ruptured her ACL, they knew little about the syndrome of injuries to female athletes, and even afterward, they knew nothing about training programs designed to prevent young women from tearing (or retearing) the ligament.

This hardly set them apart. In nearly every other realm, parents seem to know all the ways to keep their kids safe. They're highly involved in all aspects of their lives, to the point of obsession. But in sports, they either do not know the right things to be concerned about and the right questions to ask—or they just feel powerless within a culture that they know on some level is extreme. The demands of youth sports work against examined thought. You're at the tournament, checking the map, just trying to get from one field to the next. Everyone is caught up in the swirl.

On that Sunday morning, the Flamengo competed in a predictably desultory manner and were defeated by a team that looked only slightly less exhausted. It was like watching zombies play soccer. The girls on both teams were, to use Dorrance's word, shattered. Overplayed and used up. The good news was that none of them got injured.

• • •

THE DIRECTOR of the Potomac Memorial Tournament, Arnold Tarzy, a financial planner by trade, is sufficiently well versed in sports to know that the soccer extravaganza he presides over does a disservice to young athletes. He is president of the multiteam Potomac Soccer Club, its director of player development, and has coached championship high school teams in both golf and soccer. In addition, Tarzy is known in soccer circles as the man who discovered phenom Freddy Adu.

He was coaching a recreation-league team in Montgomery County, Maryland, when Adu, freshly arrived from Ghana, showed up as a member of the opposing team wearing black jeans, an orange sweatshirt, and a Mickey Mouse hat. Tarzy recruited Adu onto his travel team and mentored him as he zoomed up the ranks of U.S. soccer, and he remains Adu's close adviser.

I asked Tarzy about the heavy schedule of games, not just at his event but at others around the country. Before I could say anything more, he stopped me. "Are you asking me," he said, "why I'm doing something I know is bad for kids?"

He did not say this defensively. Like the coaches at IMG, Tarzy understands that he is giving the marketplace what it wants rather than what is good for it. And, like Dorrance, he recognizes aspects of the youth sports culture as madness. "Nobody should be playing more than one game a day," he said. "I understand that. I really do. In Europe, they don't do it. They allow ninety minutes of play a day, and if they play two games, they're each forty-five minutes. That's forward thinking: let's protect the kids from abuse.

"So why do we have a tournament in this format? The answer is, this is the way tournaments here are done. If I were to change from the norm, teams would go to another location, and we wouldn't have a tournament."

A lot of money flows through a big tournament. The three hundred teams entered in the Potomac Memorial paid between $575 and

$895 to enter, with those in the older age groups paying the most. Tournament profits went into the operating fund of the sponsoring entity, the nonprofit Potomac Soccer Club, although the money did not amount to enough, according to Tarzy, to justify all the volunteer effort.

The beneficiary of most of the entry fees was the SoccerPlex. Big tournaments like the Potomac Memorial are the raison d'être for such facilities—and also their lifeblood, because the sites charge rent, by the game, for each field. It's a simple formula: the more games played, the more money flows to the facility.

Built with $20 million in public and private funds, the Soccer-Plex is a nonprofit, as are most such facilities around the nation. But it still must be fed. There are fields and facilities to maintain, including a 3,200 seat stadium, common areas to keep up, employees to pay. With an annual budget of more than $2.5 million, the SoccerPlex began running up big deficits as soon as it opened.

The local hospitality industry also has an interest in tournaments being staged on a grand scale. The WRAL Soccer Center in Raleigh, North Carolina, site of the Raleigh Shootout and several other big annual youth tournaments, is responsible for an estimated 10,000 hotel room nights a year. In arguing for public funding for the soccer facility, a league official touted the economic spin-off of tournaments: "We average eighteen kids per team plus two coaches. Typically with these teams, three quarters of the parents come, and there often are siblings. The parents have got to entertain the kids, and we're doing the Shootout in November, which is Christmas shopping time. Most of these people are on the road, so they have got to find a place to eat, go to a movie, go shopping, or go find video games."

The syndrome here is the same as what's behind the blanket TV coverage of Little League baseball and high school football: child athletes as little profit centers. Young soccer players at an out-of-town tournament may well enjoy the experience—playing the games, at least the initial ones, before exhaustion sets in; seeing new parts of the country; hanging out in hotels with their teammates. But they are performing, in part, for someone else's financial benefit.

Traveling for an out-of-town game used to be solely the province of college athletes or high school players who advanced deep into postseason playoffs. It is now routine for many kids starting at about age ten, or even younger. This is related to what has become known as KGOY—kids growing older younger. It's a marketing term, not something that comes from a new understanding of the stages of child development. And it has opened up whole new markets—for equipment, apparel, and services.

Any effort to dial the whole thing down—to have fewer tournaments, play fewer games, play them closer to home with less travel—would work against moneyed interests. Making it all work economically is of far greater import to these interests than health concerns caused by overplay.

Tarzy said that no effort is made to track injuries at his tournament. "I don't know that there would be any value in it," he said. A field marshal monitors each game, and if a trainer is needed, the marshal summons one on a walkie-talkie. No follow-up information is sought if a player subsequently seeks treatment elsewhere.

Tarzy has coached teams of elite high-school-aged girls and seen plenty of injuries, including ACLs tears—four in the last three years, out of a group of eighteen players on his squad. "It's crazy," he said. "I have one who suffered multiple ACL injuries and surgeries, and she's been told she can't play again. Unfortunately, she was the most gifted of our players."

He did not know about the programs designed specifically to decrease the rate of ACL injuries and did not think any were in place among teams in his Potomac Soccer Club. He reasoned, somewhat bizarrely, that any effort at injury education or prevention on the part of his soccer organization might put it in legal jeopardy. "I don't want to say we're indifferent to the injuries," he said, "but you can't grow up around here without being aware of the litigiousness that surrounds us. If you put something in place, maybe you've assumed a responsibility that can't be fulfilled enough. I'm just speculating, but if somebody then gets hurt, does the parent come at you and say you didn't do enough?"

For the first time, in 2007 Tarzy gave teams in the older age groups the option of playing their first game on the Friday afternoon preceding the three-day weekend, so that only those making the semifinals would end up playing two games in a day. "It was my way of doing what I believe is right," he said. But most of the teams declined; it was too hard for them to arrive in town that soon.

Tarzy places most of the blame for overplay on parents. "They want a lot of games, in whatever conditions. It can be freezing cold and raining and the field looks like crap, it's unsafe, but believe me, you'll hear from parents if you cancel a game. There's this compulsion they have. Play, play, play, no matter what."

That is what Tarzy believes. I talked to parents who wished their kids played fewer games and would welcome tournaments with more reasonable schedules. As for the girls, they just go along and play however many games are set in front of them.

For many high-school-aged players, the lure of the tournaments is the chance that they will attract the attention of college coaches, and events are named with this in mind: the Crossroads of America College Showcase in Indiana; the Empire Cup Showcase in Rochester, New York; the Rocky Mountain Cup and College Showcase in Boulder, Colorado. It's a marketing thing. There are a couple of dozen similarly named events, but even in tournaments not specifically called showcases, the older players hope to be scouted.

On my way into the Potomac Memorial, I stopped at the table where the participating club teams had left binders for college coaches. In them were the collected resumes of their players, with on-field accomplishments, grade point averages, and SAT scores all duly noted.

The resumes also listed off-field activities, with particular attention paid to good works. One young woman stated that she had volunteered in a soup kitchen, picked up trash as part of a highway
cleanup program, and made submarine sandwiches for a Super Bowl
Sunday fund-raiser. Another touted her work in Fiji with an organization called Rustic Pathways. A senior from a private school had
traveled to South Africa and volunteered in an orphanage for children with AIDS. A few of the players listed more prosaic off-field
pursuits like scooping ice cream for an hourly wage and babysitting.

But only about 5 percent of high school athletes continue to play
in college. Some get partial scholarships, but no more than 1 percent
of high school athletes, representing just the top layer of national-
caliber players, get full scholarships. For most families, even those
whose daughters are high-achieving CDAs—girls who were captains
of the varsity team, all-county, even all-state—there is no monetary
return on the tens of thousands of dollars they have spent on team
fees, travel, equipment, and private coaching. Some parents also pay
for professional recruiting services to market their children to college teams, which can cost thousands of dollars and which most collegiate coaches consider a particular waste of time and money.

"A lot of people are delusional," San Jose State women's coach
Dave Siracusa said of the tendency of parents to believe their children are playing for some financial payoff.

Excelling at sports, though, can work to an athlete's benefit in
another way, by gaining her admissions preference to the nation's
most academically selective colleges and universities—to Harvard,
Yale, and the rest of the Ivy League, and to a couple dozen of the
most coveted liberal arts colleges. Unlike the wish for a college scholarship, it is not a fantasy.

The Game of Life, by James Shulman and former Princeton president William Bowen, published in 2001, explores in groundbreak-
ing detail how this works. Using numbers obtained from a sample of

thirty academically select institutions of various sizes, the authors demonstrated how athletic prowess is the most powerful nonacademic factor in the admissions process, well beyond all other considerations, including minority status and legacy.

The great revelation in the book is that the influence of sports on admissions decisions is far greater at midsized Ivy League universities and elite liberal arts colleges than at bigger universities, because these smaller institutions often field just as many teams—and sometimes more—but have far fewer students to fill them. Consider some examples: Penn State, with 36,000 undergraduates, sponsors twenty-seven varsity teams. Harvard, with 6,700 undergrads, fields thirty-nine teams. The University of Illinois has 36,000 students and twenty-seven teams; Williams, with just 2,100 students, fields thirty teams.

At the large universities, even the ones sometimes criticized as "sports factories," athletes are actually few and far between. It's not that common to end up in a class with one. But at Williams, or nearly any other highly selective liberal arts college you can think of— Swarthmore, Bowdoin, Amherst, Johns Hopkins, Middlebury, Pomona, Haverford, Macalester—varsity athletes make up anywhere from 25 to 40 percent of the student population.

These colleges do not sponsor teams so that their players can get pummeled. They want to win—or at the very least not be embarrassed. In order for the teams to be stocked with capable players, a high value must be placed on athletic talent in admissions decisions.

Athletes in the Ivy League and at the small NCAA Division III colleges do not receive athletic scholarships. But about half of them are recruited, meaning they are included on "coaches' lists" submitted to the admissions offices. This is sometimes referred to as a *slots* system—the slots being places in each freshman class reserved for athletes.

The applicants admitted from coaches' lists are generally excellent students judged capable of surviving demanding college coursework—no school wants to admit an athlete who is apt to flunk out—and some are stellar academic performers who do not need the athletic edge. But Bowen and Shulman showed that, on average, recruited athletes have substantially less impressive high school academic credentials than their non-sports-playing peers admitted at the same schools. They were waved in because a coach wanted them. Without that edge, they would not have been on top of the pile.

The athletic edge in admissions at these selective schools has been growing, more so for women than men, as colleges have had to fill the rosters of newly created teams. In 1989, a woman who was a recruited athlete had a 26 percent greater chance of being admitted than a female student at large, after adjusting for differences in SAT scores, according to Shulman and Bowen. That was about the same edge that minorities and legacy applicants were granted. By 1999, the value of a recruited female athlete to the admissions office had skyrocketed. A young woman on a coach's list had a *53 percent* better chance of being admitted over a similarly qualified nonathlete. The edge for male athletes was 48 percent. The minority and legacy advantage stayed the same.

Those who gain entrance through sports, Shulman and Bowen write, "have been paying close heed to the signals that colleges and universities have been sending with their admissions policies. These students have paid more attention to the schools' practices than their lofty rhetoric."

USING SPORTS as leverage to gain entry into top academic institutions is alluring to a particular demographic: families who will pay the steep tuitions of private colleges and who are from communities in which admission to selective schools bestows status. In upper-income communities across America, the hope of securing this privilege drives much of the frenzy of youth sports and a good deal of the overplay.

Title IX created the opportunity for girls to get into one of these glory schools through athletics. It's achievable, even for those who are not elite athletes. They've got to be good, of course, but no Olympic pedigree is required.

Young women have opportunities not just in soccer, basketball, and other traditional sports but in sports that are relatively new in college and do not yet have deep pools of talent, such as lacrosse, ice hockey, and water polo. Women's rowing is currently the fastest-growing NCAA sport. Eighty-six women's crew teams competed in 2007, up from thirty two decades ago. I know of a young woman, six feet tall and long-armed, an ideal build for crew, who took up the sport late in high school and was immediately besieged by college coaches. She had gold-plated academic credentials, but even some valedictorians with perfect SAT scores get rejected by their top choices. She never had to worry. She settled on Harvard but could have gone to any top-tier school with a crew team.

The Waspy, country-club sport of squash is the latest game to be targeted by parents seeking an edge through athletics. It has two primary attractions: a small pool of capable players and nothing but high-status schools seeking them. (The women's top ten in squash for the 2006–07 season: Princeton, Penn, Harvard, Trinity, Yale, Dartmouth, Williams, Brown, Cornell, and Bates, with other ranked teams including Stanford, Vassar, Colby, Smith, and Columbia.)

It is almost as if some sports have been elevated in importance to benefit a privileged population. Lacrosse? It was a Native American game, around forever, played mainly in a narrow corridor between New York and Washington. It has rapidly spread into the Midwest and West, and to high-income communities in Florida and Texas, in no small part because of new college opportunities.

Almost all the fastest-growing women's college sports are ones played primarily by white suburbanites. A coach of a club soccer team told me, "The perfect kid that coaches want is one who is a good player, doesn't complain, and has parents who pay every month and don't complain."

This coach had recruited "lower socioeconomic kids" for his team but with mixed success. "You need to pick them up. They never have their forms, their certifications, their medical documents. Elite soccer demands lots of travel and lots of money and parent commitment. It's what keeps it so white."

An argument is sometimes made that sports recruiting adds to the racial diversity of campuses, but that holds true only in football (which women do not play), basketball, and, to some degree, track and field. In most cases—and especially at the elite academic schools—sports are yet another venue for the rich to get richer. Relatively few minorities and poor children of any race are involved in rowing, squash, water polo, or lacrosse, so to the extent those sports confer admissions preference, they are not eligible.

A college campus is greatly enhanced by having athletes on campus. They are physically fit. They embrace competition. If they have achieved academically in high school while excelling at a sport, they likely have mastered one of the most important requirements for success in college: time management.

Shulman and Bowen acknowledge the value of sports but decry the practice of giving athletes such an edge in admissions, arguing that reserving so many places at the smaller colleges overvalues athletic talent at the expense of other attributes that might be pulled into the student population. In the preface to the paperback edition, they lament that many parents had missed that part of the message and were using their book as a "how-to guide" for getting their kids into top schools.

Reporter Bill Pennington of the *New York Times* wrote a series of stories in 2005 and 2006 on athletic recruiting at elite liberal arts schools. "The process gets more organized every year," Greg Kannerstein, Haverford's athletic director (now dean of the college) told him. "The parents are more savvy, the athletes are polished, and the institutions are meticulous."

Communications between academically elite colleges, high school athletes, and their parents take place largely in code, as if what is being discussed is not entirely aboveboard. It's one thing for a big-time football power like Ohio State to give an academic pass to a coveted defensive tackle, but the Ivies and the leafy liberal arts con-claves do not want to be perceived as doing the same. The eight Ivy League universities issued a manifesto that tried to make clear that it is admissions officers, not coaches, who select the freshman class, no matter how many winks and nods a prospective student and her par-ents may have picked up from the coach of her chosen sport. "Ad-missions offices at each Ivy school may offer some athletic and other candidates a 'likely' letter, which has the effect of a formal letter of admission provided the candidate continues to have a satisfactory secondary school experience," the document states. "Coaches may initiate the requests for these letters, but only the office of admission can issue a 'likely' letter."

Kannerstein was frank about how specific needs of teams figure into admissions decisions, even at a place like Haverford, which has just twelve hundred students and is annually ranked among the handful America's most selective schools. "We can and have gone to admissions and said, 'We have to admit a goalie in field hockey or we won't have a team,' " he said. "It doesn't mean they'll automatically admit a goalie, because nothing is guaranteed, but they will listen. It's a contributing factor."

The system, though, is anything but transparent, and the game is not played in the way that many parents may think. To the extent that a player travels to a tournament in the expectation of being no-ticed by a college coach, it is in most cases a waste of her time and her parents' money. There are far too many tournaments—with too many games occurring simultaneously on too many fields—for a player, even a very good one, to have much of a chance of being observed. Most college coaches have limited recruiting budgets. If they travel to a tournament, they see only a handful of games involving only the top teams. And even if a player is observed by a coach, she has to hope it is early in a tournament. "You would not want your kid evaluated in the second half of the second game of the day," Tarzy points out.

Ariana Cook was an honorable mention "all-Met" selection by the *Washington Post,* putting her among the best players in Washington, D.C., and its Maryland and Virginia suburbs. But Ariana is sure she was never observed by a college coach at a tournament. She attracted the attention of the Amherst coach at a summer soccer camp she attended.

"I was never seen at any tournament right up until the last one, when we played three games in Nashville," she said. "The reason I know is because the college coaches tell you. They let you know they were there to see you play. It was frustrating, because it was for nothing. It was definitely for nothing."

CHAPTER 13

"I'M A STRESSED
PERSON"

When your children get older, they become less visible to you, and most of the essential things they do occur out of your sight. This is inevitable and necessary and difficult. You can't take a seat in the bleachers and watch them sweat out an algebra exam (nor would you want to), and you are not invited to their social gatherings. But when they play a sport, you get to observe them doing something they love and catch a glimpse of their spirit in a way that is otherwise not often possible.

I remember a friend's response when I mentioned that my daughter planned to swim in college and would be close enough for my wife and me to go to her meets. He said he was envious. His son's last high school track meet was a sad day for him because he knew he would never again see one of his children's athletic competitions.

Parental interest can, of course, go wrong. You can become such a fan of your own sports-playing child that you forget you have a job to do and turn into a Little League parent—or worse. Child psychiatrist Ian Toffler has described the stages of parental involvement in athletics as follows: "It begins with healthy pride and support for the child's athletic achievements. At the next step, parents may take a second or third job, move closer to a gym and training facility, or send their children to 'sports hatcheries' for year-round training. At level three, the parent places increasing pressure on the child to perform, even if the child is injured or ambivalent about participation. The child becomes an instrument of adult goals. With the fourth and most ominous stage, parents become self-serving and encourage their children in endeavors that risk their physical and emotional health. Parents rationalize their actions by telling themselves that all this is done to satisfy the child's love of athletic competition. In reality, the parent's true motive is recognition or financial gain—for the parent. At this point, achievement by proxy degenerates into a form of child abuse."

While this kind of extreme behavior exists, I did not really encounter it in my research, at least not in its most grotesque form. It is far more difficult than some imagine to push a reluctant child into sports, especially at an intense level that demands a high degree of commitment. Children may acquiesce for a while, but all but the most passive or abused will eventually rebel and shut down. The truly pathological sports parent, in most cases, is a short-timer who leaves the scene when his kid quits playing.

I found a different syndrome: parents of highly motivated athletic children who are supportive of their kids' sports but bewildered by the culture. The children, as often as not, are the ones leading the way. They do not so much put pressure on themselves as they absorb it from the youth sports culture. The parents get subsumed in ways they never anticipated.

"We had no idea what we were getting into," says Rich Pierson, Janelle Pierson's father. "You just feel your way as you go. She started playing with a local team just once or twice a week, then began with the travel team, and after that it just builds on up. Before you know it, it's your whole world."

Colleen Hacker, the sports psychologist, says, "Parents' hearts are usually in the right place. I don't think anybody's saying, 'Honey, how do we screw them up tomorrow?' But the attention, judgment, and objectivity that parents bring to their work lives and other spheres of importance, they don't bring to their kids' sports."

Some of the benefits of sports are obvious. Children get in the habit of being physically active, a routine vitally important in an era of ever-increasing obesity. Several studies show that girls who play sports build bone density, which can protect against osteoporosis later in life.

But the health benefits of competitive athletics can be overstated. Exercise and sports are not the same thing. "It's a false argument to advocate competitive sports for health reasons," Nancy Theberge, the sports sociologist, says. "The best examples of physical activity for health are people involved in regular, nonextreme physical activity in a noncompetitive environment. There are particular risks to being an elite athlete. Competition exposes them to risk, and athletes whose identities are invested in their sport will push limits in ways that others will not."

As parents, we all tend to find ways to rationalize behavior that may be excessive. Some other parents, we tell ourselves, are even more extreme. Starting your child's college search and taking a tour of campuses when she's in 8th grade? It's always best to be organized, right? And besides, didn't the family down the street have their kid take the SATs in 6th grade, just to get a baseline?

I will confess my own rationalization when my daughter began to swim year-round when she was eight, then moved on to occasional "two-a-days" in her early teens—practiced at dawn, gobbled down breakfast, went to school, then got back in the pool in the afternoon for another practice. Crazy, right? But swimming, I told myself, is an endurance sport. It's *always* been a year-round thing, always a cult for obsessives. Well, OK, so what? It worked out (I think), but with one major injury that cost her nearly a full season, and too many other pursuits crowded out.

Training for young athletes, in any sport, identifies and pushes forward a handful of the most talented, hearty, and injury-resistant kids. Those who cannot withstand the regimen fall by the wayside. "You have to be careful about which part of the story you tell," Hacker said. "We hear about Tiger Woods as a prodigy at three years old. For every Tiger Woods, there are thousands of kids who never want to touch a golf club again."

Said Steve Marshall, "A coach can make his career with one kid who becomes a well-known star. But that's one in a thousand. So we take a thousand kids and throw them against the wall, hoping for that one star, and ruin a lot of them. That's the system we've created."

The Maryland suburbs of Washington, D.C., where I live, are on the doorstep of the federal government and the power centers of national politics. We are near the National Institutes of Health and the National Naval Medical Center, numerous hotbeds of high-tech and biomedical research, and several fine universities. In general, the population is financially comfortable and status-conscious, with status attaching more to achievement and education than wealth.

In its approach to youth sport, my community is typical of hundreds of other middle- and upper-middle-class communities across America. It is sports mad — or, I should say, mad for *organized* sports — with teams available for both boys and girls starting at age five or even younger.

David Cooper, a Yale-educated psychotherapist, is a good example of a parent who struggles with a sports culture that seems to spin beyond his control. He looks very much the 1960s-generation intellectual: short and slim, curly black hair, cropped beard, wire-rimmed glasses, a tiny earring in his left ear.

He is a particular subtype of sports parent—the kind who cannot believe such a kick-ass athlete resides in his household. His
daughter, Hannah, is a dynamic, all-Metro soccer player at Bethesda–
Chevy Chase High School, lightning fast and a wizard of a dribbler
who can score with either foot. The local weekly newspaper summed
up her attributes, "Impeccable footwork, speed, ball skills."

"This is a new world for me," Cooper said during lunch one day
near his office. "And I feel I am the most adrift. Other parents are in
their second or third generation of this level of sports. I love sports,
but I was never much good at them. Hannah has opened this up for
me."

Cooper tells the classic story of his daughter's skills being recognized and the whole family being rushed. Hannah started playing on
a team in kindergarten with friends from the neighborhood. She
would get the ball and dribble through everybody, scoring what
seemed like a dozen goals a game. He would think to himself, Wow,
she's really kind of something. But he did not have a frame of reference to really know. Hannah's rec league coach, a native of Turkey,
told Cooper and his wife, Amy Scott (Hannah's stepmother), "She
can do anything she wants in soccer. There's no limit."

A few years later, Hannah took a skills test to try to qualify for a
travel team. Multiple coaches wanted her and started calling the
Cooper household to make their pitch. One was adamant that Hannah should "play up," join a team of older, equally skilled players,
which would involve a greater number of games and practices.

Her parents were opposed. They asked the coach: "What if we
wait a year?" Hannah was just nine years old, but the coach replied,
"You can wait, but she'll miss out on an important year."

That set a pattern. David and Amy have tried, with intermittent
success, to "hold the reins. That's been our role." They have a younger
child at home, a boy who plays Suzuki violin and loves baseball. Amy,
wary of organized sports, is involved in "free play" days at a local park
with Hannah's younger brother. Hannah also has a twin brother who

lives with their mother in neighboring Silver Spring. "It's a compli-cated life," David says. At times, he has had to tell his daughter, "We're full up. We're doing as much of this as we can."

As Hannah was entering ninth grade, the coach of her club team convened a meeting of the parents and asked if the team should stay in league play during that fall—which would mean playing concur-rently with the high school season—or sit out a cycle and play again in the spring. David was against the team's competing in the fall, but parents who felt otherwise prevailed.

With all the practices and games, the girls on the club team were on the field six or seven days a week that season, but Hannah sat out. It was her parents' choice, not hers. She played just once that fall with the Bethesda Santos, her club team, joining her bedraggled teammates at a tournament over Columbus Day weekend. David Cooper recalls, "The other parents were saying to me, 'The kids are so exhausted. They're just worn out.' I said, 'Why didn't you vote with me?' Most of them didn't seem to even remember there was a vote."

Or perhaps they were so unused to being given a choice by a coach that they did not fully recognize when one was offered.

"My parents don't share my enthusiasm. They haven't supported my soccer as much as they could have," Hannah Cooper said not long after we sat down to talk at a coffee shop near her house. Her tone lacked any evident anger or bitterness. She was just matter-of-fact, confident in her pronouncement.

Her parents had refused to let her accept any of the repeated in-vitations she received to play ODP soccer, the Olympic development program. The practices took place in Baltimore, an hour away, more in afternoon traffic. Hannah had wanted the attention she believed ODP would bring. "You can get noticed without ODP, but it's harder. You have to fight to be seen. I think it's held me back."

Even in an area where it is common for high schoolers to be ambitious and driven, to load themselves up with multiple Advanced Placement courses along with heavy sports and extracurricular schedules, Hannah is considered by friends, teachers, and other adults who know her to be especially intense. She led her high school varsity team in scoring in her freshman season; the next year, she was nervous during tryouts about making the team again. Her father has suggested, not jokingly, that he'd like her just once to get a C in a course; she has only ever gotten A's. It's rare for team-sport athletes to enjoy long-distance running—they may occasionally run to get in shape for a season—but she takes off on eight-mile runs just to relax.

The first time we talked, Hannah was about to begin her junior year of high school, an important time for any college-bound student but even more so for an athlete hoping to be recruited. She feared suffering a major injury. Two girls on her high school team had already torn ACLs, and she knew several girls in club soccer who had done the same. (Ariana Cook was on her club team, and at that point still six weeks away from tearing her ACL.) "I'm really worried about it," she said. "If that happened to me this year, my exposure to colleges would be reduced."

But she was already injured. Like so many girls, Hannah was *always* injured. She estimated that she was on a soccer field somewhere between 200 and 250 times a year and had been for the last half dozen years, and all the running, pounding, and cutting had taken a physical toll.

"My ankles are sort of permanently sprained," she said. "The left one never fully recovers, so I play in a brace. I also have shin splints, so that hurts all the time, but I've just learned to ignore it. I also tore my meniscus, or I think I did. That's what my [club] coach thinks. I'm just trying to get through this club season before I get it looked at, and hopefully, it won't be as bad as I think. I've probably had concussions, because I've had hard collisions where I was disoriented and had headaches afterward, but I've never missed a whole game because of one. If I have to sit out, I always come back in."

David Cooper says he once heard that in pro football the injury rate is 100 percent. Judging by what he observes with his own daughter and her soccer-playing peers, "It looks to me, in girls' soccer, it's the same thing."

Sports, in theory, is a stress reliever, but it was not clear if soccer was relieving anxiety for Hannah or serving as a gathering point for it. What she likes about her sport, she said, is the feeling of scoring an important goal. "I like being the hero. I admit that." She enjoys earning the respect of her teammates and coaches and gets a special kick out of being the focal point of the other team. "I like it when the other coach says, 'Good game, number six.' You know you've made an impression. I want them to feel like I was a challenge to his team. I want to be the person they have to think about."

But when I asked why she plays, the answer was more complicated. "I can't imagine life without it," she said. "But it's a given that I'll keep playing, rather than real enjoyment sometimes. People take it so seriously, more so the adults. It's too big. It's too important."

If you think of pressure as pollen, free-floating particles that affect some people more than others, Hannah is more susceptible than most. Expectations fall on her, and she absorbs them.

As gifted in the classroom as she is on the field, Hannah has been told repeatedly that she will probably earn admission to whatever selective college she wants. "I've been told it shouldn't be a problem, but I'm a stressed person," she said. "I still worry that I won't be able to get into the kind of school I want without soccer, so that just makes it really important that I play well when I'm supposed to."

HILLARY GOLDMAN, a teammate of Hannah Cooper's on both her high school and club teams, is a less acclaimed but nonetheless accomplished player. Her long brown hair, soft features, and affection for hippie-looking bracelets and multiple rings belie the ferocity of her play. Hillary is a risk taker, a midfielder who goes for every ball, courting contact and full-on collisions numerous times a game. She spends a lot of time on the turf and experiences more than her share of head-to-head and elbow-to-head contact.

When I asked if she had soccer heroes, Hillary looked at me like I was out of my mind. "Of course," she said. "Mia Hamm."

Assigned a project in elementary school in which children had to dress like and embody a figure in history (they stood motionless at their desks, as if in a wax museum), she chose to be Hamm. In tenth grade, for a yearlong independent research project, she chose a different kind of sports-related topic. She mapped and analyzed the causes and treatments for all her various soccer injuries: Plantar fasciitis beginning in fifth grade. Back spasms beginning a year or two later. Pain shooting down her legs, probably from the back problems. Hamstring strains. Chronically sore knees. "There have been whole years," she said, "when I've always had at least one thing hurting and I've never not been in pain."

Even in a milieu in which people routinely suffer sports injuries, Hillary is known for her frequent injuries, the classic chain of them, from the feet up through the trunk. Something always hurts. Her teammates see her go down on the ground in a heap or hobble off the field and say, "That's just Hillary." They don't think she's a wimp. Just the opposite; they know how tough she is.

Hillary sees herself with three jobs: Attend school. Play soccer. Go to physical therapy. When she has had to take time away from soccer to try to heal, she hated it. "I don't care for practice, but I love the competition of the games. It's just like a beautiful thing when the team connects, when it's successful."

She has worked assiduously to build core muscle strength to try to prevent other parts of her body from breaking down and, as she began her junior year, was relatively healthy except (like Hannah) for an ankle sprain that would not heal despite repeated courses of physical therapy. She felt pressure to get back on the field. At age sixteen, she had been playing intensely for ten years, year-round, including times when school and club teams overlapped and "you would be so tired from the week, and then you'd get to the games on the weekend, and you wouldn't have any energy left."

She hoped that college soccer might actually be more fun—a reward of sorts for all her hard work. She did not want to win a place at a Division I, scholarship-granting university, because she did not want soccer to entirely define her college experience. Her plan was the one detailed in *The Game of Life*: use her sport to excite the interest of a highly selective academic institution. "I know soccer will help me get into a school I might not get into just on academics," she said.

Hillary's mother, Melissa Reitkopp Schwartz, was in the first wave of Title IX beneficiaries, a member of her high school's first girls' soccer team, then part of the first women's team at Cornell. She marvels at what her daughter and others can do on the field. "They're so much faster than we were, and more skilled, but I don't know if they're tougher. We were tomboys; we weren't sissies. We played a hard game."

But back in the early seventies, women athletes could not use sports as leverage into college the way they do now. Schwartz has been trying to market Hillary, whom she refers to as a "scholar-athlete package," to the right schools and coaches. But both mother and daughter have become frustrated. They regret that they did not start strategizing earlier—*much* earlier, like ten years ago.

Hillary and her mother believe they have been outmaneuvered by people more versed in the ways of youth sport. Team sports certainly can be cruelly subjective, with opinions on who should make certain teams being just that—opinions. Players can benefit by favoritism or because they have established a reputation greater than their actual talent.

"I don't like the political part of soccer," Hillary said. "It's all about what club team you decided to be on, and that decision gets made before you know the consequences." She told me about a friend, talented enough but with a status that in Hillary's mind derives in large part from the company she keeps on her well regarded club team. "She shows up and it's like, 'Oh, how are you, great to see you.' I'm not whining about it. I just wish I had the same advantage."

Hillary's mother explained that a team had formed all the way back in fourth grade, good players but not above Hillary's level. They stayed together, and now when they travel to tournaments, college coaches gravitate to their games. But Hillary's family had just returned from several years of living overseas and did not know the local soccer landscape. She joined a different team.

"Hillary and I were not politically savvy," Schwartz said. "We didn't do the right things. You really had to be an aggressive, plugged-in parent to know what was going on. It was all about what club you played with, who your coach was, what his reputation was, what tournaments he could get you into. I'm sorry to say, but that's how the game goes."

I pressed Schwartz. Could a decision made for a ten-year-old athlete really be that defining? "Totally. Without a doubt. I feel guilty that I didn't recognize it. You try to gain information from other parents, but by the time I started asking, it was too late. Hillary is one of the top three players on her high school team, but in club soccer, she's been marginalized."

College coaches usually scout the massive tournaments rather than high school games, because on just one trip they can see dozens or even hundreds of prospects just by walking from field to field. It's more cost-efficient. And yet because they find their way to what they consider the top games, they see only a fraction of the players at any given tournament. The club team that included Hillary Goldman, along with Hannah Cooper and Ariana Cook, contended for the state cup in Maryland and was invited to the best tournaments, including the Disney Showcase, but not into the highest brackets. It was like securing a reservation to a trendy restaurant but being seated at an undesirable table near the kitchen. The team was at the right tournaments but not on the right fields to be seen by recruiters.

Melissa Reitkopp Schwartz vowed that if the Santos went to any more tourneys, she would personally seek out the college coaches. She had learned how it was done from a parent on another club team. "You say, 'I'm the representative from so-and-so team, and here's our brochure.' Someone from our team did it once and was rejected. But it's not an offer. You don't let yourself get turned down. You just hand over the paperwork and say, 'Here it is. What college are you from?' And then you put them down on your list."

Schwartz works as a recruiter, matching PhDs with consulting jobs in the DC area. Putting her daughter and her teammates together with college coaches seems to be about the same thing. "It's very much like my sales job. I'm a headhunter. I sell people."

Rob Kurtz is Hannah's and Hillary's soccer coach at Bethesda–Chevy Chase. He wears college T-shirts to practice: Yale. Pomona. Emory. Dickinson. Haverford. "That's my market, the private, highly academic colleges," he said. "The shirts put the goal right in their faces. It reminds them about life after high school, and maybe it spurs them on to train a little harder."

The majority of U.S. high schoolers take college prep courses; their sports now are also college prep. Kurtz is a guidance counselor at a neighboring high school and also has a private business counseling athletes on how to market themselves to college coaches. He does the same for his own high school players but without charge, constantly helping them to look to the future, toward what he calls "the next level."

The intensive year-round programs have produced tens of thousands of girls with competent skills. "I don't even need to touch their skills," Kurtz said. "What I want to do is up the ante even more athletically."

Kurtz's teams, usually among the top squads in Maryland, rarely just kick the ball up the field and chase it. They play an artful style — short, crisp passes, set plays, beautiful teamwork. Lately, though, he has begun to think they are sometimes "too pretty." When two skilled, nuanced teams meet, "the tougher one wins every time. I want to build my players up to where, athletically and in terms of their mind-set, if they're going for a ball, they won't even think about it."

Kurtz said his players have become "more dynamic, more aggressive, just more overall athletic. I've got girls who can do pull-ups, can squat a hundred pounds, and bench-press their weight." He knows this is also what college coaches want — fast, aggressive young women with no fear of physical play. That's the Anson Dorrance method: assemble a team of fierce warriors and turn them loose.

So-called athleticism, though, is double-edged. Athletes rarely hurt themselves moving slowly or playing softly. This is why injury rates in games are always far higher than in practice; they go up with intensity and speed. But a girl who gets stronger and faster without enhancing her balance, running mechanics, and landing technique may be putting herself in greater peril. "It seems intuitive that if you get stronger, you're safer," said Donald Shelbourne, the Indianapolis orthopedic surgeon. "But you're not, because you're going to move faster and be more aggressive but still at times be out of control. If you have an accident, you're going to be more likely to tear an ACL, or have another significant injury, because you've generated more force."

Kurtz is cognizant of injury issues. His teams complete a dynamic warm-up before each game and practice, twenty minutes of active stretching and lunges. He does not do any specific ACL injury prevention, but in preseason workouts in the summer, he has brought in a trainer to teach girls how to land from jumps and decelerate with flexed knees. "You can see with a lot of the girls that they don't land well and they've got all these alignment issues, hips and backs. They're just crooked, some of them. To me, that's where the problems start, but I'm not trained to know how to fix that."

Hannah Cooper, his best player, has been a particular project. Focused and determined, she has spent many hours in her backyard, by herself, playing with a soccer ball. Left foot. Right foot. Juggling the ball, inventing new ways to trick opponents. It's how she has fun, and why she is so good. She is the rare player who is not primarily coach-taught.

But despite her skill and speed, Hannah, who is five-two and slight of build, rarely gets much room to operate on the field. She is constantly jostled and elbowed, bounced from one defender to another. She is strong once she has the ball, but before she can get control of it, and often while the referee's attention is elsewhere, she finds herself getting pushed out of the play.

At her level of club competition, and among the best high school teams, each opponent has at least one strong, aggressive defender who takes pride in impeding a dangerous offensive player, if necessary by physical intimidation. "Players like that are admired, or sometimes they're laughed at," Hannah said. "With some of them, you'll hear somebody say, 'She's a man. She's scary.' I imagine in college it's even worse. The play is rougher, and everybody has to suck it up. I'm ambivalent about it. I understand that it's a challenge I have to deal with, but the game is not supposed to be a bloodbath."

Hannah has the speed and skill to play major Division I college soccer but not yet the physique. "She has a strong lower body, she turns quickly, with short steps, and she's very fit," Kurtz said. "She leaves nothing exposed in her lower body. But she can barely lift a teacup."

He has told her that her opponents in college will be bigger and even more physical. "Five-foot-nine, 165 pounds, and almost as fast as you are. They'll just knock you over and keep on going."

Kurtz talked of sometimes playing Hannah at outside midfielder rather than as a striker, the team's primary offensive threat, which he hoped would serve two purposes: she would be less likely to get roughed up, and by showing the ability to play another position, he said, Hannah would "diversify her resume."

He wants her to spend more time in the weight room, building her upper body. But she is not sure she wants to. "I don't really know if I want to change my body," she told me.

Her reluctance may be part of a larger issue. A game that she started out loving feels ever more like work, full of things she must do. It is hard for her to find the joy. Her father wrote in one e-mail to me, "I just wish the game could be fun and the pressure minimal— dream on."

On October 16, 2007, Kurtz's team played its crosstown Bethesda rival, Walt Whitman High School, in a matchup that could serve as a parable of the state of women's athletics. The contest took place under the lights in front of a good-sized crowd. Both teams were stocked with superior players, serious athletes who had honed their skills over the course of many years. Most of them, in the manner of true CDAs, probably started somewhere around kindergarten.

But not everyone who wanted to play made it onto the field. Start with the girls from Whitman High: senior captain Julie McCabe could only cheer from the sideline, because in the third game of the season, she had ruptured the ACL in her left knee as she sprinted for a ball, then decelerated to turn. As her coach, Gregory Herbert, re-membered the injury, "She cut one way, and the knee went the other. She heard it pop."

Three games, and exactly two weeks later, junior Sara Schmidt tore an ACL, also in a noncontact, seemingly innocuous episode. To Herbert, it looked identical to McCabe's injury: "She turned, the knee didn't."

The next to be injured was Meaghan Doherty, another junior,

perhaps Whitman's most talented athlete and surely its most star-crossed. "A phenomenal player," Herbert said. "She was a starter from day one of her freshman season."

But not for long. A couple of weeks into her freshman season, she fractured a growth plate in her right knee. She sat out a few weeks, but when she came back, she suffered cartilage and bone damage to her other knee—possibly by changing her gait to compensate for the previous injury. She needed two surgeries on her left knee, and the rest of the freshman season was lost. Doherty's sophomore year was better: she played in most of the regular season games, but then tore a ligament in her left ankle and missed the playoffs. Then came 2007: After the two ACL injuries to her teammates, and a couple of weeks before the game against Bethesda–Chevy Chase, Doherty lifted off her feet for a header on a corner kick, hoping to redirect the ball for a goal. Teammate Emily Mason went for the same ball and Doherty slammed into her jaw, loosening two of Mason's front teeth. Doherty suffered a concussion.

She tried to come back a week later, but she either suffered another concussion or a recurrence of symptoms from the previous one. "She had the shakes," Herbert said. "She felt light-headed and nauseous." Doherty, who started playing organized soccer at age three, was ordered by a doctor back to the sidelines, and there she sat when Mason, who miraculously had *not* suffered a concussion when the two of them collided, got involved in another on-field mishap.

Mason described for me how it happened: "I was chasing a girl down, tripped, and hit the back of my head on the ground. I got up and started feeling really tired. I couldn't keep running. I thought to myself, Oh my God, why am I dying? The coach took me out, and I lay down and closed my eyes. Everything started spinning and I felt nauseous. I told my coach that I didn't feel well. Then Meaghan came over and she started talking to me, and she knew right away. She said, 'Emily, you have a concussion.' And then I really started shaking." The diagnosis was confirmed by a doctor.

Two concussions. Two ACL tears. But that was not all of the Whitman injuries. Another talented junior, Retha Koefoed, had been in and out of the lineup with back pain—after missing her entire sophomore season with a stress fracture in her back. "When she can play, she plays," Greg Herbert, the Whitman coach, explained. "She's been in and out." On this night, she could not.

Senior captain Rachel Haas did play and was her team's most visible player because of her remarkable, almost freakish ability on throw-ins. Whenever Whitman was deep in its attacking end, Rachel was able to fling the ball all the way into the goal area—a potent offensive weapon made possible by the extreme flexibility of her spine and her back muscles. You didn't need an MRI to see this; it was obvious from the bleachers. When she took the ball back behind her head to throw and arched her back, she looked like one of those old Gumby figures, the green rubberized dolls you can bend in any direction.

But Rachel has chronic back problems, which cut short each of her first three seasons of high school soccer and makes regular visits to a chiropractor. "It's been a problem every year," her mother, Gail Ross, said. "This is as far into a season as she's ever made it." Ross said her daughter and most of her teammates played a heavy club soccer schedule. "The tournaments are very hard on the girls. But there's this incredible tension because they want to be seen by college coaches. But how many games can you play?"

Herbert said that he has had girls show up for his practices and ask if they can sit out and take a nap. "Their parents want them to play in college. They play here. They play on weekends. The exposures add up. There has to be a connection. I'm concerned with the constant breakdown of their bodies. With no real season off, and no time to recuperate, it seems inevitable that you're going to suffer an injury. You just wear out, and something gives. If you're lucky, it's not a major injury."

Herbert has observed that his players do not get enough sleep, and most do not eat well. They grab a bag of chips between practices. "That in itself can't help," he said. He misses having the control that his own high school coaches exerted back in the era when school sports predominated and the rules were ironclad: during the school season, you played in no other venue. The high school coach was an autocrat, but with benign intent. "I had coaches who wouldn't let us go swimming," Herbert recalled. "It could be a hundred and five de-grees out, and they'd say, 'No, you're not allowed to go to the pool.' And we had no choice but to listen."

But if a high school coach sought to stand in the way of his play-ers' club commitments, he would risk losing his best players. Herbert has learned that there is not that much he can do. He keeps his prac-tices to no more than ninety minutes. Sometimes his team watches soccer videos rather than going out on the field. He will let an ex-hausted player take a nap. He tries to offer counsel, but it is rarely heeded, and he understands why. "I have girls practice with me and then go right off to another practice afterward. I say to them, 'You're killing yourself.' But they have obligations and they're not just going to walk away from them."

INJURIES PILE up in such a way on girls' teams that a squad with just a couple of starters out for the season—and perhaps a few others playing through injuries—can seem like a picture of good health. On the night they played Whitman, the Barons of Bethesda–Chevy Chase High School were, relative to their opponents, in far better shape.

Rob Kurtz's team had won its first ten games, but the perfect re-cord did not convey the full measure of their dominance. The B-CC girls had scored fifty-one goals, while allowing just two. Much of that record had been accomplished without their top scoring threat, Hannah Cooper, who missed all or part of six of those games with the same tender ankle that had plagued her since the summer.

Hannah was back in the lineup for the Whitman game but midway through the second half went down in pain and was carried off the field by a teammate. (One advantage of not bulking up is that you can be easily carried to the sideline.) It turned out to be just a scare. Her legs had cramped up, and she was able to stretch and return to the game.

It was a different story for Hillary Goldman. Like Hannah, she had entered the high school season with ankles that were chronically sore and prone to injury, but she survived preseason workouts and the first three games with just a minimum of discomfort. She did not feel perfect, but if she waited for that, she would never take the field.

But Hillary could not play against Whitman, nor would she make it onto the field the rest of that season. In the team's fourth game, a ball had come loose out of a scrum in the goal area and she had gone for a shot. A defender's foot made contact with the ball at the same instant, and it felt to Hillary like her right ankle, the one that had caused her so much trouble, went backward.

She was wearing a brace, "but it was just too much force for it to handle," she recalled. "The brace prevented the ankle from turning, so it just jammed. It was really violent." When her doctor examined it the next day, he asked her where it hurt. "Here, and here, and here," she replied, pointing to the top and both sides of the ankle.

Hillary was on crutches for more than a week, and the ankle stayed black and blue for three weeks. A month and a half later, it was still swollen. "My ankles are just so weak," she said. "I've done all this physical therapy to try to strengthen everything around them, but every time I get an injury, it's like a step backward."

Her doctor finally cleared her to start running and said she could try practicing with taped ankles. But she could not make it back. Her junior season was a bust. "I want to be playing. It's so upsetting," Hillary said. "This is the strongest team we've ever had."

After Bethesda won its first fourteen games, its season came to an unexpected end when the Barons were upset in overtime in a state regional final. Hannah Cooper scored both the team's goals.

Hillary, watching from the sideline, had already plotted how she would restart her soccer career. The club season and college recruiting season were starting to heat up, with big Christmas showcases approaching. Hillary decided to finally break the connection to the club team she had played with for five years.

She called her coach and let him know. "It was emotional," she said. "But it's something I had to do and probably should have done earlier than I did. My coach was really kind about it. He wished me luck on wherever I went next."

While still looking for another club team, Hillary signed on as a "guest player" with a team needing a midfielder in the big Raleigh Shootout. There was not a lot of time to waste. She was hoping for a window of good health so she could get back out there and impress recruiters.

CHAPTER 14

HEAD TO TOE

The pattern of injuries on the Whitman team would not be surprising to most players, coaches, or parents immersed in women's sports: a couple of ACLs, back problems, and serial ankle sprains. (At least two players on the field that evening for Whitman had missed previous games with ankle injuries, and Retha Koefoed, one of the girls out with back pain, had previously missed other games with ankle sprains.) Nor should it be surprising that among the injured were two girls who suffered concussions. Concussions are a major issue in women's sports, although until very recently, almost all public concern and research on head injuries in sports centered on men. But a major study published in 2007 showed that concussions conform to the same pattern as ACL injuries— women suffer them at higher rates than men playing the same sports. "Most groups comparing concussion incidence and recovery in high school and collegiate athletes focused primarily on football, with minor consideration given to other male sports or to female sports," stated the 2007 study, conducted by researchers at Ohio State University and Nationwide Children's Hospital, both in Columbus, Ohio.

Using data collected by certified trainers at high schools across the nation, the study found that female high school soccer players suffered concussions at a rate of 0.36 per 1,000 exposures (practices and games). For boys, the rate was 0.22 per 1,000. Among the high school sports studied, only football, with 0.47 concussions per 1,000 exposures, had a higher concussion rate than girls' soccer.

In basketball, the girls' concussion rate was 0.21 and the boys', 0.07 per 1,000 exposures. That finding was in line with a study that showed women in the WNBA are three times as likely to suffer concussions as the men of the NBA.

Data on concussions in college sports compiled by the NCAA show the same trends in even sharper relief. Men's football, at 0.38 per 1,000 exposures, and women's soccer, at 0.36, are statistically identical. (The preseason crucible of spring football is compiled separately and has a higher concussion rate—0.54 per 1,000.)

The NCAA sport with the highest concussion rate by far is the fast-growing sport of women's ice hockey—at a staggering 0.91 concussions per 1,000 exposures. Men's hockey is less than half that. The women's number is based on a smaller sample. Nonetheless, a researcher involved in injury prevention said to me, "If the numbers on women's hockey are even close to correct, they should stop playing until they figure out how to lower them."

Comprehensive statistics on total sports injuries are in short supply. The NCAA numbers are the best, but even they are based on just a sampling of colleges and universities. At the high school and youth level, the numbers are even less specific and reliable. Most high school studies have measured sports injuries by emergency-room visits, which usually result from traumatic events like broken bones and concussions. Even a serious injury like an ACL tear often does not lead to a visit to an emergency room; the initial examination typically occurs at a doctor's office, either a pediatrician's or an orthopedic surgeon's. Potentially debilitating syndromes like chronic ankle, knee, hip, and back pain, as well as stress fractures and shin splints—all of them more commonly suffered by female athletes—would barely register in the surveys of ER visits.

The possible connection between "nagging injuries," as they are called in sports, and acute injuries like ACL tears is also unknown. UNC's Michelle Boling is researching patellofemoral pain syndrome—pain around the kneecap—and what it may portend. "More women suffer from it," she said. "It could be a precursor to ACL injuries. It's something we don't know yet." Holly Silvers of Santa Monica Orthopaedics goes further: "Bad landing after bad landing creates low-grade microtrauma," she says. "The knee gets worn down. Those bad landings seem innocuous, but they're not."

The studies of U.S. high school athletics indicate that boys, in raw numbers, suffer more of the kinds of sports injuries that lead to ER visits. But the picture is thrown off kilter by football and by the fact that boys still represent the greater percentage of high school athletes.

One of the more ominous findings of the concussion study was that among high school soccer and basketball players of both sexes, 20 percent of the concussions were classified as recurrent. Concussions build on each other, and the symptoms are usually more severe and longer-lasting each time.

The injury can cause short-term memory loss and nausea, usually for just a few days—and headaches, sleep problems, and concentration difficulties that can go on for weeks or months. "With my female concussion patients, I also pick up more signs of depression," sports doctor Rebecca Demorest told me. "It's possible that's because I'm looking for it more, or girls are more willing to be open about it."

Just as in ACL injuries, it appears that it takes less force to cause a concussion in a female than in a male athlete. For example, for both males and females, the most common cause of concussions in soccer is player-to-player contact—usually head-to-head or elbow-to-head. Boys rarely get concussions heading the ball or falling to the turf headfirst, but for girls, those are significant causes of concussions.

The Ohio study noted females' "smaller head-to-ball ratios." A previous study of collegiate soccer players took measurements of competitors of both sexes and concluded that the women had "26 percent less total mass in their head and neck than males."

Joseph Bleiberg, a neuropsychologist and expert on brain injury, put it more colorfully. "It's like comparing an SUV and a VW bug," he said. "The same level of impact is probably not going to cause the same level of damage." The neck, he said, is the "shock absorber." If it is smaller and weaker, more of the force will be absorbed in the brain.

There is no prevention program for concussions, no training regimen in which an athlete can build up muscle groups or change the way she runs or jumps in order to avoid them. But style of play, which can be modified, is a factor. No one wants young women to play with any less determination or gusto, but they can—and should—play smarter.

For a soccer player to head a ball and make an effective pass to a teammate—especially if the header is contested—is far more difficult than playing it on the ground. Heading a ball is certainly a part of the game, a big part of it, but it should not be done just for show.

As we watched youth and collegiate games in Southern California, Holly Silvers pointed out numerous times when young women went for headers, risking violent collisions, for no tactical advantage. They had no chance of controlling the ball. Their only possible objective was to make a macho point—every ball challenged, no backing down.

Silvers gasped several times, in horror and anger. "Let the ball settle. Please, let the ball settle." Another time, when a repeat offender attempted yet another reckless play for a ball in the air: "That is just so stupid!"

At times, she seemed ready to boil over. As we watched the UCLA women play Washington State, one particularly aggressive player twice plowed over opponents from the back as the ball was in the air. It was more akin to clipping in football (which earns a penalty) than a soccer play. She was not carded. It reminded me of the lax officiating I had seen at the NCAA women's basketball championships.

This same player later scored a goal. "That is awful vindication," Silvers said disgustedly. "Just awful."

Anson Dorrance told me that he has become more concerned about concussions than ACL injuries. "The ACL injury does not come from a girl taking a risk. It's from a girl changing directions. So within the context of the game, there's nothing you can do about it."

Dorrance is a proponent of the Full 90, a protective device that looks like a headband but that some fear may promote an even greater degree of risk taking. "The thing with concussions is they can become chronic," Dorrance said. "You get one and become vulnerable to more of them. That's my big fear."

He made another distinction. "An ACL is certainly a catastrophic injury, but I don't think there's really any incredibly long-term damage. The surgery is so sophisticated now and the rehab so much better that when a girl tears it, she is basically making a one-year sacrifice."

Many who know the long-term fallout of ACL ruptures would dispute this view. The truer thing to say is that women seem more vulnerable to ACL injuries and concussions—either one of which can be a long-term nightmare.

SAMANTHA FIRSTENBERG, a junior at the private Stone Ridge School of the Sacred Heart in Maryland, plays lacrosse, a sport that follows the same model as youth soccer—and youth basketball, field hockey, baseball, swimming, golf, tennis, and all the rest. She practices and competes, indoors or outdoors, eleven months a year. In the summer, she plays in multiteam tournaments nearly every weekend, up to four games a day.

Unlike girls' soccer or basketball, girls' lacrosse is played by significantly different rules from boys.' The girls' game is less physical and, in theory, noncontact. No body-checking is allowed. The boys wear helmets and pads; the girls do not.

In September 2007, Samantha was competing in a tournament game—her second of the day—when she sprinted with the ball up the sideline and toward the opposing goal. Three girls from the other team closed on her, and she took a stick to the head—actually, three sticks to the head, she believes, because she had three separate bruises.

She did not lose consciousness and attempted to keep playing, then quickly signaled to her coach that she needed to leave the game. It was deep into the second half, not far from the end of the game and the tournament.

The instinct of most young athletes—as long as they are conscious, not gushing blood, and ambulatory—is to indicate that they're fine. That is what Samantha did, and she went back into action for the game's waning minutes.

"That's when the doctors think the damage was done," her mother, Suzanne, told me. "They said that after a blow to the head, additional damange can be caused by exertion soon afterward. Unfortunately, we didn't know."

In the days immediately following, Samantha was nauseous, dizzy, sensitive to light, and unable to think clearly or focus. When the symptoms persisted for more than a week, her parents took her to a specialist at Children's National Medical Center in Washington DC, and, several weeks later, to leading concussion experts at the University of Pittsburgh Medical Center.

"Even three weeks afterward, I was almost as bad as the day after," Samantha said. "Then the severity tapered down, but the major symptoms didn't. It was very difficult to concentrate, and I would have to take breaks from class. I couldn't focus for more than ten or fifteen minutes at a time."

In Pittsburgh, she was advised to rest her mind and cease all attempts at difficult thinking—a tough thing to ask of a college-bound eleventh grader. But she had been having no success with her schoolwork, so it was a relief to be told to stop trying. Samantha's parents talked to her school administrators and teachers, got her excused from her most difficult work, and arranged for note takers to sit in her classes so that she would not fall too far behind.

The concussion was initially graded as mild, because Samantha did not black out. "But she's gone through three months of hell," her mother said. "I can't imagine what a severe concussion looks like. At a certain point, we were close to making the decision to pull her from school. It was that bad.

"She just wants to get better. And she wants to play in college. This is recruiting season coming up. Coaches have come to watch her in tournaments already, but she wasn't able to play."

Samantha did, slowly, make progress. She was prescribed amantadine, a Parkinson's drug, and it seemed to help. The drug is being used in clinical trials to treat concussions, although Samantha was not part of a study. She began functioning at close to her normal intellectual level. She exercised but had to monitor her heart rate and stop if it got above 160. Over Christmas break, more than three months after the injury, her doctors advised that she give her brain a complete rest—she was not allowed to read or even play computer games. Emotionally, it was difficult. The spring lacrosse season, with more opportunities to be recruited, loomed. She worried about regaining her conditioning and skills—her "stickwork," as lacrosse players call it.

• • •

WHITMAN HIGH School's Emily Mason was full of bravado a few weeks after suffering her concussion. In some ways, that was to be expected. Teenagers often feel bulletproof. And even if they harbor their own doubts and fears, they do not easily betray their vulnerabilities.

In the days after the collision, Emily, a tenth grader, was more tired than she could ever remember. She couldn't do homework. She had to skip her photography class because the chemicals in the darkroom gave her splitting headaches, so she would take a seat in the back of Coach Herbert's classroom and take a nap. She observed practices from the sideline, then came home and took another nap.

She was mentally confused, even if sometimes she did not realize it until later. Before going to bed one night, she wrote "health" on her hand to remind herself to quickly dash off an assignment for health class when she got up in the morning. But when she looked at her hand the next day, she saw that she had spelled *health* completely wrong—the letters were all switched around—and it took her a moment to figure out her own reminder. "It was really weird. It freaked me out."

She could not play soccer for two weeks. "I missed ten games," she said. Ten? That seemed like a lot. "I had a tournament I missed," she explained. "That's four games. Plus two high school games, then another tournament."

Even three weeks past the concussion, she still was more tired than usual and had a hard time focusing. But she felt closer to her old self. Emily plans to change nothing about the way she approaches her sport. "I'm still going to be aggressive," she said. "That's a big thing with me. I don't care. If I get injured, I get injured. If it happens, it happens."

She repeated an old saw that generations of athletes have internalized: The aggressor does not get injured; the player who backs down does. It is one of those maxims that's always true, except when it's not.

"If somone goes in really hard at you and you don't go hard at them, you'll be the one who gets hurt," Emily said. "So you can't be the one who's not aggressive. I'm known for being really aggressive, and I'm really good in the air, heading the ball, so I can't change that."

By order of her doctor and her parents, there was one change Emily did make: she wore protective headgear on the field. She did not like the way it felt, and like 99 percent of girls who have been asked to wear a helmet, she definitely did not like the way it looked. She hoped to discard it as soon as possible.

In her first game back, it came off accidentally. "I went up to head a ball, and it fell off, and I smashed heads with someone. Luckily, I didn't get another concussion. My mom was in the stands, and I know she was like, 'Oh my God.' "

She cannot envision anything happening that would cause her to give up her sport. "If I can't play," she said, "I'm not happy. It's just what I do."

RESEARCH INTO sports concussions customarily raises the question of whether female athletes are more likely to report symptoms than male athletes, on the theory that boys may not want to risk losing playing time. The boys are presumed to be more "hardheaded," if you will.

It is a supposition difficult to prove, but one that to my mind is not based on real knowledge of how girls and women play sports. I see no indication that girls are any less desperate to stay on the field of play—to compete, keep their starting positions, and reap the fun of playing. Young athletes want to play through any kind of injury, and on this count, girls may be more, not less, determined than boys. (Keep in mind the research from military basic training that it takes a more significant injury to drive a woman out of the Army than a man.)

"I get more compliance from the boys," Dwayne Owens, the athletic trainer at St. Thomas Aquinas High School in Fort Lauderdale told me. "Boys are actually willing to sit and rest if that's what I tell them. The girls want to get back out there. They want me to tape them up and let them play."

St. Thomas's Janelle Pierson, who was so determined to get back on the field after her second ACL rupture, achieved her goal. She returned to competition in January 2008, less than six months after her reconstructive surgery—an aggressive, Amy Steadman–like rehab that allowed her to play in the Florida high school playoffs. Even highly paid professional players commonly take nine to twelve months.

Janelle's physical therapist said she was healed. Her surgeon was initially reluctant to write a letter to her school stating that she was medically cleared to resume playing, but she convinced him that she was ready. Then she suited up and played, against the better judgment of her parents. "My parents were like, 'No, you're not going to do that,' " Janelle said. "And I was, like, 'Yes, I am. This is my last year, and I want to win the state championship.' "

With a mix of resignation and pride, Janelle's father, Rich, said: "We've raised these girls to be very headstrong and independent. That's Janelle." Her mother, Maria, said she used to love to watch her daughter's games, but now she is filled with anxiety. "Oh my God, I have such a stomach ache now every time I watch her play."

But playing through pain, rushing back from injury—the Warrior Girl ethos—is ingrained in Janelle, as it is in so many female athletes. It is what she knows and what she's seen all around her. Real girls don't leave the field. A high school teammate one class above her, Kristine Rubi, endured six ankle surgeries—three in each ankle—over the course of her four years on varsity. "You're in a cast four to six weeks," Rubi explained to the *Miami Herald*. "Then you have three weeks of therapy. Then you can play."

Janelle said that her first surgery was "monumental. It felt scary. You know, it's surgery. The second one was like, OK, I know what I need to do, let's just do it. Let's have the surgery and rehab and get back out there."

CHAPTER 15

AMY: "I MISS IT SO MUCH"

When I visited Carol and Ned Steadman in Brevard, North Carolina, they insisted on showing me around the area so I could see some of the beautiful Appalachian terrain that presses up against their small town. We drove through dense forestland that opened up to reveal views of dramatic gorges and breathtaking waterfalls. Ned stopped the car at an overlook, near where Amy liked to go camping on her birthday—and where she made her dives from the fifty-foot ledge into a lake. "She loved it there so much," he said. "We'd take her there every year with her friends, and it was always boys until she was thirteen. They were the ones could keep up with her."

The tour was magnificent, and I was thankful for it. But I also sensed that the Steadmans may have wanted that moment of tranquillity before talking about Amy. They approach the subject of her injuries in different ways.

Talking to her father, it is not hard to see where Amy comes by her physical determination, and also her stoicism. Ned Steadman says that he is not an athlete, but he is a kayaker, rock climber, and hiker. He takes a quiet pride in knowing that he will challenge trails that others find too daunting.

Ned told me on the telephone, before our visit, "I'm pretty good about not looking back. What's past is past. It's harder for Carol." He said he had heard his wife crying for a long time one recent night. "She feels like she's been a bad mother, that there was something else she could have done. There wasn't, but I know she thinks that."

Ned taught chemistry for years at Brevard High School, about 200 yards from the Steadmans' house, then took his retirement from the local school system and began teaching across the border in South Carolina. Carol works as a teacher's aide at an elementary school. They are thoughtful people—sophisticated, well-read, and engaged with current events.

Her daughter's injuries and pain are not something Carol Steadman can block from her consciousness. "Not a day goes by that I don't think about Amy and her knee," Carol said over dinner. She knew that I had seen Amy not long before, and had questions. "Did she cry when she talked to you?" she asked.

I said that Amy had not cried but that I could tell she was holding back tears. I saw the same crack in Amy's stoicism each time we talked—a determined effort to keep her composure, as if at any moment her emotions could gush out with the force of one of those waterfalls back home.

Carol seems to worry that she failed to protect her daughter from pain, and having done that once, she will not raise subjects with Amy that might expose her to more pain—emotional pain. From grief and loss and regret. She does not want to get in the way of whatever Amy does to help herself move on.

"One thing I would love to ask her is about why they called her the Killer," she said. "Do you know?" I didn't. I said that I just assumed it was because of the fierceness of her play—that as a defender, she would sooner kill someone than let them score.

Carol talked about Amy crying on the drive back home from Chapel Hill after her first surgery, when she was seventeen, something she rarely did again in the wake of any of her other injuries. "She accepts pain well. Isn't that a terrible thing to say about someone that young? But that's how she always was. She was never into dolls or anything like that. She was just very tough."

Ned recalled Amy, as a high schooler, returning from a tournament in Europe with a serious ankle sprain and another competition looming, the state high school track and field championships. Amy was the top seed in the 200- and 400-meter runs but had not been able to train for weeks. She opted out of the shorter event, "her one concession," and then competed in the preliminary session of the 400 meters but ran poorly, barely qualifying for the finals.

"She came back up in the stands with us, and she was just beside herself," he said. "She was upset at her performance. In the finals, she just outgutted everybody. She was injured, she hadn't trained, but she won the state title."

Amy's parents attended each of her surgeries, and they talked to the doctors and to Bill Prentice, the team trainer. But Amy never talked much to them about any decisions, because there were none to be made. She was going to rehab and get back on the field—as quickly as possible.

When she was getting near the end of her playing career at UNC—after the last injury and the final surgery—Amy did finally include her parents in the circle of people she asked for advice. But neither her mother nor her father was forceful about insisting she give up the game. They knew that only she could make the choice.

Ned remembers her calling one night after she had made her decision. "All she said was, 'I'm not going to play anymore.' " I said to her, 'I think that's a smart decision.' "

Near the end of our time together, I mentioned to Amy's parents that when I saw her, she did not seem to be walking comfortably. I regretted it as soon as I said it. Carol Steadman looked stricken and became quiet.

I realized that Amy, Warrior Girl to the core, must summon her threshold of pain whenever she is in the presence of her mother. She sucked it up and moved like the sprightly tomboy who had bounded up and down the Appalachian trails. Her mother had no idea how much she hurt.

ANSON DORRANCE always told Amy she was going to be a multimillionaire one day, a refrain he began not long after meeting her, when she was still a teenager. She would laugh and ask him, "Anson, why do you keep saying that?"

But during his quarter-century of coaching, Dorrance had seen enough young women come through his program to be able to make good guesses about who was ticketed for some kind of grand success. In 2006, Amy graduated with distinction from UNC with a 3.65 grade-point average overall and a 3.8 in her major, economics.

Late one afternoon in the spring of 2007, she greeted me in the lobby of the high-rise Wachovia One building in downtown Charlotte. She didn't look like a college girl anymore. She wore a skirt, a blazer, and a pair of sensible pumps. She could usually make it through most of a day in those shoes before her right knee became too sore and she had to change into flat sandals. She was too modest to say, but her job, upstairs on the thirty-seventh floor, was of the type that many college graduates covet but few attain: analyst at an investment banking firm.

Her company, Edgeview Partners, was on the "selling side" for private midsized companies—Amy helped put together the thick, data-packed books that went to would-be buyers. Edgeview got a percentage of the sales price. It was high-stakes, high-pressure work and it suited her, even the crushing hours. She routinely put in six-day, eighty-hour workweeks—and even longer ones when the press of clients' needs demanded that she break her vow not to work at all on Saturdays.

She once stayed in the office until 5 a.m., drove back to her apartment, took a shower, then turned around and came back to put in another long day's work. "That was one time that I said to myself, 'My life is just awful.' But that's rare. Usually, I just love it."

On each project, she was part of a team along with a partner and an associate. They worked on deals together, strategized, traveled to meet clients. It was intense and competitive, which felt familiar. As the junior member of the team, she had to do some of the scut work, making copies at night when necessary, once having to write an apologetic e-mail to a client when something went wrong. It was not specifically her fault, but the task fell to her. It reminded Amy of being a freshman on the UNC team. "The other people have rank, and you just do as you're told," she said. "That's the way it works."

She was one of the few women professionals in the firm, but a natural at fitting into a macho atmosphere. (As we walked back toward her office after dinner that night, I noticed her unselfconsciously chewing on the toothpick she had picked up on the counter on the way out of the restaurant.)

Amy had taken up a new game, poker, which helped fill her need for competition and risk taking. On her rare time off, she sometimes played with her boyfriend and his buddies. "I think I play pretty well," she said in a sort of mischievous way when I asked if she was good at it. "The boys are impatient. If you're smart about it, you can use that to your advantage."

She stayed involved in soccer in a small way, helping to coach a team of girls, including the daughter of one of her firm's founders, on a rec-league team in Charlotte. But she desperately missed playing. "I loved the games," she said. "I loved practice. I loved being with my teammates. I loved the traveling, the competition. I really did just love it all. And not just soccer. I loved playing sports.

"As a defender, I loved the one-on-one battles. Some girl is running at me with the ball, and if she gets past me she's gonna score, so I'm just determined to take it from her. And I knew I could do that."

She has friends and former teammates on the women's national team; she had visited them at their training site in Southern California. They practice for a couple of hours in the morning and spend the rest of the day living at the beach, which seemed to Amy an even better life than investment banking.

She is drawn to watching any kind of competition—football, lacrosse, basketball. She likes watching the English Premier League soccer games on television. But watching women's soccer is more difficult. "I can't watch, and I can't not watch," she said.

Colleagues sometimes ask her to play pickup soccer, but she always declines. Even beyond the pain, she thinks it would be too frustrating to be so physically limited in a realm she used to dominate. She did once agree to play flag football, and immediately regretted it. She couldn't run without pain. She kept playing, after a fashion, but really just concentrated on staying out of the way. In the game that day, she was a person she did not recognize—the girl who primly watches the boys having their fun. She couldn't wait for it to end.

Her work colleagues know that she played soccer at the University of North Carolina but not that she was an elite, national-level player—*Parade* magazine's "best of the best" coming out of high school and, if not for her injuries, an heir to the legacy of Mia Hamm and the other greats of U.S. women's soccer.

She was one of eight analysts hired in 2006 at Edgeview out of more than one hundred interviewed. (In July 2008, she was to take a new job in the Washington DC area with a private equity firm, a company on the "buyer's side" of deals, a typical progression that often leads to business school and ever bigger jobs. In predicting great riches for her, Dorrance may have been on to something.) "We tend to hire a lot of athletes, because what we do requires people to work long hours together and fit into a team culture, which she has done with flying colors," Matthew Salisbury, Edgeview's managing partner, said. "I knew that she had played soccer at UNC when we hired her, but I didn't know much beyond that. Amy is a humble, modest person. She wouldn't be a person who would tell you how good she was."

Amy assisted Salisbury's wife coaching the girls' soccer team. "I knew her career was cut short by injuries," he said. "And I know she's still limited, because my wife said she can't really kick a ball."

There were times that I felt bad talking to Amy about her knee because it forced her to focus on such physical and emotional anguish. But over time, I came to realize that she welcomed our conversations. She did not let many people know how much her knee hurt. To her parents, she gave only hints. Her father knew she had recently been to see a couple of new doctors. "That speaks volumes to me," he said. It told him that Amy was hurting more than she let on.

Amy's pain is beyond what Advil or other over-the-counter drugs can calm. At its most intense, she said, "It's like a broken arm that hasn't been set yet."

It takes her a while to get out of bed in the morning, because her knee stiffens up when she sleeps. It gets tired and sore as the day goes on, and more painful at night. Stairs are hard for her, especially walking down them. "I can't go down stairs without hopping. It just doesn't feel stable. I feel like my knee is going to collapse under me."

She had just been to a new doctor in Charlotte, who she felt did not understand her situation. "He was like, 'Oh, no ACL, we'll put one in.' There's a lot of history I have to tell to a new doctor."

Amy has arthritis, "bone-on-bone contact," as she puts it. "It swells, not a ton, but enough that I notice it. I've also been told I have bone spurs and that the articular cartilage is deteriorating, so it's pretty much a big mess in there."

She briefly considered having another ACL reconstruction and even thought about how to do it without missing too much work: go to the office on a Friday morning, have the surgery in the afternoon, work from home over the weekend, show up in the office Monday morning, and just make sure to keep the knee elevated. The hardest part, she thought, would be not being able to eat from midnight until surgery the next afternoon. But she decided the odds of success were not good enough and also realized that she had fallen back into one of her old habits—minimizing the prospect of surgery and rehab, as if they were quick pit stops that should not slow her down for long.

"I had to remind myself that it's a big deal," she said. "You have to focus on getting back your range of motion, your balance. You can't just go to the gym for a half hour at lunch, and I don't even have that anyway."

The doctors she talked to were interested in finding a "permanent fix," she said, "because I'm so young." But there isn't one. She investigated a meniscus transplant, tissue from a cadaver to build back the cartilage that cushions the joint, but decided against it, at least for now. She had no appetite for risk on matters involving her knee. She wanted to know something was going to work, and no option gave her that assurance.

Amy knows that it is likely her knee will ultimately have to be replaced with an artificial joint made of metal and plastic. "I want to postpone it as long as I can," she said. "But in today's world, it will probably have to happen in ten or fifteen years. I'm holding out hope that at some point, they'll have some technological advance and just inject my knee with something, and it'll be good to go."

At the University of North Carolina, there are some who consider Amy a cautionary tale, a too-young player who was in too big a hurry ever to rest properly and heal. It always felt to Amy that she was going to be missing out on something. The under-nineteens were going off to Vancouver. Another college soccer season was starting.

Her parents left her soccer career and most medical decisions to the experts at UNC, where the ethos, as in nearly all elite collegiate programs, is to crash through rehab as quickly as possible and get back in uniform. It is not all that different for younger, less elite players. Youth sports have become a game of getting and keeping a foothold.

Amy sees herself that way, as a cautionary tale. "Knowing what I know now, I would definitely rehab slower. I would take my time and make sure I was as strong as I could possibly be. There's no way to know if that would have made a difference, but I wish I would have given it a chance."

She does not blame anyone else. She was so powerful and so insistent that she called the shots. "I knew what I wanted. I was focused. I was the kind of person who made it clear, I'm doing things my way, and nobody can stop me. It didn't work out the way I wanted, and of course you can question that: Why?"

One answer she has come to is that she was not as wise as she imagined. "When I got to UNC, I was very mature in some ways and very immature in others. I wasn't social. I had no friends outside my sport. I didn't have anything outside of soccer. I didn't see the need, and I didn't have an interest.

"It took all these horrible injuries to make me a more complete human being. As a person, I'm much better off. I'm not a prima donna anymore, whining about what I need for soccer. I'm more balanced. I feel better about myself. I'm not in that soccer bubble, but it's bittersweet. I miss it so much."

AFTERWORD:
PRESCRIPTIVES

To play sports is to accept the inevitability of minor injuries—sprains and bruises—and the possibility of major ones. An athlete accepts the risks because the rewards of competing are so great.

But for girls and young women, the risk-reward ratio is gravely out of balance. What happened to Amy Steadman is unacceptable, as are the nine ACL injuries out of eighteen players on Janelle Pierson's club team. For half the starting point guards in a major collegiate conference to suffer ACL tears in a span of several months is unacceptable. So is the wave of injuries endured by the 2007 Whitman High School girls—concussions, serial ankle sprains, torn ACLs, disabling back pain.

As I have established, this is an epidemic that must be recognized and stopped. But what to do? Pause to imagine for a few minutes what the parents of these girls are feeling. Many of them come close, at times, to a sense of despair and helplessness. They told me, usually in halting conversations, that they felt powerless to intervene as their daughters ran themselves ragged on the fields of play. And they also told me they had no idea that such a disproportionate risk to young female athletes exists. So here is what I believe must happen:

Parents must stop abdicating responsibility and must start protecting their daughters. They should seek out ACL prevention programs and demand that they be instituted on their daughters' club and school teams. The prevention programs are not complicated or overly time-consuming. Preliminary research on their effectiveness is encouraging. Information on the warm-up program designed by Santa Monica Orthopaedics can be downloaded at www.aclprevent.com/pepprogram.htm.

You pay your daughter's club team fees. If the coach is a paid professional, he works for you. Get together with other parents and tell the club team coach, We want you to do this, and it's not optional. If it is a school team, bring the research to the coach, athletic director, or principal, and argue for it.

There are many other programs that tout themselves as preventing ACL injuries. Some are more in the realm of personal training or off-season training for an entire girls' team, rather than a set of exercises to be integrated with in-season practices. Many of them are good; some are not. How should you sort them out?

Some advice: Be wary of training facilities that seem to specialize in working with male athletes seeking scholarships, particularly football players who want to build "explosiveness" so that they can improve their times in the forty-yard dash or their ability to lift heavy weight. Some of these facilities may have trainers who can work equally well with girls, but you will need to interview them.

Ask a series of questions of anyone seeking to offer training to your daughter: How do you train female athletes, and how do you tailor training to the individual and the particular sport? As I have demonstrated, the culture elevates and affirms a Warrior Girl mentality, so you will need to be dogged in finding coaching and training that recognizes that young women have bodies that are different from males' and that they also change throughout the teen years in different ways.

Ask what coaches and trainers know about the latest research on gender and sports injuries. Does their training for female athletes focus on core muscle strength and running, landing, and deceleration techniques, or is it just a scaled-down version of their program for boys? Anyone training your daughter should be able to speak knowledgeably about the anatomical and biomechanical differences between males and females, as well as about some of the differences in the way they approach their sports. Find out what program they are following and where it came from, and make a determination as to whether it has truly been informed by research and tailored to young women.

If you are still in doubt, seek out more resources—the athletic trainer at your high school (if there is one), a trainer at a local college or university, a physical therapist with experience in treating female athletes.

Do not be bullied into having your daughter give up her other sports in order to specialize in her "best" one. This is perhaps the most important advice I can give, because there is nothing that puts a young athlete at risk for injury like overuse and exposure—playing one sport from an early age and wearing down the same set of muscles, day after day and year after year.

Nearly every injured athlete I met in the course of researching this book played one sport exclusively, beginning at age ten or younger. Amy Steadman did run track through high school, but it was very much a sideline, and she rarely trained for it. Janelle Pierson was a good tennis player, and her mother wanted her to pursue tennis alongside soccer, but Janelle felt that she could not. "At ten years old, I had to choose," she said. "It wasn't an option to play another sport. People would question you. They'd want to know, Why would you ever want to do that?"

Bring the same thoughtfulness to your sports parenting that you use in your daily parenting. Come together with other parents to set reasonable limits and enforce them. There's strength in numbers. When our kids are young, we set their bedtimes, and as they get older, all the way through high school, we enforce curfews. Only in sports do we outsource oversight of their schedules.

There is an obvious senselessness to much of what we ask of our youngest athletes, yet we can't seem to stop. To ask a teenage girl to play multigame tournaments over two or three successive weekends is indefensible. For a club coach to expect a young player to come to an evening practice—after she has practiced in the afternoon with her high school team—is indefensible. We don't make these kinds of demands on college athletes or professional athletes.

Talk to other parents. If the team has been together for several years, try to compile a history of past injuries to determine if they occurred during times of especially heavy play. If that is the pattern (and it likely is), show it to the coach. Then work with him to establish what seems like a reasonable schedule for practices, games, and tournaments—one that builds in time for rest and physical training, as opposed to just skills acquisition. If the coach wants to play tournaments in quick succession—the most demanding thing we ask of our girls—make him justify it. What will be gained by playing two tournaments rather than just one? What is the possible reward, as opposed to the known risk?

And be prepared to walk away. If you have a coach who is insistent about too much play and warns your daughter that if she doesn't follow that direction, she'll fall behind her peers, you may be in the wrong program.

Try to give your daughters a holistic vision of body awareness, fitness, and exercise that is not derived solely from the world of competi-

tive sports. The writer Michael Pollan, in his latest book, *In Defense of Food,* recommends that we "eat real food," which he describes as what our great-grandmothers would recognize as food rather than the packaged, processed foods that come out of food-science laboratories.

Likewise, our kids' physical activity seems to come entirely out of a package. None of it is naturally occurring. A lot of our most athletic children are sedentary except for their sports. They don't walk anywhere, ride bicycles, hike in the woods, or even do yard work or help in the kitchen, because their busy sports schedules do not allow it. They don't go to traditional summer camps but rather to specialty sports camps, where they get more of the same.

Moving around is a normal and necessary part of life. It's a marvelously easy form of cross-training. A girl who continues to walk, hike, rake leaves (rather than using a leaf blower), splash around in pools even if she's not involved in a swim meet—anything that gets her body moving—is likely to be more injury resistant when she does play her sport. And probably happier too.

Another necessity: we must coach girls to pay attention to soreness, fatigue, and what may seem like minor injuries. "It seems an odd omission to me that coaches, physical education teachers, and parents don't teach young people to pay attention to their own bodies," the writer Mariah Burton Nelson says. "We teach girls how to display their own bodies, for male approval or attraction. In a sporting context, we teach them how to accomplish tasks and achieve with their bodies. But a huge missing piece is that we don't teach them how to pay attention to the day-to-day biofeedback they are getting—to recognize when they're tired or hungry, when they're sore, when they need to strengthen or rest. The only thing they hear is that they are supposed to ignore pain, and when the body is breaking down, that's the message that gets us into trouble."

And finally, prominent coaches of women's teams must speak out about injuries and campaign for more research and more public education. Parents alone can't make changes. When Tara VanDerveer, the Stanford women's basketball coach, lost a player to an ACL injury and said, "I'm numb to it. It's part of women's basketball," we can assume she did not mean to sound so cavalier or unfeeling. Perhaps she felt she had to "go to war" with her able-bodied players, as coaches sometimes say, and could not dwell on the fallen ones.

But VanDerveer and other top coaches are among the strongest voices in women's sports. They see up close the physical and emotional toll of ACL injuries. It's not enough for them to just look down the bench and call in the next substitute every time they lose a player. VanDerveer, basketball coaches Pat Summitt of Tennessee and Geno Auriemma of Connecticut, UNC soccer coach Anson Dorrance, and others should come together to lead the call for more research and public education. And they should challenge coaches and parents at the youth levels and tell them, What you're doing is hurting girls. Too many are suffering major injuries in their midteens. And those who go on to play in college arrive on campus worn down from years of overplay and ripe for injury. They know this because they see it. They should speak up.

THE BEST thing about sports is that it teaches us to persevere. You don't quit when things aren't going well or ask to sit out at the first sign of discomfort. Title IX and the women's sports revolution have opened up these lessons for our girls and given them a chance to feel ever stronger and more confident.

But that great opportunity is coupled with odds of suffering serious injuries that are needlessly grim. We can't prevent every injury, but what we are currently doing is manufacturing them. If you *intended* for a girl to suffer a major injury, you would take away all her other sports before puberty, make her play her one sport all year round, and put her in frequent five-game-in-three-day tournaments and other similarly crushing athletic crucibles. And then you would just wait.

It is time for parents to rise up and demand research, education, prevention programs, and most of all, a saner sports culture. And it should happen before too many more terrific, spirited young female athletes leave the playing field in pain and despair.

A NOTE
ON SOURCES

This book is based primarily on interviews with athletes, parents, coaches, doctors, and researchers. I relied as well on numerous written resources, which are listed below.

BOOKS

ANGIER, NATALIE. *Woman: An Intimate Geography.* Boston, New York: Houghton Mifflin, 1999.

BLAIS, MADELEINE. *In These Girls, Hope Is a Muscle: A True Story of Hoop Dreams and One Very Special Team.* New York: Warner Books, 1995.

BLUMENTHAL, KAREN. *Let Me Play: The Story of Title IX, The Law That Changed the Future of Girls in America.* New York: Atheneum, 2005.

CORBETT, SARA. *Venus to the Hoop: A Gold Medal Year in Women's Basketball.* New York: Anchor Books, 1998

CROTHERS, TIM. *The Man Watching: A Biography of Anson Dorrance, The Unlikely Architect of the Greatest College Sports Dynasty Ever.* Ann Arbor, Mich.: Sports Media Group, 2006.

Dorrance, Anson, and Gloria Averbuch. *The Vision of a Champion: Advice and Inspiration from the World's Most Successful Women's Soccer Coach.* Ann Arbor, Mich.: Huron River Press, 2002.

Hoberman, John. *Testosterone Dreams: Rejuvenation, Aphrodisia, Doping.* Berkeley, Calif.: University of California Press, 2005.

Ireland, Mary Lloyd, and Aurelia Nattiv, eds. *The Female Athlete.* Philadelphia: Saunders, 2002.

Longman, Jere. *The Girls of Summer: The U.S. Women's Soccer Team and How It Changed the World.* New York: Harper Collins, 2000.

Melnick, Ralph. *Senda Berenson: The Unlikely Founder of Women's Basketball.* Amherst, Mass.: University of Massachusetts Press, 2007.

Metzl, Jordan D. *The Young Athlete: A Sports Doctor's Complete Guide for Parents.* Boston: Little, Brown, 2002

Nelson, Mariah Burton. *We Are All Athletes.* Arlington, Va.: Dare Press, 2002.

Nelson, Mariah Burton. *Are We Winning Yet? How Women Are Changing Sports and Sports Are Changing Women.* New York: Random House, 1991.

Rhoads, Steven E. *Taking Sex Differences Seriously.* San Francisco: Encounter Books, 2004.

Richardson, Dot. *Living the Dream.* New York: Kensington, 1997.

Shulman, James, and William Bowen. *The Game of Life.* Princeton, N.J. Princeton University Press, 2001.

Smith, Lisa, ed. *Nike Is a Goddess.* New York: Atlantic Monthly Press, 1998.

Summitt, Pat (with Sally Jenkins). *Raise the Roof.* New York: Broadway Books, 1998.

Theberge, Nancy. *Higher Goals: Women's Ice Hockey and the Politics of Gender.* Albany, N.Y.: State University of New York Press, 2000.

Thorne, Barry. *Gender Play: Girls and Boys in School.* Rutgers University Press, 1995.

ARTICLES

AGEL, JULIE, ET AL. "Anterior Cruciate Ligament Injury in National Collegiate Athletic Association Basketball and Soccer: A 13-Year Review." *American Journal of Sports Medicine*, February 8, 2005.

AGEL, JULIE, ET AL. "Descriptive Epidemiology of Collegiate Women's Basketball Injuries: National Collegiate Athletic Association Injury Surveillance System, 1988–89 Through 2003–04." *Journal of Athletic Training*, June 2007.

ALEXANDER, KEITH. "Lighting Up Vegas, D.C. Style: Marc Barnes Brings the Love for All-Star Weekend." *Washington Post*, February 20, 2007.

ALTAVILLA, JOHN. "Thomas to Have Surgery Today." *Hartford Courant*, January 18, 2008.

AUSTAD, STEVEN N. "Why Women Live Longer Than Men: Sex Differences in Longevity." *Gender Medicine*, Vol. 3, No. 2, 2006.

BARR, JOSH. "Business Embraces Prep Football." *Washington Post*, September 2, 2007.

BAUMEISTER, ROY. "Should We Stop Studying Sex Differences Altogether?" *American Psychologist*, December 1988.

BLOOM, MARC. "Among Runners, Elite Girls Face Burnout and Injury." *New York Times*, April 20, 2003.

BODEN, BARRY, ET AL. "Video Analysis of Anterior Cruciate Ligament Injury: Abnormalities in Hip and Ankle Kinematics" (submitted for publication).

BOUGHTON, BARBARA. "Anterior Cruciate Ligament Tears Leave Legacy." *Pediatric News*, January 2003.

BRENNER, JOEL S. "Overuse Injuries, Overtraining, and Burnout in Child and Adolescent Athletes." *Pediatrics*, June 2007

CLINE, ALANA D., ET AL. "Stress Fractures in Female Army Recruits: Implications of Bone Density, Calcium Intake and Exercise." *Journal of the American College of Nutrition*, Vol. 17, No. 2, 1998.

DEMORAT, GENE, ET AL. "Aggressive Quadriceps Loading Can Induce Noncontact Anterior Cruciate Ligament Injury." *American Journal of Sports Medicine*, March 2004.

DIAL, JENNY. "Seeking an End to Career-Ending Injury." *Houston Chronicle*, July 26, 2006.

DICK, RANDALL, ET AL. "Descriptive Epidemiology of Collegiate Women's Soccer Injuries: National Collegiate Athletic Association Injury Surveillance System, 1988–89 Through 2002–03." *Journal of Athletic Training*, June 2007.

DRAGOO, JASON L., ET AL. "Relaxin Receptors in the Female Anterior Cruciate Ligament." *American Journal of Sports Medicine*, July-August 2003.

EAGLY, ALICE H. "The Science and Politics of Comparing Men and Women." *American Psychologist*, March 1995.

EATON, WARREN. "Sex Differences in Human Motor Activity Level." *Psychological Bulletin*, July 1986.

EMANUEL, BOB, JR. "A Contender." *Miami Herald*, January 9, 2007.

FITZGERALD, TOM. "The Scholarship Chase." *San Francisco Chronicle*, October 30, 2005.

FURLONG, JIM. "Unbended Knees." *Durham Herald-Sun*, November 29, 2002.

GEGAX, TRENT. "The Sound of the Fury." *Newsweek*, August 13, 2001.

GESSEL, LUKE M., ET AL. "Concussions Among United States High School and Collegiate Athletes." *Journal of Athletic Training*, December 2007.

GILCHRIST, JULIE, ET AL. "Exercise-Related Injuries Among Women: Strategies for Prevention from Civilian and Military Studies." *Morbidity and Mortality Weekly Report*, Centers for Disease Control, March 31, 2000.

GOFF, STEVEN. "Injuries Lead to a New Staple of Sideline Care." *Washington Post*, September 25, 2007.

GREGORY, SEAN. "Where Are the Women Coaches?" *Time*, August 16, 2007.

GROSSMAN, HILLARD. "Harris Helps Tar Heels Win NCAA Soccer Title." *Florida Today*, December 4, 2006.

GWINN, DAVID E., ET AL. "The Relative Incidence of Anterior Cruciate Injury in Men and Women at the United States Naval Academy." *The American Journal of Sports Medicine*, January 2000.

HEEREN, DAVE. "High School Soccer Injuries Growing Concern; Games Take Toll on Girls' Knees." *South Florida Sun-Sentinel*, January 25, 2007.

HELYAR, JOHN. "Dr. James Andrews Still Works on the Cutting Edge." *ESPN Magazine*, September 18, 2007.

HEWETT, TIMOTHY, ET AL. "Effects of the Menstrual Cycle on Anterior Cruciate Ligament Risk: A Systematic Review." *American Journal of Sports Medicine*, April 2007.

HEWETT, TIMOTHY, ET AL. "Anterior Cruciate Ligament Injuries in Female Athletes. Mechanisms and Risk Factors." *American Journal of Sports Medicine*, February 2006.

HOFFERTH, SANDRA, AND JOHN SANDBERG. "How American Children Spend Their Time." *Journal of Marriage and the Family*, May 2001.

HOOTMAN, M. JENNIFER, ET AL. "Epidemiology of Collegiate Injuries for 15 Sports." *Journal of Athletic Training*, June 2007.

HYDE, JANE SHIBLEY. "The Gender Similarities Hypothesis." *American Psychologist*, September 2005.

JONES, BRUCE. "Intrinsic Risk Factors for Exercise-Related Injuries Among Male and Female Army Trainees." *American Journal of Sports Medicine*, September 1993.

JONES, BRUCE. "Prevention of Lower Extremity Stress Fractures in Athletes and Soldiers: A Systematic Review." *Epidemiologic Reviews*, Vol. 24, No. 2, 2002.

KNAPIK, JOSEPH J., ET AL. "Discharges During U.S. Army Basic Training: Injury Rates and Risk Factors." *Military Medicine*, July 2001.

KRUSE, SARAH. "Building Revenue Through Kids' Camps." *Idea Fitness Journal*, May 2006.

Levesque, William R. "In the Long Run, Military Alters Its Training." *St. Petersburg Times,* June 13, 2007.

Mandelbaum, Bert R., et al. "Effectiveness of a Neuromuscular and Proprioceptive Training Program in Preventing Anterior Cruciate Ligament Injuries in Female Athletes." *American Journal of Sports Medicine,* May 2005.

McGrath, Ben. "Teen Spirit: The Sophomore Season of America's First Soccer Celebrity." *The New Yorker,* May 23, 2005.

Miller, Ed. "Title IX Plays Big Role in Rise of Women's Rowing." *The Virginian Pilot,* May 25, 2007.

Mountcastle, Sally B., et al. "Epidemiology of Anterior Cruciate Ligament Injuries in a Young, Athletic Population." *American Orthopaedic Society for Sports Medicine,* May 2007.

Myklebust, Grethe, et al. "Prevention of Anterior Cruciate Ligament Injuries in Female Team Handball Players." *Clinical Journal of Sport Medicine,* Vol. 13, No. 2, 2003.

Patrick, Dick. "Plant, Pop, Then Pain." *USA Today,* June 25, 2003.

Pennington, Bill. "Books and Bouncing Balls in a Delicate Balancing Act." *New York Times,* December 4, 2005.

Pennington, Bill. "In Winnowing the Candidates at Haverford, Every Little Thing Counts." *New York Times,* December 4, 2005.

Pennington, Bill. "One Division III Conference Finds That Playing the Slots System Pays Off." *New York Times,* December 25, 2005.

Pennington, Bill. "The Results Can Be Jarring When the Recruiting Carousel Stops." *New York Times,* May 21, 2006.

Ruibal, Sal. "World Cup Exacts a Physical Toll: Hard Hitting Has Become Crucial in Women's Soccer." *USA Today,* September 25, 2007.

Sangenis, Patricia, et al. "Girls and Women in Sport." Report to the International Olympic Committee's Women in Sport Congress, April 2002.

SASLOW, ELI. "In Prep Cross-Country, Girls Often Face an Uphill Battle; Physiological Changes Can Hinder Female Runners." *Washington Post*, September 16, 2006.

SASLOW, ELI. "Girls' Soccer Team Spends a Season in a World of Hurt." *Washington Post*, October 24, 2007.

SCHMITZ, CRISTIN. "Trial Lawyer Tops in Testosterone Study." *The Lawyers Weekly*, March 13, 1992.

SHELBOURNE, K. DONALD, ET AL. "The Relationship Between Intercondylar Notch Width of the Femur and Anterior Cruciate Ligament Tears." *American Journal of Sports Medicine*, Vol. 26, No. 3, 1998.

SHULTZ, SANDRA J., ET AL. "Absolute Serum Hormone Levels Predict the Magnitude of Change in Anterior Knee Laxity Across the Menstrual Cycle." *Wiley Interscience*, June 17, 2005.

SHULTZ, SANDRA J., ET AL. "Sex Differences in Knee Joint Laxity Across the Female Menstrual Cycle." *Journal of Sports Medicine and Physical Fitness*, December 2005.

SMITH, MICHELLE. "ACL Demons on Rampage in Pac-10." *San Francisco Chronicle*, February 8, 2007.

SOKOLOVE, MICHAEL. "Constructing a Teen Phenom." *New York Times Magazine*, November 28, 2004.

SPIOTTA, DANA. "Breaking Away." *New York Times*, July 14, 2007.

SULLIVAN, ANDREW. "The He Hormone." *The New York Times Magazine*, April 2, 2000.

THEBERGE, NANCY. "The Gendering of Sports Injury: A Look at 'Progress' in Women's Sport." *Sport in Society*, October 2006.

YU, BING, ET AL. "Age and Gender Effects on Lower Extremity Kinematics of Youth Soccer Players in a Stop-Jump Task." *American Journal of Sports Medicine*, July 2005.

ACKNOWLEDGMENTS

Amy Steadman lost her sport at far too young an age, but not her fierce determination and prodigious heart. She is a remarkable woman, and I am indebted to her for summoning memories and feelings that I know were not always easy to talk about. My thanks, as well, to Amy's gracious parents, Ned and Carol, who were so thoughtful as I sought to understand their daughter's story.

Janelle Pierson, star of the St. Thomas Aquinas Lady Raiders, let me follow her as she bravely fought back from injuries and tried to salvage the end of her senior season. Her parents, Maria and Rich, helped me interpret the world of elite youth soccer.

Gayron Berman, Ariana Cook, Hannah Cooper, Hannah and Sarah Coy, Samantha Firstenberg, Leslie Gaston, Victoria Gersh, Hillary Goldman, Emily Mason, and Rachel Young were among the dozens of other girls and young women who talked to me about their sports and, in several cases, their injuries.

Steve Marshall, Barry Boden, and Holly Silvers served as both sources and sounding boards, allowing me to come back to them repeatedly with my questions and theories. Bruce Jones opened up his fascinating work on injury patterns among men and women in military basic training. Many other doctors and scientists were generous with their time and knowledge, among them Anthony Beutler, Michele Boling, Lisa Callahan, Rebecca Demorest, William Garrett, Jo Hannafin, Bert Mandelbaum, K. Donald Shelbourne, Sandra Shultz, and Diane Watanabe. (Any errors of science or fact in the book are mine alone.)

Anson Dorrance did double duty as both a source on Amy Steadman's collegiate career at the University of North Carolina and an authority on women's athletics. Bill Prentice, the longtime trainer of UNC's women's soccer team, contributed a wealth of knowledge and historical perspective.

Several friends and professional colleagues deserve mention. Gerry Marzorati, editor of *The New York Times Magazine*, provides me and a cadre of other lucky writers with a staging ground for the best work we can muster. It was Gerry, along with my fine story editor at the magazine, Dean Robinson, who first sent me off on the subject of female athletes and injuries. My friend and fellow writer at the magazine, Jonathan Mahler, read an early draft of the manuscript and provided valuable insights.

David Rosenthal and Ruth Fecych at Simon and Schuster provided deft advice on the structure of the book.

Heather Schroder, my agent at International Creative Management, contributed her keen thinking to the substance of the book, along with all the support and advocacy a writer yearns to have. Whenever I needed her, she was there.

My deepest gratitude goes to Ann Gerhart, my fabulous wife, who endured too many weekends and holidays when I was bunkered in my office, and who amid her own challenging work buoyed me emotionally and guided me editorially. She read the manuscript and vastly improved it, as of course she would.

INDEX